Perceptions and Policy in Transatlantic Relations

G000114376

In this book, experts from both sides of the Atlantic, examine the recent tensions between Western Europe and the United States over such issues as transatlantic security, policies towards terrorism, and relations with Russia and the former Soviet Union, against the broader background of perceptions and misperceptions in transatlantic relations.

Drawing on Professor Robert Jervis' work, *Perceptions and Misperceptions in International Politics*, this book examines whether Jervis' thesis has a new relevance given the current challenges in transatlantic relations. Some of the issues examined include:

- Perceptions and misperceptions in general, focusing on US foreign policy, issues of decision-making and implementation and issues of alliance management.
- The capacity of the United States and the European Union to cooperate effectively within the broader transatlantic framework.
- Studies focusing on the 'alliance security dilemma' and the transatlantic security community.
- Case studies of transatlantic relations in the 'war on terror' and relations with Russia.
- The present and future of the 'Western alliance'.

Providing a global and multilateral analysis from American and European perspectives and exploring fields of cooperation and competition, *Perceptions and Policy in Transatlantic Relations* will be of strong interest to students of international relations, American politics, and European politics.

Natividad Fernández Sola is Professor of Public International Law and International Relations and Jean Monnet Professor at the University of Zaragoza, Spain.

Michael Smith is Professor of European Politics and Jean Monnet Chair at Loughborough University, UK.

Perceptions and Policy in Transatlantic Relations

Prospective visions from the US and Europe

Edited by Natividad Fernández Sola and Michael Smith

Routledge
Taylor & Francis Group

LONDON AND NEW YORK

First published 2009
by Routledge
2 Park Square Milton Park Abingdon Oxon OX14 4RN

Simultaneously published in the USA and Canada
by Routledge
270 Madison Avenue, New York, NY 10016

Routledge is an imprint of the Taylor & Francis Group, an informa business

Typeset in Times New Roman by
Taylor & Francis Books
Printed and bound in Great Britain by
TJ International Ltd, Padstow, Cornwall

British Library Cataloguing in Publication Data
A catalogue record for this book is available from the British Library

Library of Congress Cataloging in Publication Data
Perceptions and policy in transatlantic relations / edited by Natividad
Fernández Sola and Michael Smith.
    p. cm.
    Includes bibliographical references and index.
    1. United States–Foreign relations–Europe. 2. Europe–Foreign
relations–United States. 3. National security–International cooperation. 4.
Security, International. I. Fernández Sola, Natividad. II. Smith, Michael,
1947-
    JZ1480.A54P47 2008
    327.7304–dc22
    2008009717

ISBN 10: 0-415-45487-5 (hbk)
ISBN 10: 0-415-45488-3 (pbk)
ISBN 10: 0-203-89169-4 (ebk)

ISBN 13: 978-0-415-45487-2 (hbk)
ISBN 13: 978-0-415-45488-9 (pbk)
ISBN 13: 978-0-203-89169-8 (ebk)

Contents

Figures

Contributors

Carlos Echeverría de Jesús is Professor of International Relations at the Faculty of Political Sciences and Sociology, Universidad Nacional de Educación a Distancia (UNED), Spain. He is a specialist in the areas of defense, security, terrorism and cooperation, focusing on European, Mediterranean, Middle Eastern, Caspian and Central Asian and Sub-Saharan Africa regions. He has developed his research at the Centro Superior de Estudios de la Defensa National (CESEDEN), the Spanish Armed Forces High Research Centre, the Western European Union Institute for Security Studies, and the Institute for Prospective Technological Studies (IPTS), part of the European Commission's Joint Research Centre. He also teaches at the Escuela Superior de las Fuerzas Armadas (ESFAS) – the Spanish Armed Forces High School, and works as an Analyst for the Spanish *Guardia Civil* on issues concerning Islamist terrorism and new risks in general.

Natividad Fernández Sola is Professor of International Law and Jean Monnet Professor at the University of Zaragoza, Spain, where she coordinates the Ph.D. Programme *European Union*. She was previously Professor of European Law Postgraduate Studies at the Université Sciences Sociales and of International Law at the Institut d'Études Politiques, Université Toulouse 1, France. She has conducted research at the Council of Europe, Strasbourg, the Centre for Studies and Research in International Law and InternationalRelations, the Hague Academy of International Law, and the Council of the EU. Most recent publications: with S. Stavridis, "Is a Constitutional Framework really needed for the development of a ESDP?", FORNET, CFSP Forum, WP4/04; with C. Closa, eds, *La Constitución de la Unión Europea, Centro de Estudios Políticos y Constitucionales*, Madrid, 2005; "La restructuración de la política exterior común de la Unión Europea. With or without European Constitution", *Cuadernos Europeos de Deusto*, no. 34, 2006; "La redefinición de la relación transatlántica desde una nueva óptica europea", *La crisis del vínculo transatlántico: ¿coyuntural o estructural?*, P. Vilanova and J. Baqués (eds), IUGGM, Madrid: Thomson, 2008 (re-edition); "La projection extérieure des principes fondateurs de l'Union Européenne", *Europe, 50ème anniversaire des Traités de Rome*, PUF, Paris: Dalloz, 2008.

David García Cantalapiedra is Research Fellow on US Foreign Policy and Transatlantic Relations at the Royal Institute Elcano at Madrid, Spain. He is also Professor of International Relations, Faculty of Political Sciences Universidad Complutense de Madrid. NATO Individual Fellowship (1997–99); Spanish National Defense Award 2001, Advisor on Cyberwar for Spanish TRADOC during 2001–02. Inviting Professor at Jean Monnet and Ph.D. programs on EU at University of Zaragoza. His most recent research activity is Director, "US Foreign Policy and the future of Transatlantic Relations after 2008 Presidential Elections" 2008–09, and Coordinator and Member WG on security and energy, Asia Central Program, Royal Institute Elcano 2008–09. Among his most recent publications: *EEUU y el papel de la Inteligencia en los conflictos asimétricos: las Operaciones de Paz y la Contrainsurgencia.* UNISCI Papers no. 34 with Gustavo Díazm, October 2008; "Las relaciones transatlánticas y la cooperación entre EEUU y la UE en materia de terrorismo", in Reinares, Fernando (ed.), *¿Estamos más seguros? Democracias y terrorismo global.* RIE/Ariel, November 2008; "Transatlantic Relations after the Lisbon Treaty" with Natividad Fernández, *SSRN Working Paper Series.* International Law Forum of the Hebrew University of Jerusalem Law Faculty Research Paper Series. September 2008; "A Administração Bush e o futuro da política estratégica dos EUA: Da GWOT à 'Longa Guerra'". IPRI. Sep. 2008; "EEUU, China, Rusia: la lógica inevitable de la militarización del Espacio", RIE. May 2008; "La creación del AFRICOM y los objetivos de la política de EEEUU hacia África", RIE, June 2007; "Entering the Game for a Greater Middle East 'Vision'", *EuroFuture.* Autumn 2006.

Rubén Herrero De Castro is Professor of International Relations, Faculty of Political Sciences, Universidad Complutense de Madrid. UNISCI Senior Fellow on Transatlantic Relations. Author of the book *The Invented Reality: Decision making, Perceptions and Foreign Policy* prologued by Robert Jervis (Madrid, 2006, Plaza y Valdés). As author he is currently working on a book about J. F. Kennedy and the Vietnam War. And as editor and author he is working in an *Asia–Pacific International Relations Handbook.* He publishes in diverse academic magazines (*Unisci Discussion papers, Inteligencia y Seguridad*, etc.). He also collaborates with several Spanish media (Opinion and International sections).

Robert Jervis is Adlai E. Stevenson Professor of International Politics at Columbia University, USA. He previously taught at Harvard and UCLA after receiving his B.A. from Oberlin College in 1962 and his Ph.D. from the University of California at Berkeley in 1968. His most recent book is

American Foreign Policy in a New Era (Routledge, 2005). His *System Effects: Complexity in Political Life* (Princeton University Press, 1997) was a co-winner of the American Political Science Association's Psychology Section Best Book Award. *The Meaning of the Nuclear Revolution* (Cornell University Press, 1989) won the Grawemeyer Award for Ideas Improving World Order. He is also the author of *Perception and Misperception in International Politics* (Princeton University Press, 1976), *The Logic of Images in International Relations* (Princeton University Press, 1970; 2d ed., Columbia University Press, 1989), and *The Illogic of American Nuclear Strategy* (Cornell University Press, 1984.) He has co-edited eight other books and authored over 90 chapters and articles.

Robert J. Lieber is Professor of Government and International Affairs at Georgetown University, USA. He received his undergraduate education at the University of Wisconsin and his Ph.D. at Harvard. He has held fellowships from the Guggenheim, Rockefeller and Ford Foundations, the Council on Foreign Relations, and the Woodrow Wilson International Center for Scholars, and also has taught at Harvard, Oxford and the University of California, Davis. Dr. Lieber's latest book, *The American Era: Power and Strategy for the 21st Century*, has recently been published by Cambridge University Press. As one reviewer has described it, 'This may be the best book on American foreign policy written since September 11.' In addition, Lieber is author or editor of thirteen other books on international relations and U.S. foreign policy. Professor Lieber has lectured widely in Europe, the Middle East and Asia. In the policy realm, he has been a foreign policy advisor in several presidential campaigns and consultant to the State Department and for National Intelligence Estimates.

Alexander Marshall is Lecturer in Defence Studies at Kings College London, UK. He studied at Glasgow University and at the School of Slavonic and East European Studies, University of London. He has previously taught at the Buriat State University, at the National University of Uzbekistan, the Tashkent, Barnaul State University and at Dundee University. His major publications include: 'Turkfront: Frunze and the development of Soviet Counter-Insurgency in Central Asia, 1919–33' in Tom Everett-Heath (ed.), *Central Asia: Aspects of Transition* (London: Curzon Press 2003) pp. 5–29; 'The Russian General Staff and the Far Eastern Frontier, 1860–1910' in 'To Rule The Land: Russian State Power, Religion and Ethnicity in Historical and Comparative Perspective, 1600–2002.' Ulan-Ude, 2003; 'Russian Military Intelligence, 1905–17: The Untold Story behind Tsarist Russia in the First World War.' *War in History* Volume 11, Issue 4, (2004) pp.393–423; 'Islam in Russian and Western Security Studies, 1980–2005' *UNISCI Journal* (Discussion Papers) No. 7 January 2005, http://www.ucm.es/info/unisci/Marshall.pdf; *The Russian General Staff and Asia, 1800–1917* (London: Routledge Curzon Press 2006);

'Imperial Russian War Planning for the Eurasian Space and the Impact of the Russo-Japanese War, 1900–914' in R. Kowner and S. Ben-Ami (eds) *Rethinking the Russo-Japanese War 1904–1905: Centennial Perspectives* (Global Oriental: 2006).

Carla Monteleone is Lecturer and Research Fellow in Politics and International Relations at the University of Palermo, Italy, and also teaches at the University of Catania, Sicily. She gained her Ph.D. in International Relations at the University of Milan in 2001, and her major publications include: *Le relazioni transatlantiche e la sicurezza internazionale*, Giuffrè, Milano, 2003; "Transatlantic Cooperation in Conflict Management", with Rosa Rossi, in *Jean Monnet Working Paper*, n. 57/2004, Dipartimento di Studi Politici, Università di Catania, 2004; 'The New Transatlantic Agenda: Transatlantic Security Relations between Post-Hegemonic Cooperation and Interdependence', in *Journal of Transatlantic Studies*, vol. 1, n. 1, pp. 87–107, 2003.

Michael Smith is Professor of European Politics and Jean Monnet Chair in the Department of Politics, International Relations and European Studies at Loughborough University, UK. His most recent books on EU external policies are *International Relations and the European Union* (Oxford University Press 2005, edited with Christopher Hill) and *The International Roles of the European Union* (Routledge 2006, edited with Ole Elgström) and he has published many other books and articles in this area. His work on transatlantic relations includes *The United States and the European Community in a Transformed World* (Pinter 1993, with Stephen Woolcock), *Beyond Foreign Economic Policy: The United States and the Single European Market in a Changing World Economy* (Cassell/Pinter 1997, with Brian Hocking) and many other articles and chapters. Currently he is working on a jointly-authored volume dealing with EU–US relations (*The European Union and the United States: Competition and Convergence in the Global Arena*, with Stephen McGuire, due for publication by Palgrave in 2007), and on a longer-term project dealing with crises and crisis management in the Euro-American system.

Acknowledgements

The volume arises from the papers presented at a conference held in Madrid during July 2006. Thanks are due for the valuable support provided to the conference by the Centre for Political and Constitutional Studies (Spanish Presidency of Government) and the University of Zaragoza, by NATO, by Compostela Group of Universities; thanks are also due, in particular, to ENDESA, who provided generous sponsorship.

Abbreviations

ABM	anti-ballistic missile
AMU	Arab Maghreb Union
ARF ASEAN	Regional Forum
ASEAN	Association of South-Eastern Asia Nations
ASEM	Asia-Europe Meeting
AQMI	Al Qaeda in the Land of the Islamic Maghreb
BMD	ballistic missile defence
BRIC	Brazil, Russia, India, China
BTC	Baku-Tibilisi-Ceyhan pipeline
CBRN	chemical, biological, radiological, or nuclear materials
CDU	Christian-Democratic Union
CESDP	Common European Security and Defence Policy
CFSP	Common Foreign and Security Policy
CIA	Central Intelligence Agency
CIDEL	Citizenship and Democratic Legitimacy in Europe
CTC	Committee on Counterterrorism
EBAO	effects-based approach to operations
EDA	European Defence Agency
ENDESA	Spanish electrical Company
ENP	European Neighbourhood Policy
EPC	European Political Cooperation
ESDP	European Security and Defence Policy
ESS	European Security Strategy
ETA	Euzkadi ta Azkatasuna (Basque Homeland and Liberty)
EU	European Union
EUI	European University Institute
EU-3	France, Germany, United Kingdom
FYROM	Former Yugoslav Republic of Macedonia
G8	Group of Eight leading industrialised nations
GDP	gross domestic product
GIA	Algerian Islamic Armed Group
GICM	Moroccan Islamic Combatant Group
GMOs	genetically modified organisms

GSPC	Salafist Group for Preaching and Combat
GWOT	global war on terror
HIV-AIDS	Human Immunodeficiency Virus – Acquired Immune Deficiency Syndrome
IAEA	International Atomic Energy Agency
IEA	International Energy Agency
IMF	International Monetary Fund
INF	Intermediate Nuclear Forces
IRA	Irish Republican Army
KEDO	Korean Peninsula Energy Development Organisation
MC	Military Committee
NATO	North Atlantic Treaty Organization
NIS	New Independent States
NGO	non-governmental organizations
NTA	New Transatlantic Agenda of 1995
NSS	National Security Strategy
NSSD	National Security Strategy document
OSCE	Organization for Security and Cooperation in Europe
PNR	passenger name record
SCO	Shanghai Cooperation Organization
SDI	strategic defence initiative
SITCEN	EU Situation Centre
SPD	German Social-Democratic Party
TD	Transatlantic Declaration of 1990
TEU	Treaty of European Union
TSCTI	Trans-Saharan Counterterrorism Initiative
UK	United Kingdom
UN	United Nations
UNDP	United Nations Development Programme
USSR	Union of Soviet Socialist Republics
US	United States
USAFRICOM	US Africa Command
WEU	Western European Union
WMD	weapons of mass destruction
WTO	World Trade Organization

1 Introduction

Perceptions and Policy in Transatlantic Relations

Natividad Fernández Sola and Michael Smith

During the period of the George W. Bush presidencies, there has been continuous debate about the development of European–American relations and about the future of the Atlantic alliance. Much of this debate has been centred on the different perceptions of and dispositions towards security that can be discerned on the two sides of the Atlantic; thus we have seen the apparent opposition of 'Mars and Venus' and the often vicious transatlantic exchanges linked to successive crises, especially that over the decision to invade Iraq in 2003. On the other hand, and despite differences over specific policy issues, there has been apparent continuity and commonality of interests in a series of major policy areas spanning not just security, but trade, investment, and the future of the global economy.

How are we to square the circle of seeming opposition and apparent commonality of interests, in a way that enables us to analyse and evaluate not only the Bush years but the prospects for future transatlantic cooperation, especially but not only in security issues? This volume arises out of this question, and it proposes an approach based on perception and misperception as one way of extending our understanding of the Atlantic partnership. The conference at which the papers comprising this volume were originally presented took place in 2006; this marked the 30th anniversary of the publication of Robert Jervis' classic work on perception and misperception,[1] which gave additional point to the attempt to understand the transatlantic relationship in the terms he proposes.

The volume, therefore, brings together two strands: first, the analysis of perceptions and misperceptions in the world arena, and second, the desire to understand and evaluate the current transatlantic relationship and its possible future development. In this way, we propose, we can understand not only the operation of formal alliance, expressed especially through the North Atlantic Treaty Organization (NATO), but also the less formal ways in which transatlantic partners learn about each other, frame expectations of behaviour, and shape their policy actions. This approach promises a number of analytical payoffs. First, it introduces into the study of alliance or partnership an approach that has historically been more often used to understand those involved in adversarial relationships. This dimension is clearly of potential significance to the views we form of crises within the 'western alliance', and of the ways in which those crises are managed by the participants. The approach based on perceptions and misperceptions does not eliminate the need for analysis of institutions and the evaluation of broader international structures, but it does promise to give us an additional insight into the kinds of processes that attend alliance politics, and which can in principle be evaluated by reference to what the alliance members thought they were doing in specific situations.

Second, the approach takes us away from an analysis based solely on material interest and power, although of course it does not replace such an approach. It enables us to build into our appreciation of power and interests a sense of history through which we can assess the impact both of specific conjunctures and of the parallels or analogies mobilized by policy-makers – in other words, the impact of 'lessons of the past' and their application to the present and the future. This in turn links to the analysis of learning and adaptation by participants in the changing transatlantic relationship, and to the ways in which they shape their expectations of appropriate behaviour within it. As noted above, there has been extensive use of a perceptions/misperceptions framework in dealing with these issues as they make themselves felt in adversarial relationships, but it is our contention that alliance relationships and those of partnership, as expressed in transatlantic relations, can be usefully studied through this framework.

Both of the payoffs outlined above can be linked to a third: one that might broadly be described as the changing meaning of transatlantic relations. During the first decade of the twenty-first century, those relations have been put under enormous pressure, but we must remember that 'terminal' crises for the transatlantic relationship have been identified almost on a one-per-decade basis since the 1950s. What a perceptions/misperceptions approach promises is that we can place these crises and their outcomes into a framework dealing with the development of diverse – and often competing – meanings held by the participants. Not only this, but we can address an arguably more fundamental issue: the nature of security itself as perceived by the members of the 'transatlantic community'. To understand this aspect of the relationship, we need to be aware of developments not only at the transatlantic level, but also within the broader global arena and within the domestic contexts of decision-making on both sides of the Atlantic. When we build these developments at various levels into our analysis of perceptions and misperceptions, such an analysis is enriched with a heightened awareness of the constraints and opportunities perceived by policy-makers, and thus we are enabled to gain an understanding of the ways in which alliance tensions can be dealt with or exploited.

The volume thus engages in a distinctive way with some of the key questions that have been raised by the turbulent years of the George W. Bush presidencies. Why have American policy-makers taken unilateral and apparently dismissive positions on the development of transatlantic relations? Why have European policy-makers been apparently incapable of developing consistent and collectively agreed policies towards the United States? Can the Bush years be taken apart from the broader development of the transatlantic relationship over the past 60 years? Are there really fundamentally different perceptions of power and security on the two sides of the Atlantic? How much might or might not change when the Bush years are gone and we are faced with a new President? How do US and European policy-makers respond – and how might they respond in the future – to key challenges such as those posed by a newly assertive Russia, or the persistent threat of global terrorism?

The chapters that follow address all of these issues in a variety of ways. In line with the aims of the volume, we begin with the views of Robert Jervis himself on the ways in which theories of perception and misperception might help us to understand recent US foreign policy and transatlantic relations. This is followed by the 'European' view of Rubén Herrero de Castro, which focuses not only on the application of theories of perception and misperception, but also on the ways in which they can be applied to the policy clashes that have characterized recent transatlantic relations. In Chapter 4, Robert J. Lieber advances a robust argument about the ways in which transatlantic relations express enduring commonalities of interest and perception, but also notes a number of the enduring imbalances that characterize the 'western alliance'. Michael Smith, in Chapter 5, sets out to explore the ways in which theories of perception and misperception can be used to understand the historical evolution of transatlantic relations in the light of broader international relations approaches, and suggests that these ways can be extended to explore notions of alliance learning and institutionalization. In Chapter 6, Natividad Fernández Sola explores the specific issue of the European collective presence within transatlantic relations, and asks whether current and recent tensions have led to the empowerment of the European Union as a major participant in the relationship.

In Chapter 7, David García Cantalapiedra presents a detailed study of the ways in which ideas of perception and misperception can be related to problems of security and to the kinds of 'alliance security dilemmas' that emerge from the pursuit of alliance in a rapidly changing global arena. Carla Monteleone, in Chapter 8, takes the analysis further by focusing on the broader social foundations of transatlantic relations and relating these to processes of change in international structure and domestic interests – a key dimension in the social context of policy-maker perceptions. The two final chapters in the volume, by Carlos Echevarria Jesús (Chapter 9) and Alex Marshall (Chapter 10), focus on two key current policy issues: the 'war on terror' and responses to change in Russia. They note important disparities of perception between European and US policy-makers, and argue for the need for the reappraisal of policies and institutions in the light of changing contexts.

The result of these several and different 'cuts' at the problem of perceptions and policy in transatlantic relations is perhaps a sharper set of questions for further research and analysis, rather than a definitive set of answers to the key questions set out earlier in this Introduction. It does appear that transatlantic relations can be explored through the lens of perception and misperception, and that this gives a new perspective on the evolution and functioning of the 'western alliance'. This general conclusion gives rise to a number of more specific conclusions: that history does matter in transatlantic relations; that policy-makers can not escape easily from the structural and material constraints within which they work; that divergent perceptions in key policy areas can coexist with strong underlying perceptions of common interest; that self-perception on the part of the Europeans and the Americans is a key element to a richer understanding of the ways in which transatlantic relations work; that the nature of power, security, society, and global change are important in shaping perceptions within the transatlantic relationship; and that dealing with specific challenges to transatlantic solidarity will remain a key dimension of the relationship for the foreseeable future. It is our contention that long-established theories of perception and misperception can thus be applied with fresh impact and insight to this most enduring yet turbulent partnership.

Notes

1 Robert W. Jervis, *Perception and Misperception in World Politics* (Princeton, NJ: Princeton University Press, 1976)

2 Alliances, Perceptions, and Current Frictions

Robert Jervis

> Nothing is so dangerous as an ignorant friend; better a predictable enemy.
>
> La Fontaine

Alliances and Perceptions

Most of the work on perception and misperception deals with actual or potential adversaries. Perhaps the crucial question has been how the state determines whether the other side is hostile and, relatedly, how the other is likely to respond to threats or to conciliation. Much less attention has been paid to how allies perceive each other. I think this is part of a broader pattern in the distribution of our attention in that for every book or article on relations between or among allies, there are ten such books on relations between adversaries.[1] Furthermore, most of the scholarship on relationships among allies implicitly or explicitly argues that these relationships are very strongly influenced by how the allies are relating to adversaries in the system. That is, the obvious argument from Realism is that states cooperate with each other to the extent that they have a common adversary. This is not entirely true; liberal theories stress the role of domestic politics, and social constructivism focuses on the role of norms and identities. Nevertheless, the basic point holds – relations among allies seem undramatic if not unproblematic, and are explored most when they change dramatically.

The role of perception is similarly underdeveloped in the discussion of alliance relationships.[2] Since by definition an alliance means that relations between two countries are fairly smooth, it is easy to assume that each country understands the other fairly well. This is particularly true for alliances among democracies. Most scholars now believe – on the basis of very little evidence – that democracies are able to both signal and perceive relatively clearly. That is, they can make their intentions clear and make commitments because their political processes are relatively transparent and because powerful groups and public opinion will be offended if the state acts contrary to its word. Democracies do better in perceiving accurately as well; they foster the free flow of information, competitive analysis, and relatively honest debate. By contrast, dictators must sharply restrict the flow of information about the outside world, set their intelligence services into unhealthy competition with one another, and discourage if not kill those who bring bad news. So it is particularly hard for dictatorships to understand other countries, and we therefore should not be surprised that alliances among dictatorships are hard to maintain, not only because of the leaders' overweening ambitions, but because they lack the ability to understand others.

There is something to this view, but we should not exaggerate. It is at least as accurate to say that democracies are very noisy as it is to say that they are transparent. That is, the open, competitive, and complex politics that characterizes democracies provides outsiders with so much information, much of it conflicting, that it may be extremely difficult to pick out the signals from the noise.[3] Even native observers of the American political scene often have trouble figuring out what is going on; it is even more difficult for those from other countries to do so. Similarly, the argument that democracies are particularly likely to live up to their signals and commitments needs to be questioned. In the nineteenth century, the opposite was conventional wisdom: democracies were seen as inconstant and flighty. Indeed, the very role of public opinion that proponents of democracy cite can contribute to democracies abandoning their commitments when the costs of maintaining them prove unexpectedly high. Furthermore, many commitments are made when much of the public is paying very little attention and, if the issue increases in salience, negative opinion may be brought to bear.

It is doubtful that the role of public opinion always will be to sustain good relations among allies. Leaders are particularly sensitive to the diplomatic considerations involved; the public will react more viscerally, for better or for worse. I suspect that relations within NATO (North Atlantic Treaty Organization) would be more smoothly managed if public opinion were not involved. Although British and French leaders have many sources of friction, British leaders rarely call their counterpart 'frogs' anymore. The public often does. The media enjoys baiting allies, and ridiculing friendly countries for their cultural habits, as well as their politics, is often popular.

I do not mean to exaggerate, but only to suggest that the topic of perceptions and misperceptions among allies (including if not especially among democratic allies) deserves much more attention than it has been given.

On this and many other topics, research is skewed by the tendency to look mainly at crises and other dramatic events. That is, we may overestimate the extent of misperception and misunderstand the underlying processes because we look most closely at cases in which things go wrong. Everyday relations, especially among allies, are quite smooth and therefore seem uninteresting and so go unstudied. For example, in the study of Anglo-American relations we have a full shelf of books on the Suez crisis and several studies of Skybolt, but aside from general studies of the 'special relationship' we do not have extensive research. Thus from reading what is available one would think that Anglo-American relations were characterized by great friction and a series of misunderstandings. It is as though we were trying to understand the way cities function by looking at the police records. The results are interesting and do indeed answer some questions, but do not present a well-rounded picture.

Neither does this approach get at the question of causation. That is, if after looking at cases of friction and crises we locate certain perceptual errors, we cannot jump to the conclusion that those factors played a causal role without seeing if they were present in cases when perceptions were more accurate and relations were smoother. Thus, some of the bureaucratic man-oeuvrings and differences in perspective that Richard Neustadt so skilfully maps surely played a role in the Suez and Skybolt fiascos, but they may be present almost all the time.[4] In other words, while they may be a necessary condition for things to go wrong, they may be far from sufficient. This means that in order to tell us what factors discriminate between cases in which relations run quite smoothly and cases where they do not, we have to look at the former as well as the latter.

Politics within an alliance, like general international politics, is often por-trayed as a game of chess or poker. But these are misleading; a better starting place is the Japanese story and movie *Rashomon*, which has as its central point the fact that each actor sees the world very differently and that people rarely realize this. Of course, allies communicate much more extensively and openly than do adversaries, but this creates problems of its own in that the countries – both elites and general populations – are likely to overestimate the extent to which they understand the other. This was one of the causes of the Suez crisis: British and American leaders were sure they understood their opposite numbers quite well. Prime Minister Macmillan was confident that President Eisenhower would not block the invasion, while Eisenhower was quite sure that the British would never do something so foolish as to invade, espe-cially because he 'knew' that they understood that the US would not permit this.

Alliances in general, and the current Western alliance represented by NATO in particular, are prone to what can be called a compound mis-perception. The partners not only often misperceive each other, but each partner tends to be confident that the other sees it accurately. This makes them less vigilant than they should be for things going wrong, and they take less care than they should to see that their messages are being interpreted as they are intended.

In all this we should not assume that misperceptions always lead to bad relations or, even more, that mutual understanding automatically leads to good relations. In many cases, the conflict of interest is real and will not be dissipated by an appreciation of what each side wants. As all diplomats know, as do students of interpersonal relations, good working relationships not only often coexist with mutual misunderstandings, they are nurtured by them.

The idea that relations can proceed well not despite but because of major misunderstandings is not a hypothetical one. I believe it was true for the Western alliance during Eisenhower's presidency. Declassified documents reveal the extent to which European cabinets feared that the US would pull its troops out of Europe in the near future, despite American pledges to stay. What is surprising here is not the doubt, but the degree of suspicion and the vehemence of some of the anti-American sentiments. If I had seen only these documents, I would have argued that this shows the sort of exaggerated fears – if not paranoia – that can develop within alliances among unequals. But as those who have read Marc Trachtenberg's fine account know, the Europeans were essentially correct.[5] From the beginning of his administration, Eisenhower was committed to helping the Europeans become strong enough so that they would not need American forces to protect them. As many suspected, this was the driving impulse behind the American support for the European Defense Community. Later in his term, Eisenhower turned to nuclear weapons, hoping to establish either independent nuclear forces or, better yet, a Europe-wide force that would permit the US to withdraw. I wonder whether the alliance would have survived if the Europeans had understood Eisenhower's policy.

Perceptions and relations between allies can be complicated by differences in national styles. Most famously, Anglo-French relations and understandings were made more difficult by the discrepancy between British pragmatism and French legalism. Although the difference is exaggerated in stereotypes, most analysts conclude that the difference is indeed real. Furthermore, this real difference has not always been fully grasped by the participants – although most accounts discuss this less, it has not always been fully grasped by the participants. Even when understood in outline, the parties have found it difficult to adjust to one another. I believe that further research will reveal many occasions when each side misinterpreted the other because it could not fully appreciate the style in which the other was operating.

If the central question potential adversaries must ask is whether the other is aggressive or seeks security, the central fears and perceptual problems among allies turn on the linked but opposite dangers of abandonment and entrapment.[6] Both larger and smaller partners have to ask whether the other, by design or through incompetence, is likely to embroil them in an unwanted conflict with the adversary. A smaller state especially also has to assess the likelihood that its larger partner will abandon it in a moment of danger and need. The policy dilemma is that measures designed to reduce the probability of entrapment involve distancing the state from the ally and so increase the danger of abandonment, and measures that make this danger less likely tie the state more closely to the ally and so are likely to increase the chances of entrapment.

In addition, allies must try to estimate their partner's or partners' strength, resolve, and trustworthiness, as well as the partners' willingness to take their interests into account and the partners' propensity for under- and over-reaction.

The Current Western Alliance

Turning to current relations within the Western alliance, it is important to start with underlying structural causes for differences in policy and perspective.[7]

There are of course many idiosyncratic factors at work, including personalities and factors that are in some sense accidental as events caused by personalities and factors could have occurred differently. One important and fascinating case that deserves close study is the misperceptions between France and the US in the months leading up to the Iraq war, especially the apparent French failure to understand that the US was going to invade whatever happened at the UN or the inspections, and Vilepin's surprise attack on Powell at the January 2003 Security Council meeting. But we must understand that the US and the countries of West Europe are positioned very differently in the international system. It is not bragging to say that the US is the only remaining superpower whereas the European states can have much less influence on events. (This would, of course, change were Europe to be politically united, but of this there is no prospect.) This power disparity does not determine the substantive views of any of the states, but does indicate that they will see the world quite differently. The superpower has many fewer external restraints on it, and standard Realism indicates that it then will be less restrained in its behaviour.[8] Since the Europeans cannot mount significant military power it is to be expected that they will denigrate this instrument.

In his well-known book, Robert Kagan argued that 'Americans are from Mars, Europeans are from Venus' because of their different post-war experiences. Also frequently mentioned is the European distaste for the crude and bullying American style ('Bush is just a cowboy'). There is something to these positions, but are Europeans really so opposed to force and wedded to law? When faced with domestic terrorism, Germany and other European countries did not hesitate to employ unrestrained state power that John Ashcroft would envy, and their current treatment of minorities, especially Muslims, does not strike these minority populations as liberal. The French continue to intervene in Africa unilaterally, join other European states in playing as fast and loose with trade regulations as does the United States, and for some time has disregarded legal rulings to drop their ban on British beef. Most European states favoured the war in Kosovo despite the absence of UN sanction, supported the US in Afghanistan, and had they been attacked on September 11 might not have maintained their aversion to the use of force.

Even more glaringly, the claims for a deep cultural divide overlook the fundamental difference between how Europe and the United States are placed in the international system. The fact that the latter is hegemonic has three implications. First, only the US has the power to do anything about problems like Iraq; the others have incentives to ride free. Second, the large European states have every reason to be concerned about American hegemony and sufficient resources to seek to constrain it. This is not traditional power balancing, which is driven by security fears; the French are not afraid of an American attack, and the German worry is that the US will withdraw too many of its troops. But they both, and Europeans in general, do fear that a world dominated by the US would be one in which their values and interests would be served only at American sufferance. It is hardly surprising that an April 2002 poll showed that majorities within many European countries – often overwhelming majorities – felt that American policy towards Iraq and the Middle East was based 'mainly on its own interests'.[9] Condoleezza Rice had forgotten her knowledge of basic international politics when she expressed her shock that 'there were times that it appeared that American power was seen [by France and Germany] to be more dangerous than, perhaps, Saddam Hussein'.[10] The US may be correct that American dominance serves Europe and the world, but we should not be startled when others beg to differ. The US probably is as benign a hegemon as the world has ever seen. Its large domestic market, relatively tolerant values, domestic diversity, and geographic isolation all are helpful. But a hegemon it remains, and by that very fact it must make others uneasy.

Third, the Europeans' stress on the need to go through the Security Council shows less their attachment to law and world governance than their appreciation of power. France especially, but also non EU countries such as Russia and China (two countries that are not from Venus), will gain enormously from the principle that large-scale force can be used only with the approval of the Council, of which they are permanent members. Indeed, Security Council membership is one of the few major resources at these countries' disposal. The statement of a Russian leader that 'if someone tries to wage war on their own account, ... without an international mandate, it means all the world is confusion and a wild jungle'[11] would carry more moral weight if Russia did not have a veto in the mandate-granting body. When the Europeans – including those not on the Council – argue that intervention is only legitimate if carried out with a consensus or widespread international support, what is meant is widespread European support, not Russian, Chinese, or Third World approval.

More importantly, the US is acting like a normal state that has gained a position of dominance.[12] There are four facets to this argument. First, and most general, is the core of the realist outlook which is that power is checked most effectively – if not only – by counter-balancing power. Thucydides put these words into the mouths of the Athenians in the famous Melian dialogue, and while he disapproved and knew the attitude would bring ruin, he probably agreed with the generalization:

> Our opinion of the gods and our knowledge of men lead us to conclude that it is a general and necessary law of nature to rule wherever one can. This is not a law that we made ourselves, nor were we the first to act upon it when it was made. We found it already in existence, and we shall leave it to exist for ever among those who come after us. We are merely acting in accordance with it, and we know that you or anybody else with the same power as ours would be acting in precisely the same way.[13]

It follows from the propensity of states to use the power at their disposal that those who are not subject to external restraints tend to feel few restraints at all. As Edmund Burke put it, and a position endorsed by Hans Morgenthau: 'I dread our *own* power and our *own* ambition; I dread our being too much dreaded. It is ridiculous to say that we are not men, and that, as men, we shall never wish to aggrandize ourselves.'[14] With this as the driving idea, Waltz saw the likelihood of America's current behaviour from the start of the post-Cold War era:

> The powerful state may, and the United States does, think of itself as acting for the sake of peace, justice, and well-being in the world. But these terms will be defined to the liking of the powerful, which may conflict with the preferences and the interests of others. In international politics, overwhelming power repels and leads others to try to balance against it. With benign intent, the United States has behaved, and until its power is brought into a semblance of balance, will continue to behave in ways that annoy and frighten others.[15]

Parts of the Bush Doctrine are unique to the circumstances, but it is the exception rather than the rule for states to stay on the path of moderation when others do not force them to do so.[16]

Second and relatedly, states' definitions of their interests tend to expand as their power does.[17] It then becomes worth pursuing a whole host of objectives that were out of reach when the individual state's security was in doubt and all efforts had to be directed to primary objectives. With increases in power and security, states seek what Arnold Wolfers called 'milieu goals'.[18] The hope of spreading democracy and liberalism throughout the world has always been an American goal, but the lack of a peer competitor now makes it more realistic – although perhaps not very realistic – to actively strive for it. Seen in this light, the administration's perception that this is a time of great opportunity in the Middle East is the product not so much of the special circumstances in the region as of the enormous resources at America's disposal.

More specifically, the quick American victory in Afghanistan perhaps contributed to the expansion of American goals. Bush dropped the modifier 'with a global reach' from his war on terrorists and the US sent, first, military trainers, and then a combat unit to the Philippines to attack guerrillas who posed only a minimal threat to Americans and who had no significant links to Al Qaeda. Similarly, the easy military victory in Iraq initially encouraged thought of a wider agenda, and perhaps threatening force against other tyrants ('moving down the list' was the phrase often employed).[19]

A third structural explanation for American behaviour is that increased relative power brings with it new fears. The reasons are both objective and subjective. As Wolfers explained in his classic essay on 'National security as an ambiguous symbol', the latter can diverge from the former.[20] In one manifestation of this, as major threats disappear, people elevate ones that previously were seen as quite manageable.[21] Indeed, Americans seem to be as worried now as they were during the height of the Cold War despite the fact that a terrorist or rogue attack, even with weapons of mass destruction (WMD), could cause only a small fraction of World War II's devastation. But there is more to it than psychology. A dominant state acquires an enormous stake in the world order and interests spread throughout the globe. Most countries are primarily concerned with what happens in their neighbourhood; the world is the hegemon's neighbourhood, and it is not only hubris that leads it to be concerned with everything that happens anywhere. The result is a fusion of narrow and broad self-interest. At a point when most analysts were worried about the decline of American power, not its excesses, Waltz noted that for the US, 'like some earlier great powers ..., the interest of the country in security came to be identified with the maintenance of a certain world order. For countries at the top, this is predictable behavior. ...Once a state's interests reach a certain extent, they become self-reinforcing.'[22]

The historian John S. Galbraith explored the related dynamic of the 'turbulent frontier' that produced the unintended expansion of colonialism. As a European power gained an enclave in Africa or Asia, usually along a coast or river, it also gained an unpacified boundary that had to be policed. This led to further expansion of influence and often of settlement, and this in turn produced a new area that had to be protected and a new zone of threat.[23] There were few natural limits to this process. There are not likely to be many such limits now. The wars in Afghanistan and Iraq have led to the establishment of US bases and security commitments in central Asia, an area previously beyond reach. It is not hard to imagine how the US could be drawn further into politics in the region, and to find itself using force to oppose terrorist or guerrilla movements that arise there, perhaps in part in reaction to the American presence. The same dynamic could play out in Colombia and, according to recent reports, in Africa.[24]

The fourth facet can be seen as a broader conception of the previous point. As realists stress, even states that find the status quo acceptable have to worry about the future.[25] Indeed, the more an actor sees the current situation as satisfactory, the more it will expect the future to be worse. Psychology is important here too: prospect theory argues that actors are prone to accept great risks when they believe that they will suffer losses unless they act boldly. The adoption of a preventive war doctrine may be a mistake, especially if taken too far, but is not foreign to normal state behaviour, and it has special appeal for states that have a valued position to maintain. However secure states are, only rarely can they be secure enough, and if they are currently very powerful they will feel strong impulses to act now to prevent a deterioration that could allow others to harm them in the future.[26]

All this means that under the Bush Doctrine the US is not a status quo power. Its motives may not be selfish, but the combination of power, fear, and perceived opportunity lead it to seek to reshape world politics and the societies of many members of the world community. This tracks with and extends old ideas of the US as a revolutionary country. As the first modern democracy, the US was founded on principles of equality, progress, and a government subordinate to civil society that, while initially being uniquely American, had universal appeal and applicability. Indeed, not only Bush today, but many Americans in previous eras believed that because a state's foreign policy is inseparable from its domestic regime, a safe and peaceful world requires the spread of these arrangements.[27] Under current conditions of terrorism and WMD, tyrannical governments pose too great a danger to be tolerated. The world cannot stand still. Without strong American intervention, the international environment will become more menacing to America and its values, but with strong leadership the US can increase its security and produce a better world. In a process akin to the deep security dilemma,[28] in order to protect itself the US is impelled to act in a way that will increase or at least bring to the surface conflicts with others. Even if the situation is satisfactory, it cannot be maintained by purely defensive measures. Making the world safe for American democracy is believed to require that dictatorial regimes be banished, or at least prevented from acquiring weapons of mass destruction.

Under current circumstances, the US does not have to worry much about either entrapment or abandonment, but its allies have to worry about both. The form entrapment takes in the 'war on terror' is different from the past, but the basic dynamic is the same: allies fear that the heavy-handed US response to the threat is creating more terrorism and focusing it on them as well as the US. But they also worry that the US will withdraw from Europe, if not from foreign affairs, and leave them exposed to terrorism, Russia, and each other. This means that they must scrutinize American history, American behaviour, and – particularly important – American domestic politics in order to perceive and predict whether the US is likely to endanger them in either of these ways. Contrary to the currently popular claims that democracies are relatively transparent, easy to predict, and able to bind themselves to behaviour consistently and cooperatively in the future, American allies know that it is hard to tell what the US will do.

Do these uncertainties and the current frictions mean that the Western world (plus Japan) no longer constitutes a security community (i.e. a group of countries among which war is unthinkable)? I do not believe so. Note that the existence of a security community among the world's leading country is unprecedented and constitutes a truly revolutionary change in world politics.[29] Some scholars believe that the current intra-alliance tensions put it in doubt and others argue that it would disintegrate if the US were to withdraw its forces from Europe, but this is unduly alarmist. The forces that make it inconceivable that the allies would fight each other are very deep and very strong. This does not mean the end of intra-alliance disputes, manoeuvrings against each other, and the need to try to estimate what partners will do. Indeed, the very fact that, even in the worst case, war will not occur can sharpen disputes since the states are not restrained by the fear that war can result if they overstep. So the existence of a security community means that intra-alliance relations will have a somewhat different character than such relations had in the past when everyone knew not only that the alliance might break (that is still the case), but that if it did, its members might fight each other. But conflicts of interest and perceptual differences will remain, and they may interfere with attempts to realize the gains from cooperation. So the existence of biases conducive to misperception is still important.

Perceptions and Beliefs

As with all perceptions, two fundamental kinds of biases can be located. One set are 'cold' or cognitive biases. These represent instances in which the person or state is trying to be fully rational, but given the complexity of the world, needs to employ short cuts to rationality that can lead us astray. The other category are 'hot' or motivated biases and stem from factors other than reality appraisal, particularly the need for psychological and social adjustment. Let me talk briefly about each.[30]

Cognitive Biases

Many of our beliefs are dominated by the need to understand our environments and almost all of them embody an element of this objective. What is central is the fact that the world is so complex and our information processing capabilities so limited that in significant measure people must be theory-driven. Beliefs are hard won from our world and so it is not only ego that leads us to be quite attached to them. Although this model of people as 'cognitive misers'[31] needs to be modified by the findings that people will deploy more cognitive resources in areas that are most important to them, that people vary in the extent to which they are theory-driven, and that people who are more open to discrepant evidence tend to make more accurate predictions,[32] there remains much to the basic argument.

Four implications follow for how beliefs operate. First, people are strongly influenced by their expectations: people tend to see what they expect to see. In international politics perhaps the most striking examples come from cases of surprise attack.[33] The Israelis were certain that Egypt lacked the military strength to attack in 1973 and so misinterpreted what in hindsight were obvious tip-offs that an attack was coming; in April 1940, the British and Norwegians were so sure that Germany would not expose its forces to British naval superiority that they were unmoved by Germany's sinking a transport containing German soldiers who told them that they were on their way to invade Norway; when Secretary of War Stimson was told of the Japanese attack on Pearl Harbor, he said 'My God, this can't be true. This [message] must mean the Philippines,' which was where he had expected the attack; when a Soviet front-line unit reported (June 1941) coming under German artillery fire as the latter country attacked, it received the reply, 'You must be insane. And why is your signal not in code?'[34]

Of course these cases are selected on the basis of the dependent variable because we are looking only at instances where surprise occurred. This makes it impossible for us to say that this cognitive bias is a central cause of the error. Indeed most correct conclusions are also strongly influenced by expectations, leading to the second implication of the role of theory-driven beliefs, which is that an inference is most likely to be accepted when it is seen as plausible – i.e. when it fits with more general beliefs. This is why almost everyone interpreted the scattered and ambiguous evidence as showing that Saddam Hussein had vigorous WMD programmes.[35] This inference made a great deal of sense, as the regime had used gas against Iran and its own Kurds, pursued nuclear weapons before the 1990 Gulf War, initially tried to maintain these programmes despite UN sanctions, and engaged in a great deal of denial and deception. Without this background, the intelligence reports would have been read very differently.

The third general proposition is that judgements of plausibility can be self-reinforcing because ambiguous evidence often is taken not only to be consistent with pre-existing beliefs, but to confirm them. Logically, the latter is the case only when the evidence both fits with the belief and does not fit with competing ones. But people rarely probe the latter possibility as carefully as they should, assuming it instead.

The fourth implication of theory-driven processing is that the model of Bayesian updating cannot fully apply.[36] The basic point of Bayesianism is that people should and do modify their beliefs according to the likelihood that observed new events or information should occur if the prior beliefs are correct. The difficulty is that people who hold different beliefs will see the new event or information in different ways and there is no objective arbiter to which we can appeal for verification. This is not a problem when we are trying to adjust our estimate of whether a jar has more blue balls than red ones when balls are drawn out at random. The evidence of a ball's colour is clear enough so that people can agree on it irrespective of their prior thoughts. But this is usually not true in politics. For example, supporters of the Bush administration would argue that the events in countries like Lebanon and Egypt in the months following the Iraqi elections in January 2005 show how the American policy is reshaping the Middle East. Those who disagree not only argue that their beliefs need not be changed because they are underpinned by so much other evidence, but dispute the interpretation of these events themselves, seeing them as either superficial or as products of internal politics. In other words, the inevitable impact of priors on the understanding of new 'facts' undercuts the thrust of a significant part of the Bayesian model.

Although – and because – we need theories, strong beliefs, and expectations in order to make any sense of our complex and contradictory world, reality appraisal can lead us astray. But, more importantly, this is not the only impulse shaping our beliefs, as Smith, Bruner, and White (1956) so clearly showed.

Functions of Beliefs

The fact that beliefs serve functions other than reality appraisal casts doubt on their causal role. A full understanding of how beliefs operate requires backward as well as forward linkages; we need to look for the causes as well as the consequences of the beliefs in order to see whether the connection between beliefs and behaviour is spurious with both being driven by a common third factor. Beliefs may be rationalizations for policies as well as rationales for them. When social, political, and personal needs are strong, the results can be summarized by the saying, 'If you want something really bad, you will get it really bad.' The explanations for why a policy is adopted and why it was carried out so incompetently often are linked, as the need to see that it can succeed will diminish reality appraisal and draw the actor into a conceptual and perceptual world that, while comfortable, cannot provide good guidance for behaviour.

If the discussion of reality appraisal and how it goes wrong is linked to cognitive biases, the functions of beliefs are linked to motivated ones.[37] People's need to work with others, further their political goals, and live with themselves tap into their emotions and drive them to certain beliefs. A classic demonstration is the study by Hastorf and Cantril, 'They saw a game' (1954).[38] Purely cognitive biases cannot explain why students at Dartmouth and Princeton who viewed films of a penalty-filled game between their two football teams saw the other side as at fault. When we look at elite beliefs and decision-making, we see four overlapping areas in which motivated biases are at work and beliefs are highly functional. These are the hesitancy to recognize painful value trade-offs, the psychological and political need for people to see that their policies will work, the impact on beliefs of goals and feelings of which people are unaware, and the propensity of people to infer their own beliefs from how they behave.

One can reply that these sorts of functional pressures are unlikely because they imply knowledge of the very cognitions that people are trying to ward off, if not the conclusions to which they are being steered. At times, the line between awareness and lack of it is very thin. People often say things like, 'I don't think that this is something I want to hear about', or 'That is a subject we are better off not analyzing.'[39] But beyond this borderline, a great deal of cognitive processing is preconscious and the understanding that a certain position *must* be affirmed can affect the person's thinking without their being aware of it. One does not have to accept Freudian notions of the unconscious and repression to conclude that we can be strongly influenced by impulses of which we are unaware. The requirement for bolstering beliefs can be triggered by the implicit realization that the decision is a hard one and that more thorough analysis could lead to high conflict. When people lack good choices, they are likely to imagine that the one they select is better than it actually is.

Varied forms of self-deception are common in politics, but they are not unique to this realm – as novels make clear. Scientists also feel the same social and psychological pressures, and Richard Feynman famously said to his fellow-scientists: 'The first principle is that you must not fool yourself – and you are the easiest person to fool.' This is one reason why errors in science are often detected by people not involved in the original discoveries and why it might be argued that the scientific community cannot be trusted to make unbiased judgements about the danger of experiments and technologies in which it has a large stake.

Avoiding Painful Trade-Offs

In difficult political and psychological situations, reality appraisal – far from pointing the way out – can be a menace to the person or political actor if the reality it points to is too painful to contemplate. My first discussion of the tendency to avoid value trade-offs[40] treated it as cognitive, but this was a mistake because its roots are primarily motivated or functional. Although people often have to make trade-offs – budgets, for example, force them on us – avoidance is often possible and necessary.[41] People are especially prone to shy away from trade-offs when dealing with incommensurable realms and moral choices,[42] which explains why those who oppose the use of torture on moral grounds resist the argument that its use might save lives. I would similarly predict that if Bush and his colleagues decide that the prospect of Iranian nuclear weapons is truly intolerable, they will come to see the negative consequences of an air strike as quite small.

The desire to avoid trade-offs is clear in the discussion of Iraq. As a soldier's mother put it: 'I know my son's there for a reason. And whatever might happen, that's the way it's supposed to be. And if I took it any other way, I'd be in a funny farm.'[43] Elites do not put it this revealingly, but their beliefs often serve the same functions. Thus proponents of the war had more reasons than they needed to support the war: they believed that Saddam might give Al Qaeda weapons of mass destruction, that he could not be deterred from regional adventures if he acquired nuclear weapons, that the war would be easy, that the US had to show its military might and resolve in order to shock terrorists, that the political reconstruction of Iraq would go well, and that this project would produce wide-ranging and favourable effects in the region. Opponents of the war differed on all these points. What is crucial in this context is that these beliefs were not logically linked, which means that if reality testing were shaping them, then there should have been many people who believed that while the war was necessary, it would be very costly, or who thought that while threat was present, opportunity was not (or vice versa), or that the war would be cheap, but was not necessary. But these positions are uncomfortable, and so it is not surprising that we do not find people taking them. For political leaders as well as the mother quoted earlier, if they took it any other way, they'd be in a funny farm.

Policies Call Up Supporting Beliefs

The second and relating functional source of foreign policy beliefs is the pressure generated by policies. One reason why political leaders are slow to see that their policies are failing is that good reality appraisal would force them to acknowledge the high costs and risks they are facing. Thus building on the psychological work on defensive avoidance, Richard Ned Lebow and others have shown that if the actor is committed to proceeding, even highly credible threats by the adversary are likely to be missed, misinterpreted, or ignored.[44] This is one reason why attempts to explain wars as the product of rational choices on both sides will often fail, just as the policies themselves fail.

One of the hallmarks of the functional source of beliefs is that planning on the surface looks meticulous, but in fact is terribly deficient because it is built on unrealistic and unexamined assumptions. As Isabel Hull notes in regard to German thinking about colonial warfare in the early twentieth century, 'realistic planning would have revealed the impossibility of the grand goals; rather than giving these up, planning itself was truncated'.[45] Indeed, when a part of the organization does engage in effective reality appraisal, it may be neutered, as was the case with a planning division in the Japanese army in the 1930s.[46] It is tempting to dismiss such failings as the product of military culture, but the US Forest Service, committed to stamping out all forest fires, disbanded its research arm when it showed that healthy forests required periodic burning.[47]

British planning, throughout the 1930s, for the bombardment of Germany illustrates the ways in which beliefs supporting the efficacy of a policy can be shielded from reality appraisal. The incredible costs of fighting World War I not only contributed to the subsequent appeasement policy, but also convinced the British that if war were to come, they could not fight it as they had done before. A way out was strategic bombardment that could deter devastating German air attacks on Britain and win the war without having to suffer the horrendous losses of ground warfare. It then *had* to be true that an effective bomber force could be developed, and supporting beliefs were called up to meet this demand. So it is not surprising that British planners convinced themselves that the bomb loads their planes could carry would be sufficient to do grave damage to German industries and cities, that British bombers could fly without protection from fighter escorts, that the aircraft could readily find their targets, and that bombing would be accurate. Although many plans were cranked out, these central assumptions were never scrutinized. In fact, even rudimentary questioning and military exercises would have revealed that German cities were obscured by clouds much of the year, that navigation systems were not adequate to direct planes to them, that bombs would miss their targets, and that even direct hits would rarely put factories out of action for long.[48] A history of Bomber Command notes that 'seldom in the history of warfare has a force been so sure of the end it sought – fulfillment of the Trenchard doctrine [of strategic bombardment] – and yet so ignorant of how this might be achieved as the RAF between the wars'.[49] In fact, the certainty with which the ends were espoused and the ignorance about means were closely linked. Reality appraisal was unacceptable because it would have called the highly valued goals into question.

The same pressures for beliefs to support policy explain many of the deficiencies in American planning for the aftermath of the overthrow of Saddam. Reality appraisal would have been politically and psychologically painful; to have recognized that reconstruction was likely to be long, costly, and uncertain would have been to give ammunition to the war's critics. When confronted with the Army Chief of Staff's estimate that it would take several hundred thousand troops to garrison Iraq, Deputy Secretary of Defense Paul Wolfowitz told Congress: 'it's hard to conceive that it would take more forces to provide stability in post-Saddam Iraq than it would take to conduct the war itself. ... Hard to imagine'.[50] This was indeed a failure of imagination, but under these circumstances imagination could not be allowed free rein. It is hard to ask important questions and conduct unbiased analysis when the answers may be unacceptable.

Beliefs Supporting the Established Order

The third function of beliefs is much broader, consisting of people's conceptions of the political and social structures that gratify them. In his pioneering study, Walter Lippmann argued that stereotypes form not only because they permit 'economy of effort', but because they 'may be the core of our personal tradition, the defenses of our position in society.' Marxists – and cynics – analyse the beliefs of the ruling classes in this way.[51] During the Cold War, members of the political and economic elite who incorrectly said that the establishment of revolutionary regimes anywhere in the world would menace American security interests were not lying. Rather, the knowledge that such regimes would adversely affect their economic interests led them to believe that American national security was at stake as well. People in the upper income brackets can cite many reasons why cutting their taxes would benefit the entire economy and pull others out of poverty. These beliefs, which can involve somewhat complicated economics, are not insincere, but they nevertheless derive from personal interest.

Beliefs about what is right just may have similar roots. E. H. Carr famously showed how the morality espoused by status quo states nicely justified the prevailing arrangements that suited them so well;[52] most Americans join President Bush in believing that the vigorous exercise of American power abroad is in the world's interest. Looking within US society, trial lawyers believe that unimpeded access to the courts for liability and class action suits is the best way to control rapacious companies; police officers believe that the establishment of civilian oversight boards will encourage criminals to produce false claims and defy the police; professors believe that government support for universities in general and their specializations in particular will produce a stronger and better society (but that government direction of research harms these goals). Some or all of these beliefs may be correct, but they are remarkably convenient.

Beliefs Produced by Actions

In contrast to the usual method of explaining actions by the beliefs that we think generated them, the previous pages have discussed how beliefs form to provide rationalizations for actions. In the final category of cases, actions not only produce beliefs, but, once formed, these new beliefs influence later actions. The theory was developed over 30 years ago by Daryl Bem, and the basic point is related to the one noted above that people often do not know why they act as they do. They then implicitly analyse their own behaviour in the same way that they analyse that of others and ask what beliefs and motives could have been responsible for it.[53] Answers like inadvertence, fleeting impulses, the desire to do something and get on with it, all seem inappropriate if not frivolous and, although often correct, are rejected. Instead, the person looks for more serious and lasting beliefs and motives, and then attributes their own behaviour to them. This would be no more than a psychological curiosity if the effects stopped there. But, once formed, these explanations guide future behaviour. If I think that I gave money on one occasion because I am a generous person, I will give more in the future; if as a national leader I ordered the use of force to free hostages, I must believe that this instrument is efficacious and therefore should respond similarly in other situations; if as president I gave a stiff response to another country, it must be because that state is deeply hostile and that deterrence if not force is required to meet it.

The last example is not hypothetical but is the foundation for Deborah Larson's fascinating analysis of the psychological origins of American Cold War policy.[54] Most scholars have seen Truman's containment policy as growing out of his steady response to increasing Soviet provocations. Revisionist scholars disagree, seeing the impulse as being generated by the need to keep the world open to capitalist penetration, but they too explain Truman's actions as following from his beliefs, albeit ones that were formed by the functional process noted previously. Larson argues that both these views fail to see that Truman was at first unsure of himself and inconsistent, and that his position hardened only after he came to interpret his hesitant steps as implying that the Soviet Union was aggressive and could only be countered by firmness. Having attributed these beliefs to himself, Truman then acted on them more consistently.

Conclusions

Alliance relations, like the rest of international politics – and indeed of human life – are characterized by differing perspectives and perceptual distortions. We can understand international interactions only by taking account of the multiple forces that produce individual and national beliefs. What people see in the world, in others, and in themselves is driven heavily by their expectations and their social and psychological needs. The 'objective situation', although rarely irrelevant, is also rarely determinative. As the members of the Western Alliance learn to make their way in a new world, they will have to cope with not only their differences in interests, but also in perceptions. Indeed, misperceptions are perhaps more dangerous among allies than among adversaries because allies have high expectations of mutual understanding and cooperation. As Neustadt puts it in his study of Anglo-American relations: 'paranoid reactions are associated with relations bearing something like the burden of an unrequited love'.[55] This is something that we as scholars and the leaders of the Western Alliance would be well advised to bear in mind in the coming years.

Notes

1 The best book on alliance is Glenn Snyder, *Alliance Politics* (Ithaca, NY: Cornell University Press, 1997); also see George Liska, *Nations in Alliance* (Baltimore, MD: Johns Hopkins University Press, 1962).
2 The best collection is in the special issue of *Intelligence and National Security*, vol. 13, Spring 1998, also published as Martin Alexander, ed., *Knowing Your Friends: Intelligence Inside Alliances Coalitions From 1914 to the Cold War* (London: Frank Cass, 1998).
3 Bernard Finel and Kristin Lord, eds, *Power and Conflict in the Age of Transparency* (New York: Palgrave, 2000).
4 Richard Neustadt, *Alliance Politics* (New York: Columbia University Press, 1970), R. Neustadt, *Report to JFK: The Skybolt Crisis in Perspective* (Ithaca, NY: Cornell University Press, 1999).
5 Marc Trachtenberg, *A Constructed Peace* (Princeton, NJ: Princeton University Press, 1999).
6 Snyder, *Alliance Politics*.
7 This section draws on my *American Foreign Policy in a New Era* (New York: Routledge, 2005).
8 Robert Jervis, *American Foreign Policy in a New Era* (New York: Routledge, 2005).
9 Adam Clymer, 'European Poll Faults U.S. for its Policy in the Mid East', *New York Times*, 19 April 2002.
10 Quoted in David Sanger, 'Witness to Auschwitz Evil, Bush Draws a Lesson', ibid., 1 June 2003.
11 Quoted in John Tagliabue, 'France and Russia Ready to Use Veto Against Iraq War', ibid., 6 March 2003.
12 Thus it is not entirely surprising that many of the beliefs mustered in support of US policy towards Iraq parallel those held by European expansionists in earlier eras: Jack Snyder, 'Imperial Temptations', *National Interest*, No. 71, Spring 2003, pp. 29–40.
13 *The Peloponnesian War*, Rex Warner, trans. (Harmondsworth, Middlesex: Penguin, 1954), p. 363. I should note that this generalization, although apparently secure, rests to a considerable extent on our searching on the dependent variable. That is, we are drawn to cases of such expansion because they are dramatic, especially when they come to grief, and lack a systematic way of looking for instances in which a state had the ability to expand its sphere of influence but declined to do so.
14 Quoted in Hans Morgenthau, *Politics Among Nations*, 5th edn, revised (New York: Knopf, 1978), pp. 169–70, emphasis in the original.

15 Kenneth Waltz, 'America as a Model for the World? A Foreign Policy Perspective', *PS: Political Science and Politics*, vol. 24, December 1991, p. 69; also see Waltz's discussion of the Gulf War: 'A Necessary War?' in Harry Kriesler, ed., *Confrontation in the Gulf* (Berkeley: Institute of International Studies, 1992), pp. 59–65. Charles Krauthammer also expected this kind of behaviour, but believed that it would serve the world as well as the American interests: Krauthammer, 'The Unipolar Moment', *Foreign Affairs, America and the World, 1990–91*, vol. 70, No. 1, pp. 23–33; also see Krauthammer, 'The Unipolar Moment Revisited' *The National Interest* 70 (Winter 2002): 5–17. For a critical analysis, see James Chace, 'Imperial America and the Common Interest' *World Policy Journal*, vol. XIX, No.1, Spring 2002. As Waltz noted much earlier, even William Fulbright, while decrying the arrogance of American power, said that the US could and should 'lead the world in an effort to change the nature of its politics': quoted in *Theory of International Politics* (Reading, MA: Addison-Wesley, 1979), p. 201.

16 Alexander Wendt and, more persuasively, Paul Schroeder would disagree or at least modify this generalization, arguing that prevailing ideas can and have led to more moderate and consensual behavior: Wendt, *Social Theory of International Politics* (New York: Cambridge University Press, 1999); Schroeder, *The Transformation of European Politics, 1763–1848* (New York: Oxford University Press, 1994), and 'Does the History of International Politics Go Anywhere?' in David Wetzel and Theodore Hamerow, eds, *International Politics and German History* (Westport: Praeger, 1997), pp. 15–36. This is a central question of international politics and history that I cannot fully discuss here, but I believe that at least the mild statement that unbalanced power is dangerous can easily be sustained.

17 See, for example, Fareed Zakaria, 'Realism and Domestic Politics: A Review Essay', *International Security*, vol. 17, Summer 1992, pp. 177–98; Robert Tucker, *The Radical Left and American Foreign Policy* (Baltimore, MD: Johns Hopkins University Press, 1971), pp. 69–70, 74–77, 106–11; Stephen Van Evera, *Causes of War: Power and the Roots of Conflict* (Ithaca, NY: Cornell University Press, 1999), p. 86. This process is also fed by the psychological resistance to giving up any position once it is gained: see Jeffrey Taliaferro, *Balancing Risks: Great Power Intervention in the Periphery* (Ithaca, NY: Cornell University Press, 2004). For a discussion of alternative possibilities suggested by American history, see Edward Rhodes, 'The Imperial Logic of Bush's Liberal Agenda', *Survival*, vol. 45, No. 1, Spring 2003, pp. 131–54.

18 Arnold Wolfers, *Discord and Collaboration* (Baltimore, MD: Johns Hopkins University Press, 1962), ch. 5.

19 The process may also work in reverse. The Soviet foreign policy advisor Georgi Arbatov is reported to have said that 'our very poor military performance in Afghanistan saved Poland. If we had been able to achieve our goals in Afghanistan reasonably quickly, I have no doubt we would have invaded Poland too': quoted in David Arbel and Ran Edelist, *Western Intelligence and the Collapse of the Soviet Union, 1980–1990* (London: Frank Cass, 2003), p. 89. The declassified records reveal other considerations (see the articles and records in *Cold War International History Project Bulletin*, Issue 11, Winter 1998 (Washington, DC: Woodrow Wilson Center for Scholars, 1998), pp. 3–133), but this factor may have played a role as well. Similarly both President Kennedy and his brother Robert said that had the Bay of Pigs not led him (the President) to mistrust military advice and military solutions, he probably would have used force in Laos: Nigel Ashton, *Kennedy, Macmillan, and the Cold War: The Irony of Interdependence* (New York: Palgrave, 2002), p. 41; Edwin Guthman and Jeffrey Shulman, eds, *Robert Kennedy: In His Own Words* (New York: Bantam, 1971), pp. 13, 247.

20 Arnold Wolfers, *Discord and Collaboration: Essays on International Politics*, Baltimore, MD: The Johns Hopkins University Press, 1962, ch. 10.

21 John Mueller, 'The Catastrophe Quota: Trouble after the Cold War', *Journal of Conflict Resolution*, vol. 38, September 1994, pp. 355–75; also see Frederick Hartmann, *The Conservation of Enemies: A Study in Enmity* (Westport, CT: Greenwood Press, 1982).

22 Waltz, *Theory of International Politics*, p. 200.

23 John S. Galbraith, 'The "Turbulent Frontier" as a Factor in British Expansion', *Comparative Studies in Society and History*, vol. 2, January 1960, pp. 34–48; idem, *Reluctant Empire: British Policy on the South African Frontier, 1834–1854* (Berkeley, CA: University of California Press, 1963). Also see Ronald Robinson and John Gallagher with Alice Denny, *Africa and the Victorians: The Official Mind of Imperialism* (London: Macmillan, 1961); John LeDonne, *The Grand Strategy of the Russian Empire, 1650–1831* (New York: Oxford University Press, 2004). Chalmers Johnson notes the great spread of American military bases throughout the world: *The Sorrows of Empire: Militarism, Secrecy, and the End of the Republic* (New York: Metropolitan Books, 2004). A related imperial dynamic that is likely to recur is that turning a previously recalcitrant state into a client usually weakens it internally and requires further intervention.

24 Craig Smith, 'U.S. Training African Forces to Uproot Terrorists', *New York Times*, 11 May 2004.

25 Dale Copeland, *The Origins of Major War* (Ithaca, NY: Cornell University Press, 2000); also see John Mearsheimer, *The Tragedy of Great Power Politics* (New York: Norton, 2001). For important conceptual distinctions and propositions about preventive war, see Jack Levy, 'Declining Power and the Preventive Motivation for War', *World Politics*, vol. 40, October 1987, pp. 82–107 and, for a study that is sceptical of the general prevalence of preventive wars but presents one example, Levy and Joseph Gochal, 'Democracy and Preventive War: Israel and the 1956 Sinai Campaign', *Security Studies*, vol. 11, Winter 2001/02, pp. 1–49. On the US experience, see Robert Art, *A Grand Strategy for America* (Ithaca, NY: Cornell University Press, 2003), pp. 181–97. Randall Schweller argues that democratic states fight preventively only under very restrictive circumstances: 'Domestic Structure and Preventive War: Are Democracies More Pacific?' *World Politics*, vol. 44, January 1992, pp. 235–69, and notes the unusual nature of the cases involving Israel. For the argument that states are generally well served by resisting the temptation to fight preventively, see Richard Betts, 'Striking First: A History of Thankfully Lost Opportunities', *Ethics and International Affairs*, vol. 17, No. 1, 2003, pp. 17–24. For a review of power transition theory, which in one interpretation is driven by preventive motivation, see Jacek Kugler and Douglas Lemke, *Parity and War: Evaluations and Extensions of The War Ledger* (Ann Arbor, MI: University of Michigan Press, 1996).

26 Waltz sees this behaviour as often self-defeating; Mearsheimer implies that it is not; Copeland's position is somewhere in between.

27 Bush would endorse Wilson's claim that America's goal must be 'the destruction of every arbitrary power anywhere in the world that can separately, secretly, and of its single choice disturb the peace of the world', just as he would join his predecessor in calling for 'the spread of his revolt [i.e. the American revolution], this liberation, to the great stage of the world itself!' 'An Address at Mount Vernon', 4 July 1918, in Arthur Link *et al.*, eds, *The Papers of Woodrow Wilson*, vol. 48, *May 13–July 17, 1918* (Princeton, NJ: Princeton University Press, 1985), pp. 516–17.

28 Robert Jervis, 'Was the Cold War a Security Dilemma?' *Journal of Cold War History*, vol. 3, Winter 2001, pp. 36–60; also see Paul Roe, 'Former Yugoslavia: The Security Dilemma That Never Was?' *European Journal of International Relations*, vol. 6, September 2000, pp. 373–93. The current combination of fear and hope that produces offensive actions for defensive motives resembles the combination that produced the pursuit of preponderance in the aftermath of

World War II: Melvyn Leffler, *A Preponderance of Power: National Security, the Truman Administration, and the Cold War* (Stanford, CA: Stanford University Press, 1992), especially pp. 50–52.

29 I felt this point was so important that I made it the subject of my adress as president of the American Political Science Association in 2001 and included it as the first chapter of *American Foreign Policy in a New Era*.

30 This discussion is drawn from my 'Understanding Beliefs', *Political Psychology*, forthcoming.

31 See for example Susan T. Fiske and Shelley E. Taylor, *Social Cognition* (New York: McGraw-Hill, 1991).

32 See for example Shelley Chaiken, 'Heuristic Versus Systematic Information Processing', *Journal of Personality and Social Psychology*, vol. 39, 1980, pp. 752–66; and Philip Tetlock, *Expert Political Judgment: How Good is It? How Can We Know?* (Princeton, NJ: Princeton University Press, 2005).

33 The literature is very large: key works include Richard Betts, *Surprise Attack* (Washington, DC: The Brookings Institution, 1982); Barton Whaley, *Codeword Barbarossa* (Cambridge, MA: MIT Press, 1973); Roberta Wohlstetter, *Pearl Harbor: Warning and Decision* (Stanford, CA: Stanford University Press, 1962); also see Robert Jervis, *Perception and Misperception in International Politics* (Princeton, NJ: Princeton University Press, 1976), ch. 4.

34 Quoted in Harry Ransom, *Central Intelligence and National Security* (Cambridge, MA: Harvard University Press, 1958), p. 54; quoted in John Erickson, *The Soviet High Command* (London: Macmillan, 1962), p. 587.

35 Robert Jervis, 'Reports, Politics, and Intelligence Failures: The case of Iraq', *Journal of Strategic Studies*, vol. 29, February 2006, pp. 3–52.

36 For a good review of research on Bayesianism and political attitudes, see Alan Gerber and Donald Green, 'Bias', *Annual Review of Political Science*, vol. 2 (Palo Alto, CA: Annual Reviews Press, 1999), pp. 189–210.

37 On the difficulties and possibilities of separating kinds of biases, see Chaim D. Kaufmann, 'Out of the Lab and Into the Archives: A Method for Testing Psychological Explanations of Political Decision Making', *International Studies Quarterly*, vol. 38, December 1994, pp. 557–86; Philip E. Tetlock and Ariel Levi, 'Attribution Bias: On the Inconclusiveness of the Cognition-Motivation Debate', *Journal of Experimental Social Psychology*, vol. 18, 1982, pp. 68–88. For a general discussion of motivated processing, see Steven Spencer, Steven Fein, Mark Zanna, and James Olson, eds, *Motivated Social Perception: The Ontario Symposium*, vol. 9 (Mahwah, NJ: Erlbaum, 2003).

38 Albert H. Hastorf, and Hadley Cantril, 'They Saw a Game', *Journal of Abnormal and Social Psychology*, vol. 49, 1954, pp. 129–34.

39 The importance of pre-conscious processing helps explain why many decisions, including ones that prove to be very successful, are made quickly and intuitively rather than on the basis of prolonged calculation: Deborah Larson, 'Truman and the Berlin Blockade: The Role of Intuition and Experience in Good Foreign Policy Judgment', in *Good Judgment in Foreign Policy: Theory and Application*, eds, Deborah Larson and Stanley Renshon (Lanham, MD: Rowman & Littlefield, 2003), pp. 127–52; Malcolm Gladwell, *Blink: The Power of Thinking Without Thinking* (New York: Little Brown, 2004). This also means that the person's sense that there are no viable alternatives to their policy that triggers the functional pressures may be incorrect and that a fuller and less biased search could have led to a better outcome, as we will discuss below. Under US law, being wilfully blind to facts or the likely consequences of one's actions can make the person legally culpable and the 'ostrich' defence is of questionable value: Jeremy Baker and Rebecca Young, 'False Statements and False Claims', *American Criminal Law Review*, vol. 42, 2005, pp. 427–62; William H. Simon, 'Wrongs of Ignorance and

Ambiguity: Lawyer Responsibility for Collective Misconduct', *Columbia Public Law & Legal Theory Working Paper*, No. 0480, 2004.

40 Jervis, *Perception and Misperception*, pp. 128–42.

41 For strongly political interpretations that argue that leaders sometimes can succeed in avoiding trade-offs, see Barbara Farnham, *Roosevelt and the Munich Crisis: A Study of Political Decision-Making* (Princeton, NJ: Princeton University Press, 1997); Richard E. Neustadt, 'Presidents, Politics and Analysis', paper presented at the Graduate School of Public Affairs, University of Washington, Seattle, 1986. Although there are obvious political reasons why people would want to downplay the costs of their preferred policies even if they were aware of them, the beliefs discussed here seem to have been sincere and were expressed in private as well as in public.

42 A. P. Fiske and P. E. Tetlock, 'Taboo Trade-Offs: Reactions to Transactions that Transgress the Spheres of Justice', *Political Psychology*, vol. 18, 1997, pp. 255–97.

43 Quoted in Sasha Abramsky, 'Supporting the Troops, Doubting the War', *The Nation*, 4 October 2004, p. 11.

44 Irving Janis and Leon Mann, *Decision Making: A Psychological Analysis of Conflict, Choice, and Commitment* (New York: Free Press, 1977); Richard Ned Lebow, *Between Peace and War: The Nature of International Crisis* (Baltimore, MD: The Johns Hopkins University Press, 1981); Robert Jervis, Richard Ned Lebow, and Janice Gross Stein, *Psychology and Deterrence* (Baltimore, MD: Johns Hopkins University Press, 1985).

45 Isabel V. Hull, *Absolute Destruction: Military Culture and the Practices of War in Imperial Germany* (Ithaca, NY: Cornell University Press, 2005), p. 143; see Holger H. Herwig, 'Germany', in Richard F. Hamilton and Holger H. Herwig, eds, *The Origins of World War I* (Cambridge: Cambridge University Press), p. 155 for a similar discussion of German planning for World War I.

46 Michael Barnhart, *Japan Prepares for Total War* (Ithaca, NY: Cornell University Press 1987), pp. 200–202, 240, 258.

47 Ashley L. Schiff, *Fire and Water: Scientific Heresy in the Forest Service* (Cambridge, MA: Harvard University Press, 1962), pp. 169–73.

48 John R. Carter, *Airpower and the Cult of the Offensive* (Maxwell Air Force Base, AL: Air University Press, 1998); Robert Jervis, 'Deterrence and Perception', *International Security*, vol. 7, Winter 1982/83, pp. 3–30.

49 Max Hastings, *Bomber Command* (New York: Dial Press 1979), p. 44.

50 Quoted in Peter Slevin and Dana Priest, 'Wolfowitz Concedes Iraq Errors', *Washington Post*, 24 July 2003.

51 Walter Lippmann, *Public Opinion* (New York: Macmillan, 1922), p. 95.

52 E. H. Carr, *The Twenty Years' Crisis: 1919–1939* (New York: Harper Torchbooks, 1946).

53 Daryl J. Bem, 'Self-Perception Theory', in *Advances in Experimental Social Psychology*, vol. 6, ed. Leonard Berkowitz (New York: Academic Press 1972), pp. 1–62.; also see Eldar Shafir, Itamar Simonson, and Amos Tversky, 'Reason-Based Choice', *Cognition*, vol. 49, 1993, pp. 11–36.

54 Deborah Larson, *Origins of Containment* (Princeton, NJ: Princeton University Press, 1985).

55 Neustadt, *Alliance Politics*, p. 56.

3   Foreign Policy and Transatlantic Relations

A Matter of Perceptions, Images, Objectives, and Decisions

Rubén Herrero de Castro

In international relations, as in everyday life, relations between actors exist both in terms of social interaction and in terms of interactions between images of the actors. The manner in which actors manage and project their images will thus inevitably play a key role in the field of foreign policy and transatlantic relations. The key word here is perceptions, and related to this concept, according to Robert Jervis, we can point to the existence of two environments:[1] first, the operational milieu: reality as it truly exists, in which the policies will be carried out; second, the psychological milieu: reality as the actor perceives it.

The fabric of international reality is thus made up of perceptions that result from a perception process, which is an integrative process whereby inputs/stimuli from operational reality are interpreted by actors as a result of the integration of those inputs and stimuli with the previous knowledge and ideas of the actor.[2]

The main question that arises from both terms (operational milieu and psychological milieu) is how can actors relate effectively to each other if they perceive the world in different ways. The answer is that actors tend to operate within what we define as acceptable operational perceptive limits. That is, our perceptions related to the operational environment fluctuate within an acceptable range for everyone's individual perception boundary. The perceptions occurring within that boundary can vary, but they are similar and have a similar content that allows actors to know, with some degree of certainty, what images the other actors perceive.

The mechanism described – the creation of reliable expectations and perceptions – is the one operating in transatlantic relations, although when it happens it may cause either minor or major misunderstandings between partners/ actors. For example, the shared perception is that nowadays, Iran is a threat, but the perceptions about how dangerous a nuclear Iran is (or could be) vary from those perceived by the United States to the ones perceived by some European countries and the European Union as a collective international actor. So, there is an opportunity for some kind of misunderstanding to arise.

Another likelihood is that some actors could generate perceptions that go beyond the established limits; these same actors may thus be distanced from the operational environment. The main effect of this distancing will be the generation of a poor (and/or incomplete) background for decisions, resulting in low-quality decisions, because while the images, arguments, and decisions could seem, real, well founded and effective in the environment perceived, they will be used and implemented in the operational reality that truly exists. Ultimately, the results anticipated from decisions made in the context of a mistakenly perceived reality will dramatically vary once the decision is made and applied in the reality that truly exists. This last situation is not the most common between the transatlantic partners, but this does not mean that at times such a situation does not happen. For example actions and decisions made on the premise of some misperceptions (and misinformation) involving the concept of appeasement have occurred before and after the two recent Gulf wars.

It is important to point out that apart from the development of acceptable margins of perception, there are other elements that are used by actors as a way to check/verify the perceptions and foreseeable actions of the other actors in a set of relationships. Apart from the information collected and elaborated about the international arena, and about the images and behaviour of actors within it, we can mention two further elements, namely signals and indexes.[3] Signals are actions the meaning of which is established as a result of mutual and tacit understanding (i.e. a speech, attendance at a meeting, a symbol, etc.), while indexes are actions that carry some inherent evidence about the fact that an image is correct because indexes are intrinsically linked to the intentions of the actor that emits them (i.e. signature of a treaty, military deployment, etc.).

Signals and indexes are very important tools to measure and transmit messages within the framework of transatlantic relations; for example, when the current President of Spain, José Luis Rodriguez Zapatero, did not stand up behind the US flag during the military parade celebrated in Spain (commemorating Spain's national day) on 12 October 2003.[4] At that moment he was issuing a signal expressing his protest about the second Gulf War and indicating a future (and possibly critical) attitude towards the US and its war on terror strategy, an attitude he put into practice by announcing the withdrawal of the Spanish troops from Iraq days after winning the 2004 election. The response, in the form of another signal, came from the White House during George W. Bush's second term: no official meeting between Mr Zapatero and Mr Bush was scheduled between 2004 and 2008.

Normally after situations like this one in which misunderstanding and mutual misperceptions arise, it is recommended that indexes are used as a way to demonstrate, for instance, a change of attitude – as the government of Mr Zapatero did by sending Spanish troops to Afghanistan from 2004 onwards, and most recently to Lebanon. The final result of this case, is that while the personal relations between both leaders were negatively affected at the beginning, the relations between Spain and the US have improved and currently work at a proper and effective level, although without the necessary and useful personal contact between the two leaders (which is necessary and useful for increasing/improving the effectiveness of the relations).

Other situations in transatlantic relations have changed because of an intelligent use of signals and indexes, for instance in the case of the relations between France (after the election of Nicolas Sarkozy as President) and the US. This example shows quite clearly how these tools can be used not only to improve understanding and mutual relations, but also to reshape the general framework of transatlantic relations.[5] The main achievement of this reshaping has been a reciprocal effort regarding the exploration and establishment of common principles to address global issues/problems such as international terrorism and the threats posed by some rogue states.

Related to signals and indexes, in an effort to avoid misunderstandings, the actor that analyses images and actions of other actors should take into account that the information that is managed may be erroneous or imperfect because of political-psychological dynamics inherent to the information and decision-making processes.[6] The actor receiving the information should also be vigilant about the possibility of both elements being tampered with either by the actor emitting them and/or by those interpreting and submitting information to the receiving actor. Having said that, it is proper to add that political (i.e. the democratic political system), moral (i.e. lying to allies), and practical (i.e. the costs of being discovered) restrictions operate when temptations to tamper arise, besides which to tamper with indexes is expensive because these ones imply the allocation and commitment of resources (political, economics, etc.).

This discussion leads us to the concept of image as a key element of the integrative process of perception. Because human beings are generally quite visual/graphic,[7] the logical results of this process are images that are understood as mental representations of perceptions. But images are not just empty representations without meaning. Images are structures charged with content, which help the actors in their interaction with the environment. Once an image is set and loaded with content it will be quite difficult to change. So when the US presents the image of Iran, or previously Iraq, as a clear and present danger, it is necessary to know and understand the process whereby that image has been formed. The same principle is applicable to the European Union (EU) or individual countries of Europe when their images related to the same cases are not loaded with the same content. Thus, in order to underpin reliable mutual perceptions, the transatlantic allies have to share with each other the elements that lead them to perceive and form the images that motivate them to act in different ways.

It is important to mention here that, apart from the impact of images, there are other factors, such as the learning process and the aforementioned information-acquisition process, that help actors in the task of forming reliable perceptions. The goal of the learning process is the acquisition of knowledge and assimilation of experiences that together with perceptions, images, ideas, and emotions will produce models that will help the actors, first, to understand and then to make decisions. Those things, and matters

learned, experienced, lived and/or experimented with, make possible understanding, adaptation, and interaction with the environment, and contribute
to explain the perceptions and decisions of the actors. Etheredge refers to
two key elements supporting the learning process:[8] first, intelligence, in the
sense of gaining a more accurate perspective of reality and being able to use
it in the decision-making process; and, second, effectiveness, or becoming
more successful in achieving what is valued.

Once actors have the images that they consider that they need concerning
the environment, decisions will be taken as a way to influence, modify, and
even transform the environment.

One implication of this discussion is that decision-makers should be careful
when perceiving because of the risk of misperceptions. We have mentioned
this term, misperceptions, before without explaining it. Misperceptions occur
when the perceptions of the actors diverge from the operational environment
and beyond acceptable operational perceptive margins. The greater the
divergence worse for the decision the making processes of the actors, because
they are operating/acting on a reality that only exists for them. Effectively,
they are acting according to the invented reality[9] that they have constructed.
One of the most important misperceptions that could arise in the international scenario is the dynamic called wishful thinking. This is a psychological
and political process whereby the actor relates ideas with wishes (or vice
versa) and thinks, 'that the world is benign enough so that his values will be
protected even if he remains passive'.[10]

Returning to the relationship between images and decisions, it is important to add here that images, understood as result of the perception process,
become quite important in the decision-making process through three
stages.[11] The first of these stages is *framing*: a process through which the
actor activates their specific knowledge (composed of images, information,
and experiences) related to the situation in question. The second is *adoption
of objectives and plans*: related to objectives, the actor will, in relation to
objectives, activate a screening process in order to set objectives and to
decide if these objectives are reasonable and/or worthy. In relation to plans,
the actor will imagine plans for achieving the objectives proposed and their
respective results. Actors will thus build mental images of possible futures.
The third stage is *progress monitoring*: once a plan has been selected, an
actor has several alternative courses of action. If the plan has been selected
but not implemented, the actor will try to project more precise images about
what will happen. If the plan has been implemented, the actor will compare
the images that they perceive/receive with those expected/imagined before the
implementation. Another and complementary definition of images arises
from these stages – as cognitive structures that summarize all the actor's
knowledge about what, why, and how they should pursue the objectives
proposed and the results desired.[12]

Linked with these three stages in the relationship between images and
decision-making, we can identify three types of images[13] that are clearly

related to the foreign affairs decision-making process. The first type is *value images*: these are related to the standards, values, ideas, and beliefs that represent principles (see below). The question that these images try to answer is 'why?'. Within the general category of value images we have to distinguish between *central and peripheral beliefs*. Central beliefs are the result of the actors' own experiences, they show resistance to change and the central beliefs exercise a powerful influence on other principles and ideas. Peripheral beliefs are more malleable and are used for specific situations. Another distinction that we have to mention is the one between primary and secondary principles. Between primary and secondary principles whose characteristics are broadly equivalent to those of central and peripheral beliefs. The main difference between beliefs and principles[14] is that principles have an imperative character, prescribing what should and should be not done, and influencing notably desired objectives and acceptable plans.

A second type of images is *trajectory images*. These configure the actor's agenda towards the future because they are focused on their objectives. The question that these images try to answer – in two ways – is 'what?'. First, what does the actor want to achieve? And second, what does the actor expect to happen?

A third type of images is *strategic images*. These are focused on the several plans designed and displayed. This type of image represents the actor's timeline and overall perspective in which different plans can and do run simultaneously. In relation to this type of image we can distinguish four further concepts. First, there are *plans*: these can be defined as abstract strategies, and as abstract strategies, and also as the anticipated sequence of activities. As images, they unfold in the actor's mental timeline and finish – successfully, modified, or rejected – according to the images produced by the actor. For instance, if the images show the failure of the plan, it will be abandoned. Plans should be constructed on the basis of knowledge of the past (history), the characteristics of the present (situation), and (well-founded) forecasts about the future. *Tactics* represent specific behaviours that come from abstract plans. Their effects will be much better if they are flexible, admitting some degree of change, especially if they are going to be implemented in complex and changing environments. *Policies* are pre-designed plans that the actors may use when they identify the context they are facing as similar to others that have happened before. Again, flexibility should be incorporated because it is quite unlikely that there will be an exact repetition of any situation or context, which means that policies can not be implemented exactly as they were in the past. *Forecasts* enter into play once a plan is adopted and when the actor has to foresee the result of the plan. This requires the capacity to construct possible futures. The actor has to 'see both controllable and uncontrollable facts'. Then, when comparing the expected future with the desired future, the actor should be able to estimate the feasibility of the different plans. And once the plan or plans selected are implemented/executed, the actor will repeat the process of evaluation to check their progress towards the proposed objectives.

In order to go deeper into the relationship between images, perceptions, and decisions, we have to add two further key concepts: ideas and the ideas system. According to Voss and Dorsey, an idea is the information – both general and specific – that an actor has about other actors' behaviour.[15] We agree with John Elster when he says that ideas arise from a need for meaning because human beings seem to have a deep need to have sufficient reasons for what they do'.[16] At times this political and psychological 'necessity' provokes the actor involved in both perception and decision processes to search not for the correct idea, but for the one that answers and justifies their perceptions and actions.

But having ideas in some kind of vacuum makes no sense; therefore to improve their relationship with the environment, the actor will integrate all their ideas in a system of ideas. This can be defined as an overall view composed by images of the past, the present, and the future, plus all the organized knowledge that the actor has about themselves, the other actors, and the surrounding environment. In the words of Ole Holsti, a system of ideas can be conceived 'as a lens/eyeglass through which all the relevant information is perceived'.[17] So the ideas system orientates the actor and motivates their acts/decisions towards the environment. Thus a bi-directional relationship between images and the ideas system is established. That is, actors use images to make decisions; but in the process of forming images, the actor's system of ideas will play a key role. And once an image is formed – if considered relevant – it will become part of the system of ideas.

Images then are an essential subpart of a whole that is the system of ideas, the main tasks of which are to organize the general and specific knowledge of the person; to organize the images; and to set the objectives and the order of preferences. The next step will then be to establish the relationship between ideas and the perception process.

Ideas influence the perception process through their relationship with the expectations of the actor. Ideas set expectations, and when facts happen we are prone to interpret them according to our expectations. So again there is a risk regarding misperception because when the actor is eager to relate facts and expectations, important pieces of information can be missed. There is a tendency to reject and/or ignore important and reliable information that does not fit with previous ideas of the actor, while they will accept small pieces (even weakly backed) that fit with their expectations, hopes, and wishes. If that is the case, then, as already noted, a psychological dynamic called wishful thinking can emerge, whereby the actor reduces their perception of the costs of their decision because they perceive a reality that fits with their images, values, and interests.[18] As Robert Jervis states: 'unfortunately, however, once we have established an idea of how the world works or an image of others in our mind, we do not examine new information or re-examine old information in an unbiased manner. Instead, we assimilate this information to our pre-existing beliefs, thereby reinforcing them'.[19]

This last statement is one that has considerable relevance in the context of transatlantic relations, especially after the Cold War. After the Cold War the European allies of the US felt that they no longer needed the protection of their former and powerful ally, so they began to form their own ideas, perceptions, and images about the international arena. They did so because they wanted to conduct a different type of foreign policy through which the most important countries of Europe and the EU itself could be relevant actors in the global arena, thus taking over (partially at least) the role of the US and proposing multilateralism instead of the American trend to unilateralism.

On the other hand, the US reinforced the ideas, perceptions, and images that they had been using during the Cold War, and that had backed strategies such as Eisenhower's Massive Retaliation or Reagan's Peace through Strength, and these emerged into George W. Bush's doctrine of Peace through Primacy. Besides following the main tenets of this last strategy, the George W. Bush Administration developed new images about the current global challenges and threats (especially after 11 September) with all of the images based on the self-perception and the idea that the world needed a strong and benign ruler, namely the US.

So in this process, both sides perceived, formed, and loaded new images that heavily influenced their respective decision-making processes and the plans, strategies, and policies derived from them. And due to political and emotional attachment to these ideas, perceptions, and images, they have played (more than might be considered desirable) a justifying role for motivations and actions (as outlined above by reference to John Elster) and have contributed, especially from 2001 onwards, to misunderstanding rather than common understanding and action to identify, measure, manage, and order the affairs of the world.

Images and Foreign Policy

Until now we have focused on the importance of images when perceiving and making decisions. In this section the discussion moves on to deal specifically with foreign policy. From the discussion above it can be assumed that in order to build a strong foreign policy, and to be able to communicate with other actors, decision-makers will need to be aware of how they manage and project images and how they perceive and assimilate the images coming from the international stage.

In relation to international actors we can define images as 'those ideas and beliefs about other/s actor/s that affect our own forecasts about the other/s actor/s behaviour under specific circumstances'.[20] So, for any international actor the design and projection of their own image will influence how others perceive/see them and, more importantly, their forecasts concerning future decisions. Because of the possible benefits for their interests and the achievement of the objectives of their foreign policy that this fact makes possible, actors may use the process of projection of images as a way to influence the perception and decision processes of other actors. In doing so, they will be influencing their expectations and forecasts about the actor's behaviour and future actions.

Related to the management of the elements and factors included in the image projection process we have to mention the theory of deception which is based on the psychological offensive-defensive behaviour of lying. We can not be naive, and we have to accept that lies are an intrinsic part of the international system, but we have to keep in mind that the aforementioned behaviour has its limits, as does the manipulation of indexes and signals. Thus the intention to deceive has to take account of a number of complicating factors. First, because of the complexity of the international stage, there are a lot of actors to convince. Second, as we saw before, actors are prone to adapt the incoming images to match their expectations. Third, the ideas, beliefs, and images of the other actors tend to be quite resistant because the actors behave quite sceptically when perceiving, analysing, and assimilating the images that other actors are sending/projecting. As a result, most international actors can not be cheated easily because they are aware of the possibility that other actors may send manipulated images. Further, if some actors play this game – and it is discovered – their overall image and interests will be seriously harmed as will their credibility. But if we want to play fairly – as we should do – and because of the likely initial resistance to the image projected, then we can use elements such as indexes and signals as a way to convince the other actor/s about the credibility of our image and intentions.

Earlier in this chapter we said that when analysing and studying signals and indexes, manipulation was possible, but we have also to consider that both can represent a true and honest way to send an image and to declare intentions. So when managing our image we should use all tools available to 'broadcast' it to other actors. Actors also have to make the effort to transmit the images that they are sending as clearly as they can if their goal is to avoid being misunderstood and misperceived. In trying to avoid other actors' misperceptions, the actors of international society, and specifically those involved in transatlantic relations, should keep in mind, for instance, the concept of evoked set, whereby actors are prone to think that the matters that worry them and/or they are focused on, are the main focus of attention of other actors. For instance, the US should not currently take for granted that all their European allies are worried and focused on the development of the Iranian nuclear programme, as the US is. Doing so without checking clearly before first sending signals and indexes to their European allies (and to the international community), and then acting in consequence, could lead to miscommunication, confusion, and mutual misperception about the decisions and actions of both Americans and their European allies towards Iran.

The influence of the evoked set could turn out negatively, for example, when the actors assimilate and evaluate information and perceive according to a small but active part of their mind/memory. In this case the actors could miss relevant information if it is not related to the matters that worry them. When an actor is especially focused/worried about a specific matter a kind of tunnel vision is created whereby information is examined with fewer resources than usual and the actor assumes that the other actors will share their worries and attribute to them most of the consequences that the actor is facing. So if this behaviour occurs, communication between actors will be harmed and a variable degree of confusion will appear. The actor will emit information (focused on the matter with which they are concerned) that will not be properly assimilated and analysed by the actors receiving it, so the response from the receiving actors will not make sense to the first actor, nor will it correspond with the expectations of the actor-emitter expectations. If, because of this situation, a conflict arises, the parties involved will blame the other/s, but not themselves.

For instance, if an actor thinks that a current situation has clear similarities with a past one, this actor could be prone to think that the remaining actors are establishing the same historical analogy. As a result, this actor will perceive and emit specific information – and what is more important, will make decisions – thinking that all their perceptions and actions are not only appropriate to the situation, but are quite clear to and shared by the remaining actors. For example, when backing the decisions that led to the second Iraq War, the US, was thinking – among other things – that the argument of negative effects of appeasement[21] could be applied to Saddam Hussein's regime, would be clear for the main actors in international society, and especially for the most important states of Europe, in particular France and Germany.

The notion of the evoked set is related to the policy agenda and, as we have determined before, currently the transatlantic friends have agendas of their own. There is also a tendency to suppose that the issues that worry the different countries involved in transatlantic relations are the main preoccupation too for other countries. Most important, the parties think that they are perceiving and addressing the global issues in an appropriate manner. So, from 2001, the actors involved in transatlantic relations have proceeded – for the most part – by thinking that their ideas and objectives were widely shared and accepted. Because of the great support received after 9/11 and in the Afghanistan War, the US thought that it was clear to everyone that their next goal/step was to erase the global threat of a nuclear Iraq by overthrowing the tyrannical regime of Saddam Hussein. At the same time, their European allies were thinking that the US was aware that the 'wave of help and solidarity' extended only to Afghanistan, whilst in respect of Iraq, the solution should be one agreed multilaterally, through dialogue and based on peaceful methods, such as, international pressure on Saddam's regime, inspections and reports of the International Atomic Energy Agency, and combined sanctions from the EU and the UN.

Why Different Perceptions and Decisions?

If we sum up the argument so far, we can express it in terms of a question: why do actors have different perceptions and make different decisions when exposed to the same environment and facts? To explain this phenomenon we have to consider several potential causes. First, in history we can find some answers about the construction and evolution of the perceptions that guide behaviour and decisions. When reviewing the decision-making processes we have to consider the concept of learning process, as discussed earlier. In this case, ideas of learning can illuminate and explain the nature and evolution of historical experiences and facts lived and experienced. So, specific historical situations, experiences and/or historical lessons derived from history can lead to perceptions that will motivate and substantiate decisions that are then explained by reference to some historical events. For instance, the decisive role of the US in Germany's defeat during World War II, their subsequent contribution to the reconstruction of Western Europe, plus the new-born threat of the Soviet Union, contributed to positive perceptions by Western Europe countries (leaders and populations) about the necessity of a strong link with the US, acceptance of US protection, and recognition of the US role as leader of the free world against the threat of communism.

Second, actors may have different and/or opposing objectives. For example, during the Cold War it was quite logical that the US and the Soviet Union had different perceptions and made opposing decisions in circumstances where a race for world power was underway. So the situation demanded different ways for each actor to achieve its objectives and goals. Similarly, in the current world arena the different designs (and objectives) expressed and implemented through the several foreign policies of the participating countries can explain the different decisions made by actors involved in transatlantic relations.

Third, actors may develop different images of the international arena because of different sets of perceptions, images, and ideas that result in opposing systems of ideas. This may be the case when, for example, the leader and/or ruling elite of a dictatorial religious regime examines reality through the lens of its system of ideas that is highly influenced by religious thoughts and beliefs. Obviously the images resulting from that process will vary from the images formed by leaders of true democratic systems.

Fourth, the management of the information acquisition process, through all or specific phases: recollection of information available, processing, analysing, assimilation, and evaluation of information, may significantly influence actors' perceptions. This is a key issue: the quantity, the quality, and the origin of both the information that the leader is receiving and – just as important – the information that they do not receive. The proper working of the information and intelligence services, plus the collision of interests of the different organizations involved, play a very important role in the management of information. The question related to information, which we could pose when examining the behaviour of several leaders towards the same environment, is what information do they have at their disposal, and how are they using it?

Fifth, political factors, such as the political system in terms of democratic states versus non-democratic states, can shape the perceptions of decision-makers in important ways. In international society, one important distinction bearing on this issue is that between legal and rogue states. Legal states respect basic freedoms and follow international law. Rogue states, on the other hand, do not respect basic freedoms and tend to conform to international law when it suits their interests.[22] The main difference is that where they have behaved incorrectly, democratic states accept that they are and can be found responsible for their actions and will accept and fulfil the punishment legally imposed.[23] The other side of the coin are rogue states (dictatorial regimes), which systematically violate their own people's basic rights and challenge the international order and security, neither accepting any responsibility nor complying with any international and legal decision against their behaviour (for example, the rejection by the Saddam Hussein and Mahmoud Ahmadinejad regimes of nuclear inspections in their territories and sanctioned by the United Nations).

Further differences between legal and rogue states can be expressed in terms of morality (in the sense of goodness): thus legal states, normally, will refrain from dishonest behaviour, such as lying (for example image projection, not respecting and fulfilling a treaty, etc.), while rogue states will use any tool, mainly dishonest ones (such as lying in any of its forms[24]), to achieve their objectives. With reference to differences about perceptions and decisions between legal states, the stress could be put on the nature and characteristics of their political systems. So different political cultures, political processes, and decision-making procedures can lead to different decisions, even among a set of legitimate, democratic states.

Sixth, the personality of the leader and those involved in the development and implementation of the foreign policy can shape distinctive decisions and patterns of action. Personality can be defined as the ways in which individuals are different from each other.[25] The influence of this element is key when explaining political behaviour. This statement rests on the premise that no political behaviour exists in a void – it happens in a specific environment – and no political behaviour exists independently from a person.[26] So the existence of different personalities can help to explain different decisions that are related to the same environment.

Seventh, and linked to personality, we can identify the emotions, ideas, beliefs, and principles involved in perception and decision-making. As we saw before, all these elements are part of the actor's learning process and combine to create the lens (system of ideas) through which the actor forms perceptions and later makes decisions.

Finally, it is clear that perceptions among groups of actors must be viewed in relation to the objectives, goals, interests, and means of the actors. Even when objectives are shared among members of international society, these members can have different means to achieve their goals. Therefore, decisions will vary from actor to actor in the light of their capacities and inclinations to act in specific circumstances. For instance in the case of Islamic terrorism, most of the actors agree that it is a very important problem that has to be faced. The difference is where and how, and this has been a significant element in recent transatlantic relations.

All these factors and dynamics will influence what decisions are made, why they are made, and how they are made. Obviously, if actors have different perceptions, decisions will be different. But even where actors operate within what we earlier termed the acceptable operational perceptive margins – generating similar perceptions at the overall level and containing their differences – their decisions could be different. The explanation could be found in the interaction of all or some of the factors discussed here.

Perceptions, Images, Decisions and Transatlantic Relations: Mirror, Mirror on the Wall ...

With reference to transatlantic relations, we can appreciate that on the basis of the preceding arguments there are different perceptions and images of the international arena that have been translated into some key disagreements between the US and the EU. These are mainly about the world role of the US, about the nature of the ties inherent in the transatlantic relationship, and about the best way to address and resolve the problems that threaten the world. The main effect of these disagreements is that perceptions, specifically those framed by European countries, are changing, and, hence, decisions made by those countries are widening the rift, especially in matters of security and world-order management, between the US and their (at other times) staunch European allies.

Unlike Snow White's stepmother who had a magic mirror to know everything – 'Mirror, mirror on the wall, who is the loveliest lady in the land' – we do not have a magical artefact to distinguish who is really right from who is really wrong in their perceptions, images, objectives and decisions. In the current world, we might assume that both sides (the US and the European countries) should perceive correctly the main challenges, the images, and the information originating from the international stage. It is true that there are different perceptions, but they occur within the limits of what we termed earlier the acceptable operational perceptive margins. Because of that, there are not significant distances between the mutual perceptions of various countries, but obviously the slight differences in perceptions and images influence and help to explain why both parties (the US and Europe – mainly the EU) are perceived and behave in the way they do. Related to this last statement, it is important – as we have noted – to consider other facts that influence, motivate and shape different perceptions and images, such as historical factors, political factors, emotions, principles, ideas, attitudes, and the interests at stake, that influence and contribute to motivate and shape different perceptions and images.

Historical Facts

After World War II, the Western European countries joined the primacy strategy designed by the US,[27] and that was understood as a shield against the Soviet Union and as an instrument for economic development.

Because of this strategy, both parties created a shared system of norms with the aim of countering the Soviet threat and avoiding future wars in Europe. This framework provided the US with political, military, economic, and normative primacy. The ruling perception between the allies, at that time, was that this primacy was fair and necessary. The world leadership of the US was accepted without major reservations, mainly as a consequence of the Western European countries' self-perception of weakness in the face of the power of the Soviet Union (and the communist bloc) and their loss of confidence in their own skills and capabilities (political, military, economic, and normative) to exercise world power.

The perceptions that stemmed from World War II were also influenced by emotional facts, such as feelings of gratitude and admiration towards the country that initially contributed substantially to freeing them and then decisively contributed to winning the war against the Nazi regime. This emotional basis for acceptance of US dominance was most apparent in the Western European countries because at the end of the war they needed protection against the Soviet Union. These kinds of feelings help us to explain the success of the spreading (or willing importation) across Western Europe of the American way of life[28] immediately after World War II. In our opinion this emotional predisposition plays a key role in influencing the perceptions (in a positive way) of Western European populations in relation to the US.

Transatlantic relations under the premises of US strategic supremacy and extended deterrence[29] were reinforced during the Cold War period and the European integration process. This last process was quite well received and endorsed by successive US administrations who perceived it as a way for Europe to improve its economic and military capabilities, and thus make Europe a more effective ally against communism and in pursuit of world order. If Europe could defend itself and/or effectively manage its internal affairs, the US could divert more resources to world primacy. But when the collapse of the Soviet Union and subsequently the Eastern Europe communist bloc happened, new perceptions that had been growing across the Western European countries became apparent. At that time, the basis of extended deterrence was kept, but the new perceptions put in doubt the nature and fairness of the transatlantic tie, as well as the role of the EU and the US in world management. In less measure, these new perceptions were related to the transatlantic shared values and interests.

These new perceptions were supported by a number of factors. First, the end of the communist threat generated the feeling and perception that the need for US protection was also reduced. Second, the success of European integration generated the feeling and perception that internal security within Western Europe was guaranteed, and reinforced the idea that the EU was able, and would continue to be able in the future, to cope with European problems. Third, the economic development of Europe made it increasingly difficult for Europeans to accept a secondary role in relation to the US. Because of these facts, the EU countries developed self-perceptions of confidence in their capabilities, which led to discussion about and challenges to perceptions about the distribution of power, the normative pre-eminence of the US, and the common values and interests established by the primacy strategy. As a result, the EU began to seek and to promote a more active, autonomous, and influential role in world affairs. In that sense we can point to the development of the Common Foreign Security Policy, complemented and completed by the European Security and Defence Policy.

From the end of the Cold War, the EU felt itself more secure and capable, so the transatlantic tie was put in doubt as a symbol of prosperity and security.

Political Factors

The US is a political entity as a whole, while Europe is not. This fact is quite important, for instance in the case of foreign policy. While the US has, in principle, a single constant foreign policy, Europe has not. In the case of the US (as for the United Kingdom (UK)), it can also be argued that the main tenets of foreign policy do not depend on political changes. All the administrations of the US, especially from the end of World War II, have designed and implemented a strong foreign policy with the objective of supremacy. From the doctrines of 'Containment of communism' and 'Massive nuclear retaliation' until the most recent doctrines of 'Peace through strength' and 'Peace through primacy', all the doctrines used (theoretically and practically) to back and guide the actions of the US administrations have at their core the tenets of their own primacy and – as part of this – the reinforcement of the transatlantic alliance on the basis of extended deterrence.

The case of Europe is different. Whilst the EU has a developing 'foreign policy', all the member countries continue to develop their own foreign policies. So we can anticipate that this will lead to different positions towards the US and different orientations in respect of the international arena, depending on the country and the ruling government. With reference to specific countries, we can note that the foreign policy goals of several states, such as Poland and most of the ex-Soviet republics (even though they are members of the EU), differ importantly from the aims of some Western European countries and of the EU as an entity. This can be appreciated, for instance, in issues such as the different decisions made about the war against terrorism led by the US (some countries, such as the UK, backing the US' position, and some rejecting it) and about the US proposal of an anti-ballistic missile defence shield in Eastern Europe. It is quite striking to observe how the US is receiving its highest rates of approval and most significant promises of collaboration from Eastern European countries. Once again, perceptions are playing in favour of the US – this time in countries that were formerly and for a long period under Soviet dominance. During the long period of subordination, the common perception was that while the Western European countries and the EU were predominantly looking after their own interests, there was just one country that was really concerned about their sad situation and set out to help them, namely the US. The US in this context not only meant and means the most admired values and way of life, but also meant protection against the Soviet Union in the past and means protection against the Russian Federation nowadays.

For these reasons the Eastern European countries are (as were the Western European countries in the past) in favour of reinforcing the transatlantic alliance and thus accept the world leadership of the US and back its major plans, strategies and policies.[30] It is not surprising then that the US had a great interest in the incorporation of these countries into the EU, knowing that once they had entered the EU the most critical voices regarding the actions of the US would lose some of their strength and impact.

In considering how orientations, perceptions, and decisions may vary, depending on the ruling government of different European countries, one of the most illustrative examples is the changing orientation of the foreign policy of Spain which was clearly pro strong transatlantic ties during the government of Prime Minister Jose María Aznar (1996–2004). In March 2003, in the Azores Meeting, Spain supported the position of the US, willingly joined the alliance built for the war on Iraq, and embraced the tenets of the war against terrorism that was designed by the George W. Bush Administration. Rather different was the foreign policy of Spanish Prime Minister José Luis Rodriguez Zapatero (elected in 2004), which clearly changed the direction of Spanish foreign policy. Zapatero's first decision as Prime Minister was to withdraw the Spanish troops from Iraq in 2004; he went on to propose an alternative to war on terrorism, the 'alliance of civilizations', and to pursue a policy far from pro strong transatlantic ties and that was focused on joining the axis of Paris and Berlin.

More recently, we have seen that even a country with one of the most consistent foreign policies in Europe, and not characterized by its support for the transatlantic alliance – France – is now considering (because of the new government of Nicholas Sarkozy) rejoining the North Atlantic Treaty Organization (NATO), reinforcing the transatlantic alliance, and rethinking its position towards the war on terror doctrine. Sarkozy has also hinted at departing from the official position of the EU towards Iran, and threatening this country with war if it does not abandon the development and implementation of its nuclear programme. Linked to this last issue, the French Foreign Affairs Minister, Bernard Kouchner said: 'We will negotiate until the end. And at the same time we must prepare ourselves ... for the worst. ... The worst, it's war.'[31] A few days later while visiting Washington, he said: 'A more powerful Europe is not incompatible with a transatlantic relation.'[32]

So it can be seen that not only is the foreign policy of the EU not a constant one because of the differences between its members, but also that individual states face difficulties and challenges in developing a constant and consistent foreign policy because of the tendency to change direction depending on the political orientation of their governments. So this is a source for different perceptions, making it more difficult to establish a new and long-lasting transatlantic tie.

As already noted, another political fact must be considered: that there is only one political system in the US versus (at least) 28 in Europe (one from the EU plus 27 from the EU's current members). Clearly, the more members, the more complexity there will be, specifically in four aspects. The first of these reflects the different procedures of decision-making. As we have seen, this issue also links with the processing of information (gathering, selection, transmission, and assimilation). The more information networks, the more confusion, and the result will be different perceptions and images coming from the very same environment. A second and related factor reflects the number of institutions linked to the decision-making in relation to, the elaboration, and the control of – which in the case of Europe is quite high – and which reinforces the inevitable diversity of different national governments. A third factor is the number of political parties with an interest in foreign policy. In the case of the US, there are two political ruling parties sharing a broad perspective on foreign policy, while in Europe there are more than 100 parties (either ruling parties or those with the capacity to influence ruling parties), each with widely differing perspectives about the objectives, development, and implementation of their respective country's national foreign policies and about how things should be done on the international stage. Finally, it is important to mention public opinion.[33] While US administrations face one public opinion, all governments of EU Member States face their own public opinions. This factor, which is related to each individual political system, helps us to explain why parties involved in transatlantic relations can perceive events and trends differently. It also raises another possibility, namely that although the states and leaders implicated do share common perceptions, their decisions could be unalike, for example because of the pressure of domestic public opinion.

We think that the range of political factors explained here contributes to a certain degree of confusion when European countries are perceiving and making decisions. This translates into a variety of different foreign policy goals and objectives that vary from country to country, almost from government to government, and that, depending on the situation, collide or agree with the general guidelines of the European Common Foreign and Security Policy. As a result, when one attempts to find common ground for a transatlantic alliance, relating European foreign policies to the comparatively solid and steady US foreign policy, there is no one solid EU foreign policy (because of the inner tensions of the countries involved, not just as members but as individual actors).

Emotions, Principles, Ideas, and Attitudes

A range of additional, complementary factors can play a role, reflecting different situations and policy needs. A first such factor is the psychological characteristics of public opinion. In the US, public opinion is more prone to support the government in time of crisis.[34] In Europe, public opinion tends to back political parties and particular points of view rather than the government (the UK being an exception). A second factor is the psychological characteristics of the head of state or government. A US president's personality, perceptions, images, ideas, and beliefs are very important when designing and making foreign policy decisions. There is a personal style in US foreign policy, which is not so prevalent in the foreign policies of the European countries (again, the case of the UK is an exception, with prime ministers such as Winston Churchill, Margaret Thatcher, and Tony Blair), not even in the cases of France or Germany.

A third factor can be the contest of wills and projection of images, signals, and indexes linked to the geopolitical and psychological concept of 'strength'. This is a behaviour often displayed by the US because of its dominant position in the world order. The US, when viewed from this perspective, cannot be defeated or it will lose its image as unbeatable world power. The will to maintain and use predominant world power as a tool for defending its national and global interest is a very important influence when forming perceptions and images, setting foreign policy objectives, and making decisions. In this context we can also point to the psychological (and additional) pressure on presidents of the US about not being the first president to lose a war or being considered guilty of weakness in the face of those actors disputing hegemony, power, and interests with the US.

We can say that the US has the means, the will, the power (military and economic), and the commitment to protect and defend its national interest anywhere in the world. Besides the influence of the political and psychological factors explained earlier, the EU (and European countries) faces problems when trying to develop and implement policies aimed at exercising regional power and/or defence of their interests. Illustrations can be found in the war in the Balkans[35] or in the limitations shown in pursuit of the project of a common European Foreign and Defence Policy. Both cases (and others similar in the broad range of EU foreign policy activities) are linked to the desire to exercise or develop military power, but this concept is not considered politically correct in Europe although it is completely acceptable and positively valued in the US (by leaders, political parties, public opinion, etc.). Thus the nature and influence of emotions, principles, ideas, and attitudes can provoke different decisions even if the images and perceptions are the same or quite similar. In June 2004, a survey of transatlantic opinion found broad consensus between American and European public opinions on the seven most significant international threats (international terrorism being at the top of the list). Just one issue showed clear differences: the use of force, in respect of which 82 per cent of US citizens and only 41 per cent of Europeans believed that sometimes war is necessary to obtain justice.[36]

In the case of the US the psychological factors mentioned contribute to tougher and straighter actions/decisions even against the background of the same or similar perceptions and images as those held by the European countries. For instance, the US shows markedly less patience than European countries when facing extended conversations or negotiations with rogue states/actors, as was shown in meetings with the Iraqi regime before the second Iraq war and nowadays with the Iranian regime about the development of the latter country's nuclear programme.

The Interests at Stake

The US has global interests while the EU and even the most important individual countries within Europe do not – with the limited exceptions of Britain and France. Significant differences linked to perceptions arise when designing and developing a specific foreign policy under the pressure of having national interests at stake all over the world. This contrasts with the situation in which other countries find themselves: for the US, interests are growing and being constantly threatened, whilst others have to take care of a smaller sphere of interests. Depending on the interests at stake, the decisions made on the basis of similar perceptions and images can vary. When your own vital interests are in danger, for instance, time is a very demanding factor and obviously will affect why and how a decision is made.

Nowadays this situation is changing, and the EU is trying to gain influence in the international arena, but this does not mean that direct interests are involved, although it is true that the interests of the EU are growing around the world. Because of this European quest, we can talk about the EU challenging the US. The EU is trying to change the distribution of power, but their position is not supported by new capabilities (especially military ones). The differences concerning European perceptions on what is the influence of the EU and its place in the transatlantic alliance, according to its interests and capabilities, are a key issue that helps to explain the existing rift between US and some European countries.

Conclusions

According to the argument developed here, transatlantic relations are divided by different perceptions and images; and shaped by different objectives, means, and decisions. This fact may find explanation in some of the factors developed previously. Images that result from divergent decisions, attitudes, and behaviours could lead us to think that there are more factors that might loosen the transatlantic tie instead of tightening it. But we would argue that this is not the case. The challenges of today really require a strong transatlantic alliance. In order to achieve this, the actors involved in transatlantic relations should not try to project images harming the image of other allied actors. Reciprocal trust has to be reinforced through honest signals and indexes. The path to sharing objectives and the means of achieving them, which would benefit all the parties, is easier to take from a situation of mutual respect and confidence. For instance, the US decisively contributed to the solution to the Balkans crisis in the 1990s, even when its interests were not involved. The US did it because of two facts: first, the EU could not find a common agreement to intervene because of conflict of interests and its lack of a proper and well-equipped military force; second, there was a perceived need to preserve the solidarity of the transatlantic alliance.

With reference to this last point, it might have been expected that the US should have received more support from the EU when its national security and interests were in danger in the Middle East. In the framework of transatlantic relations, the EU complains about the unilateralism of the US. Reciprocity could be, among other measures, the key to reducing unilateralism. Equally, given the key role of images, they should be used in transatlantic relations as tools for understanding, not for confrontation, between allies. Each party should try to perceive accurately what is really happening on the international stage and try not to emit images that might harm its allies. Building on the common ground regarding the main challenges that the Americans and the Europeans confront, there has to be understanding and the actors involved have to perceive accurately the key challenges, allies, and capabilities.

This proposed understanding could be articulated around the concept of 'democratic peace' in the sense established by Kant in his book *Perpetual Peace*. This conceptual meeting point could invigorate the relationship, offering a basis for perceptions of the international environment, and adding legitimacy to the actions and means of the transatlantic alliance. This concept worked effectively in the past, and consensus around it should be constructed again. The end of the Cold War changed the dynamics of the international arena, including general and particular interests of the United States and their European allies, but a consensus has to be built on the security model (that includes a shared view about the strategic interests of the alliance) and the normative frame because the international system will continue to be anarchic and unstable, with presenting threats and challenges (Islamic terrorism, rogue states, weapons of mass destruction, and at a certain level climate change).

If such analysis and actions are undertaken, the United States and their allies should agree about doing what is best for everyone on the basis of an agreed division of labour. Nowadays, the EU, for instance, could use its soft power in favour of the transatlantic alliance while the US could use its hard power. In the process of doing that, both parties could learn from the other, and then seek to refine and improve their weak points. By doing so the interaction between allies will improve, and the benefits for them and their respective allies will increase. So the weight and positioning of the parties to the transatlantic alliance could be revised according to essential common interests, the common strategic interest, and the contribution of those involved in securing the resulting benefits, not just on the basis of self-perceptions or self-interests. In sum, perceptions, images, objectives, capabilities, and decisions should be used as bricks for a bridge, not for a dividing wall.

Wishful thinking might bring comfort but not security. Call this strategic challenge, call this as I do, axis of evil … call it by any name, but let us speak the truth, if we ignore this threat, we invite certain blackmail, and place millions of our citizens in grave danger.

(George W. Bush, German Bundestag, 2003)

Notes

1 Jervis, Robert, *Perception and Misperception in International Politics* (Princeton, NJ: Princeton University Press, 1976), p. 13.
2 Voss, J. F. and Dorsey, E., 'Perceptions and International Relations', in Singer, Eric and Hudson, Valerie, eds, *Political Psychology and Foreign Policy* (Boulder, CO: Westview Press, 1992), p. 8.
3 Jervis, Robert, *The Logic of Images in International Relations* (Princeton, NJ: Princeton University Press, 1970), p. 5.
4 At that time, Mr Zapatero was not Prime Minister, but the leader of the main opposition party to the government of Mr José Maria Aznar.
5 Due to the fact of the international influence of France, once it has introduced some changes in the orientation of its foreign policy after the election of Nicolas Sarkozy as new president, there is a subsequent (MS) influence on the EU, meaning a more positive attitude towards the US's actions, policies, and strategies.
6 More about these dynamics can be found in Herrero de Castro, Rubén, 'Influencia de variables políticas y psicológicas en los procesos de información y decisión', *Inteligencia y Seguridad: Revista de análisis y prospectiva*, Plaza y Valdés, vol. I, issue 2 (November–July 2007).
7 Images are quite powerful tools for understanding and behavioural processes. For instance, would Americans have the same perception about terrorism without the terrible image of the twin towers collapsing?
8 Etheredge, L. S., *Can Governments Learn?* (New York: Pergamon Press, 1985), cited by Voss J. F. and Dorsey E., in Singer, Eric and Hudson, Valerie, eds, p. 21.
9 The concept 'invented reality' is explained and developed in detail in Herrero de Castro, Rubén, *La realidad inventada. Percepciones y proceso de toma de decisiones en Política Exterior* (Madrid: Plaza y Valdés, 2006), especially in Chapter IV.
10 Jervis, *Perception and Misperception in International Politics*, p. 366.
11 Beach, L. R., *Image Theory: Decision Making in Personal and Organizational Contexts* (New York: Wiley, 1990), p. 4–7.
12 Beach, p. 4.
13 Ibid., p. 8–29.
14 It is important to point out that the term 'principle' by itself does not mean virtue or goodness. There are good and bad principles. Some imperatives could be ignoble and motivate actions/decisions (i.e. cruelty, selfishness).
15 Voss, and Dorsey, p. 11.
16 Elster, Jon, *Political Psychology* (New York: Cambridge University Press, 1993), p. 14.
17 Holsti, Ole, 'Cognitive Dynamics and Images of the Enemy', in Farell, John and Smith, Asa P., *Image and Reality in World Politics* (New York: Columbia University Press, 1968), p. 18.
18 Jervis, *Perception and Misperception in International Politics*, p. 366.
19 Jervis, 'Foreword', in Herrero de Castro, Rubén, *La realidad inventada. Percepciones y proceso de toma de decisiones en Política Exterior* (Madrid: Plaza y Valdés, 2006), p. 15.
20 Jervis, *The Logic of Images in International Relations*, p. 5.

21 This argument, among others, was used by the George Bush Administration before the first Gulf War when it released a publicity campaign, which showed on posters and stickers the pictures of Stalin, Hitler, and Saddam Hussein with the text, 'Oh no he is back again!'.
The effect of appeasement is a recurring argument used to justify US foreign policy actions. This argument was used again by the George W. Bush administration through all the process leading to the overthrow of Saddam Hussein's regime.

22 García Picazo, Paloma, ¿*Qué cosa es esa llamada Relaciones Internacionales? Tres lecciones deterministas y algunas consideraciones indeterministas* (Madrid: Marcial Pons, 2000), p. 240.

23 As it was for those soldiers of the US Army who were involved in the Abu-Ghraib cases.

24 For instance, never ending negotiations conducted with the intention of gaining time or of cheating; or signing a treaty with the hidden intention of not fulfilling it.

25 Greenstein, Fred I., 'The Study of Personality and Politics: Overall Considerations', in Greenstein, Fred I. and Lerner, Michael, *A Source Book for the Study of Personality and Politics* (Chicago, IL: Markham Political Science Series, 1971), p. 16.

26 Barner-Barry, Carol and Rosenwein, Robert, *Psychological Perspectives on Politics* (Englewood Cliffs, NJ: Prentice Hall, 1985), p. 19.

27 An in-depth study about the formulation and evolution of the Primacy Strategy can be found in, Garcia Cantalapiedra, David, 'Peace Through Primacy', *Unisci Discussion Papers*, n. 30, (Madrid: Unisci, 2004).

28 We can define 'American way of life' as an assortment of economic (i.e. free market, liberalism, capitalism), political (i.e. democracy, human rights, and basic freedoms) and psychological (i.e. certain aesthetic look and outlook, etc.) dynamics that reflect the main values and everyday routines of the US. In a certain sense, we can refer to the American way of life as a sort of soft power from the US, which is used as a way to influence perceptions, images, and decisions and to 'hide' those harsh aspects of its primacy that initially could be perceived as threats to sovereignty.

29 That prevented an attack on the allies in general and also distributed power among Western European countries in such a way as to guarantee security between them.

30 These concepts are used in the sense of the definitions put forward at the beginning of this chapter.

31 16 September 2007; http://news.bbc.co.uk/2/hi/europe/6998602.stm.

32 21 September 2007; http://www.univision.com/contentroot/wirefeeds/usa/7263722.html.

33 Population plus mass media.

34 For example, the support received by President F. D. Roosevelt before and during World War II and, more recently, the re-election in 2004 of George W. Bush when the post-war situation in Iraq was being strongly criticized.

35 Solved by the intervention of NATO and the US Army, to resolve the crisis in that area.

36 Möttölä, Kari, ed., *Transatlantic Relations and Global Governance* (Washington, DC: Centre for Transatlantic Relations-Johns Hopkins University, 2006), p. 47.

4 An American View of Transatlantic Relations

Robert J. Lieber

Despite widespread predictions on both sides of the Atlantic that the United States and Europe are bound to experience a widening political, economic, social, and even cultural rift, no such rupture is likely to occur. To be sure, any number of disagreements exist, some typical of disputes that arose during the Cold War, while others are of more recent vintage. Nonetheless, four underlying realities are likely to preclude a fundamental divorce. First, there are shared threats. Radical Islamism, terrorism, and weapons of mass destruction pose a long-term danger to all Western societies, and there is no separate peace to be had. Europe needs the US as an ally and as insurance against future threats. NATO (North Atlantic Treaty Organization) enlargement, as well as the extensive cooperation in intelligence and security that has taken place since the 11 September 2001 attack on the US, are evidence of this. Second, despite being competitors, the EU and the US share fundamental interests. These include not only the maintenance of an international economic order in which each is the largest investor and trade partner of the other, but also a shared interest in the stability of the international system and its institutions. Third the cumbersome structure of the 27-member EU, the absence of true sovereign unity, and policy and structural differences among its members diminish the power and military potential that Europe's size, population, and wealth would otherwise provide. Fourth despite real differences, Europe and America share the values of the enlightenment and of Western liberal democracy, including liberty, the rule of law, freedom of speech, religious tolerance, and the rights of women and minorities. As a result, and despite the sometimes bitter controversies of recent years, the transatlantic relationship remains robust.

In this chapter, after identifying some common myths about the subject, I address these four underlying realities in order to explain why the American–European relationship has endured and why it is likely to continue for the foreseeable future.

Myths About Past and Present

Myths about the Atlantic relationship abound. In the acrimonious climate that developed during the early years of the George W. Bush administration, and in relationship to the American decision to use force against the Iraqi regime of Saddam Hussein, a distinctive narrative about Europe and America – past, present, and future – emerged. Versions of this narrative differ, but they tend to share common elements. They begin, typically, by depicting the Cold War years as a halcyon era in which close transatlantic collaboration, multilateralism, and mutual consultation prevailed. This era of partnership is said to have flourished until the end of the Cold War removed the Soviet threat which had helped to bind the partners closely together. However, harmony largely prevailed until the presidency of Bush-the-younger. The former Texas governor came to office with a Texas swagger, a shoot from the hip mentality, and an aggressive unilateralist approach to foreign policy. America's past habits of restraint, self-binding to common institutions, and deference to the views of its European partners were then abruptly discarded. The 11 September 2001 terrorist attacks on New York and Washington subsequently provided the occasion for the administration to give full rein to these belligerent instincts and a pretext for violating international law and launching an aggressive war in Iraq in defiance of wise European voices calling for restraint.

This narrative not only offers an account of America's past and present roles, but also a picture of Europe's present and future. In this account, an expanding, increasingly unified, and self-confident EU was emerging as a major actor in world affairs, not only as a force for international law and institutions, but as an increasing counterweight to the US. With its enlargement to 27 member countries, a total population of 490 million people, a common currency among a majority of its Member States, and plans for a common foreign and defence policy, Europe would no longer be a partner of the US, but instead would provide geopolitical balance. Disputes, not only about Iraq, but over the Kyoto Protocol, trade issues, genetically modified organisms (GMOs), and matters of human values – for example the death penalty and the role of religion in society – seemed to provide evidence that Europe and America really were pursuing divergent paths. The then President of the European Commission, Romano Prodi, described the EU's goal as one of creating a European continent that stands equal to America. The then President Jacques Chirac expressed the new sentiments more bluntly in saying, '[w]e need a means to struggle against US hegemony', and that the EU needed its proposed constitutional treaty because without it, 'Europe would not be strong enough against the big powers'.[1]

Nor were such views confined to European politicians and journalists. Among scholars, predictions of the Atlantic partnership's demise were increasingly heard. For some, this was chiefly a product of the end of the Cold War and resultant changes in the international distribution of power. Thus as early as 1990, Kenneth Waltz, expressing a view that would become increasingly shared among structural realist scholars, observed, 'NATO is a disappearing thing. It's a question of how long it is going to remain as a significant institution even though its name may linger on.'[2] More recently, at the height of what seemed to be Europe's moment, another academic author proclaimed that NATO 'is soon to be defunct'.[3]

In short, until the Americans came to their senses, repudiated the so-called neoconservative cabal that had manipulated the country into war, and returned to the true path of multilateralism and respect for the UN and international law, Europe would be the principal force for the global common good, the embodiment of the world community, and a model to other countries and regions.

In the months just before and immediately after the start of the second Iraq war, versions of this geopolitical story gained a wide audience among sections of the foreign policy elites and chattering classes on both sides of the Atlantic. Yet, with the passage of time, it has become apparent that such views were greatly overstated, and much of this depiction of both past and present rested on shaky foundations if not outright hyperbole. For one thing, the account of postwar history had been much too romanticized. Throughout the Cold War, there had been numerous and often acrimonious disputes over a wide range of security, economic, political, and even cultural issues. To cite just a few examples, there had been arguments over German rearmament, France's 1954 rejection of the proposed European Defense Community, the Anglo-French invasion of Suez in 1956, restrictions on exports of frozen chickens to Germany, America's engagement in the Vietnam War, Middle East policies and the Arab oil embargo that followed the October 1973 Yom Kippur War, the decision to station intermediate-range nuclear forces in Europe in the early 1980s, and much else besides.

Moreover, American policy had not been so clearly multilateralist as depicted. For example, in 1950, President Truman sent American forces to Korea prior to UN authorization; in 1962, President Kennedy appeared ready to use force against Soviet missiles in Cuba; four American presidents (Kennedy, Johnson, Nixon, Ford) used force in Indochina; Reagan employed US troops to oust a junta in Grenada; and George H. W. Bush overthrew a dictator in Panama. In addition, at the end of the Cold War the elder President Bush pursued German unity over the objections of President Mitterrand of France and Prime Minister Thatcher of Britain. In another conspicuous case – the Clinton administration's 1999 use of force against Serbia to halt murder and ethnic cleansing in Kosovo – the US and NATO proceeded without UN Security Council authorization because it was widely understood that Russia would have vetoed any resolution authorizing the action.

Nor was American policy so uniformly unilateralist after 9/11. In fact, the US continued to play an active role in multilateral institutions such as the World Trade Organization (WTO), NATO, the International Monetary Fund (IMF), World Bank, and UN Security Council, as well as to pursue multilateral initiatives, including an expanded foreign aid programme and an extensive international initiative to combat HIV-AIDS.

The Importance of Shared Threats

The end of the Cold War and the collapse of the Soviet Union brought to a close a period of more than four decades in which Western Europe, the US, and Canada substantially agreed about a common threat to their security, national interests, and way of life, even though there had by no means been a uniformity of views about specific policies. The hope that a post-Cold War world would see the end of meaningful threats proved illusory, as did the belief that traditional matters of war and peace, the need for military forces and alliances, and even national sovereignty itself had become increasingly outmoded in human history.

In reality, international agreement via the UN Security Council and Resolution 678 (1990) authorizing the use of force to oust Saddam Hussein's forces from Kuwait, was not the harbinger of a new world order, but an exception. Ethnic cleansing and mass murder in Bosnia and parts of the former Yugoslavia (1991–95) and in Kosovo (1999), as well as genocide in Rwanda (1994), exemplified the weakness and incapacity of the UN. These and other cases served as a reminder of the unique role that only the US could play in the face of the most urgent and deadly perils. This was apparent not only when America became engaged, but also when it did not.

In the aftermath of 9/11, it became evident that the US and its allies now faced an unprecedented threat from the combination of radical Islamism, terrorism, and the menace of weapons of mass destruction. Numerous indications had appeared earlier, the most notable among them being the 1993 truck bomb attempt to destroy the World Trade Center, the interrupted 1994 hijacking of Air France Flight 8969 by Algerian radical Islamists who had planned to crash the plane in Paris, an abortive1995 plot (the 'Bojinka' plan) to blow up 11 wide-bodied aircraft over the Pacific, the 1998 suicide truck bombings of the American embassies in Dar es Salaam, Tanzania, and Nairobi, Kenya, the October 2000 attack on the *USS Cole*, and the plot, foiled by German police in December 2000, to bomb the cathedral in Strasbourg France. But, the new and lethal dimensions of the threat emerged full force on that September morning, and in the following years, train bombings in Madrid and London on 11 March 2004 and 7 July 2005 respectively, as well as a number of mass casualty attacks thwarted by authorities in Germany, France, Britain, and elsewhere, showed that any hopes of a separate peace were illusory.

A number of authors, including prominent academic 'realists' have sought to connect terrorism and the war in Iraq with America's support for Israel, or even to elaborate a kind of neoconservative conspiracy theory that portrays the Bush administration's decision to use force against Saddam Hussein's Iraq as the product of influential pro-Israel policy-makers and lobbyists.[4] But this allegation does not provide an accurate analysis of the Bush administration's decision to use force in Iraq and of America's Middle East policy, nor a valid understanding about the sources of radical Islam and the deep-seated factors from which radical Islamism emerges.

While solutions to the deadly insurgency and instability in Iraq and the ongoing Israeli-Palestinian conflict would be highly desirable in themselves, neither would be likely to produce a significant respite from the shared long-term danger of Islamist terrorism. The 9/11 attacks had come before the US led the invasion of Iraq, and suicide terrorism against American installations abroad had occurred during the 1990s at times when the Israel–Arab peace process seemed most fruitful. Suicide bombings in Bali, Istanbul, Jakarta, Tunisia, and Morocco, the brutal murder of the Dutch film-maker Theo Van Gogh, murderous reactions to the Danish cartoon incident, an attempt to blow up the Indian parliament, and the destruction of the Shiite golden dome mosque in Samara, along with lethal Sunni-Shiite violence in Iraq, were evidence of much more profound and lasting kinds of threat.

In essence, the bin Laden and jihadist movements derive from sources that had little to do with the Palestinian problem. Bin Laden's 1998 *fatwa* emphasized the American presence in Saudi Arabia and oppression of Iraq, and his October 2001 video invoked 80 years of Muslim 'humiliation' and 'degradation' at the hands of the West.[5] Some of the most knowledgeable authorities on the subject, including Bernard Lewis and Fouad Ajami,[6] have cited four centuries of decline experienced by the Arab-Muslim world and the sense of humiliation that this has engendered, and they and others point to the frustration of those who have become detached from one world and yet unable to be accepted in another. Al Qaeda itself was formed not in reaction to the Arab–Israeli wars of 1948, 1956, 1967, or 1973, but as a movement growing out of the war in Afghanistan against the Soviets and at a time when the Israeli–Palestinian peace process seemed to be proceeding towards an eventual conclusion. As Olivier Roy has observed, 'Al Qaeda's fighters were global jihadists and their favored battlegrounds have been outside the Middle East: Afghanistan, Bosnia, Chechnya and Kashmir. For them, every conflict is simply part of the Western encroachment on the Muslim ummah.'[7] Osama bin Laden did opportunistically add Israel to the list of adversaries to be fought, but the Jewish state remained of lesser priority than the US, the 'head of the snake'.

If the Israeli–Palestinian conflict is ever solved, some of the animus directed at the US for its support of Israel would diminish. Nonetheless, the impetus for jihadism would remain in most of its essentials. Thus Josef Joffe has pointed out that even in a '[w]orld without Israel', rivalries among Arab and Muslim states, clashes between different religious tendencies (not only Sunni versus Shiite, but involving Wahabi's Copts, Alawites, and others), ideological rivalries, the lure of reactionary utopia versus modernity, as well as intrinsic problems of despotism, the oppression of women, rule by mullahs, and obscurantism, would remain or even intensify.[8]

In addition to arguments that attempt to explain radical Islamism in terms of the Palestinian problem or as primarily about Iraq, there is an altogether different interpretation offered by a number of European observers. They seek to downplay the lethality of the post-9/11 threat by suggesting that the terrorism associated with it is not necessarily more profound or dangerous than the terrorism with which Europe has previously coped, including the Irish Republican Army in Britain, Bader-Meinhoff in Germany, the Basque

ETA in Spain, and the Red Brigades in Italy. Yet these earlier types of attacks were not at all comparable in the type of danger they posed, nor in the prospect of mass casualties and political disruption. Particularly dangerous now is the lethal risk of attacks involving chemical, biological, radiological, or nuclear materials (CBRN). An estimation of this peril can be found in the responses of some 85 national security and non-proliferation experts to a survey conducted by the US Senate Foreign Relations Committee staff for its then Chairman, Senator Richard Lugar of Indiana, and published in June 2005. Asked to estimate the likelihood of a CBRN attack occurring anywhere in the world within the following ten years, their average probability estimate was 29 per cent for a nuclear attack, 40 per cent for a radiological attack, and 70 per cent for some kind of CBRN event.[9]

In weighing this danger, it is also worth recalling the words of America's bipartisan 9/11 Commission, which observed: 'The catastrophic threat at this moment in history. ... [is] Islamist terrorism.' Yet among some observers, though more so in Europe than in the US, there is an inclination not to take sufficiently seriously the lethal danger posed by radical Islamists and to dismiss the ranting and conspiracy theories of its leaders and documents as inconsequential merely because they are often nihilistic, irrational, or delusional. Nonetheless, as the social scientist Robert Merton long ago observed, if people define things as real they are real in their consequences.[10] In this regard, the suicide terrorism of 9/11, London, Madrid, and elsewhere, along with a number of massive terror plots that have been disrupted, provide compelling evidence that there is no shortage of individuals and groups willing to act on these fanatical ideas. And even when it is only a question of belief rather than action, large numbers of people may hold deeply irrational notions. For example, a June 2006 Pew poll in six Muslim countries, and among Muslims in Germany, France, Britain, and Spain, found that in none of these populations did a majority believe that Arabs carried out the 9/11 attacks.[11]

In response to shared threats, cooperation among American and European security and intelligence services has become exceptionally close. This collaboration has flourished, even at times when relations between the Bush administration and the governments of France under President Chirac and Germany under then Chancellor Gerhard Schroeder were at their most bitter. One example was the successful creation and functioning of a major US–France anti-terrorism unit based in Paris. As yet another indicator of the strong Atlantic security tie, NATO – far from becoming extinct – has taken on new members. In 1999 it added the Czech Republic, Hungary, and Poland, and in March 2004 it admitted Bulgaria, Estonia, Latvia, Lithuania, Romania, Slovenia and Slovakia.

Shared Interests

Shared threats provided a strong motivation for allied cooperation and partnership, but common interests constitute a fundamental source of solidarity as well. To be sure, as evident in the rivalry between Boeing and Airbus or in the fierce competition to sell modern weapons to the oil-rich Saudis, Europe and America are commercial competitors on a grand scale. Yet we share common interests that underpin the modern international economic system and indeed the international order more broadly.

In the aftermath of World War II and in the decades that followed, the US, Britain, and many of the countries of Europe created the institutions and understandings through which trade, finance, investment, intellectual property, transportation, communications, civil aviation, and the myriad other dimensions of a globalized world now operate. French political leaders may sometimes rail against foreign competition and challenges to the country's language and tradition, but the leading French corporations are world-class actors that are deeply engaged in the American economy and even conduct their internal business in English.

Not surprisingly, disagreements and disputes do erupt, pertaining to trade protectionism, regulatory and technical standards, the environment, agricultural policies, and monetary and fiscal policies. Yet Europe and America remain leading investment and trade partners of each other. The Atlantic countries share a common interest in the successful maintenance of the arrangements and institutions that sustain their economies, and any disruption of these regimes would be a lose-lose proposition for both sides.

Europe's Own Limits

With the January 2007 enlargement to Bulgaria and Romania, the EU has 27 member countries, 490 million people, and a gross domestic product (GDP) exceeding that of the US. The creation of a zone of peace on the continent after three centuries of devastating interstate competition and war stands as an extraordinary human achievement. The EU has become a formidable world actor in the economic realm and at times in other sectors, such as environmental policy, and the Euro has gained growing acceptance as an international currency alongside the dollar. If the EU possessed a real central government with genuine sovereign power, effective democratic institutions, and decision-making authority over the most important political, foreign policy, and security issues, then Europe would in fact be a true world power on a scale comparable to or even exceeding the US.

The reality, however, is different. Europe does not have an actual central authority at the head of a federal system. The EU's accomplishments have been remarkable and truly historic, but there is no United States of Europe, and until or unless such a body is established, the international weight of the EU will remain limited. The proposed constitutional treaty meant to provide a more efficient basis and stronger institutions for the enlarged EU was to have been a modest step in that direction, but its decisive defeat in Dutch and French referenda during the spring of 2005 brought this effort to at least a temporary halt.

An EU grown to 27 Member States has become cumbersome and unwieldy in its institutions, and although many policy areas now depend on decisions made in Brussels, national identities, interests, and priorities continue to play a prominent role. European Member State governments remain divided, sometimes profoundly so, on issues large and small. The protection of agriculture, community budget priorities, economic and trade policies, corporate mergers, taxation, GMOs, whether to admit new members including Turkey, and the degree to which the EU should become more truly federal in its institutions are all subjects in which wide disagreements exist among member governments.

Foreign and military policies have been major subjects of dispute too. It is well to recall that rather than having been unified in opposition to the use of force in Iraq, a majority of member governments initially supported the Bush administration's decision, and a number of them sent troops or other security personnel to Iraq. Much of this early support in Iraq has fallen away, but most European countries continue to privilege NATO rather than the EU as the primary means of assuring Europe's security. Time and again, and despite a combined total of armed forces personnel larger than that of the US, European countries have found themselves lacking in anything like the capacity to project power abroad that their population, wealth, and technological sophistication should otherwise dictate. Their aging populations, looming demographic problems, and relatively modest defence budgets serve as additional constraints.

Europe thus needs America as a partner, not only for wider regional contingencies, but in coping with instability, security threats, or dire humanitarian emergencies in the wider world. At the same time, the US needs Europe. Whether in the Balkans, Afghanistan, or in far flung areas, such as the Congo or East Timor, where immediate American interests have been less engaged, America finds it essential to engage its European partners, whether for the purposes of peacemaking, peacekeeping, stability operations, or efforts to combat terrorism and weapons proliferation. Afghanistan is an example where NATO has taken charge of military operations in the southern part of the country and American troops have been placed under a NATO command, led by a British general, for the first time since World War II.

Shared Values

Differences about cultural norms, religiosity, nationalism, and the efficacy and legitimacy of the use of force have gained increased currency in recent years. Robert Kagan's noteworthy essay, invoking the image of America as Mars and Europe as Venus attracted widespread attention,[12] and critics have emerged on both sides of the Atlantic variously depicting the Europeans as weak-willed, duplicitous, postmodernist appeasers presiding over societies that are losing their dynamism and failing to replenish their own populations due to collapsing birth rates. Americans in turn have been portrayed as crass, materialistic and yet excessively religious, reckless gunslingers, overly ready to use force, apply the death penalty, ignore environmental degradation, and willing to ride roughshod over international opinion and international law.

Both of these portraits involve considerable exaggeration and tend to oversimplify subtle differences and to personify the alleged traits of individual national leaders. On the European side there is also a long tradition of anti-American caricature, most evident on the political left, but with antecedents that include the political right and can be identified as early as the eighteenth century, as described by Philippe Roger in his writing on French anti-Americanism.[13]

These depictions and the subtle differences that do exist should not, however, be allowed to obscure the enormous commonalities shared by Europeans and Americans. These Atlantic societies share a heritage stemming from the Enlightenment and Western liberalism, including traditions of political liberty, freedom of speech, the rule of law, minority rights, religious liberty, women's rights, scientific rationality, and social tolerance. These commonalities seem particularly evident when contrasted with values in many other regions of the world. Moreover, these shared values are threatened by the precepts of radical Islamism as well as the policies evident in other authoritarian systems.[14]

The American Role

Shared threats, interests, and values, as well as Europe's own limitations, do not exhaust the reasons for the continuing Atlantic partnership. An additional key dimension concerns America's unique capabilities. In response to the events of the 1990s, and especially turmoil in the Balkans which neither the Europeans nor the UN proved capable of resolving, the Clinton administration was given to referring to the US as the indispensable nation. In the post-9/11 world, America's unmatched strengths became especially pertinent. Indeed, on the most pressing and lethal international problems, and much else besides, the alternative to American leadership or engagement is not that some other country or institution will respond, but that no one will do so. Elsewhere, Michael Mandelbaum has described the US as the world's principal provider of collective goods. These dimensions include order, security, and economic stability. He concludes his depiction of this role with an insightful observation:

> About other countries' approach to the American role ... whatever its life span, three things can be safely predicted: They will not pay for it; they will continue to criticize it; and they will miss it when it is gone.[15]

Similarly, in reference to the post-9/11 world, in which threats are real, lethal, and likely to persist for a very long time, Niall Ferguson has cautioned those who are uneasy about America's unipolar status to be wary of the dangerous and even deadly character of the alternative – 'apolarity' – in a world from which American power was absent.[16]

The Future of Transatlantic Relations

As a further sign that rancorous disputes about Iraq did not fundamentally undermine the foundations of the Atlantic relationship, collaboration between the US and Europe has actually improved since 2002–03. On both sides of the Atlantic there has been an awareness of the need for cooperation and engagement to deal with common problems. For example, the US and France have worked closely together on Lebanon since 2004, seeking to restore the sovereignty of that country. Together they secured passage of UN Security Council Resolution 1559 calling for the restoration of Lebanese government control over its territory, the disbanding and disarming of Hezbollah, and in effect the withdrawal of Syrian forces. And in response to the Hezbollah-Israel war in July–August 2006, they obtained Resolution 1701 aimed at restoring the Lebanese government's control of its southern border area and reducing the threat posed by Hezbollah as a state within a state.

The US also deferred to Britain, France, and Germany (the EU-3) in attempting to negotiate compliance by Iran with its obligations under the Nuclear Non-Proliferation Treaty, and seeking to deal with Iranian violations in its nuclear programme identified by the board of the International Atomic Energy Agency (IAEA). There was agreement that if diplomacy were unsuccessful, the US and Europeans would cooperate in seeking sanctions via the UN Security Council. Neither diplomacy, nor – in view of Chinese and Russian opposition – efforts at the UN have successfully brought a change in Teheran's conduct. Nor, for that matter, have UN resolutions on Lebanon been successfully implemented vis-à-vis Hezbollah and the role of Syria. Yet the existence of close US–European collaboration on these common problems has at least been present. Other areas of cooperation can be identified as well, both on Europe's periphery, as in the Balkans and in aid to the 'Orange Revolution' in Ukraine, and in the case of Afghanistan.

Ironically, obstacles to effective coordination have less to do with American inhibitions than with European limits of capability and, at times, political will. Many European governments have lacked either the ability to send significant numbers of troops and equipment to Afghanistan, despite the formal NATO operation there as the alliance's first true ground war, or they have been unwilling to allow their personnel in that country to be deployed into areas where direct combat – and casualties – are likely to occur. Combat troops have been provided primarily by Britain, the Netherlands, Canada, and even Australia, but other European governments have been reluctant to send their personnel into harm's way.

Despite these shortcomings, the foundations of the Atlantic relationship remain durable. They include not only the existence of common threats, but shared values and interests as well as the prospect that for the foreseeable future, the EU will continue to lack the attributes of a genuinely unified federal state, while the US will continue to possess unique capabilities that no other country can match. There are bound to be mutual disappointments, and new controversies and disagreements will arise, but there will be no fundamental rupture in the relationship for a very long time to come.

Notes

1 Chirac quoted in *The Economist*, 26 April 2003, and in *Washington Post*, 15 April 2005.
2 Waltz, Kenneth, US Congress, Senate, *Relations in a Multipolar World*, Hearings before the Committee on Foreign Relations, 102nd Congress, 1st Session, 26, 28, and 30 November 1990 (Washington, DC: Government Printing Office, 1991), p. 210, quoted in Gunther Hellman and Reinhard Wolf, 'Neorealism, Neoliberal Institutionalism, and the Future of NATO', *Security Studies*, vol. 3, no. 1 (Autumn 1993), p. 17.
3 Kupchan, Charles, 'The Waning Days of the Atlantic Alliance', in Bertel Heurlin and Mikkel Vedby Rasmussen, eds, *Challenges and Capabilities: NATO in the 21st Century* (Copenhagen: Danish Institute for International Studies, 2003), p. 25.
4 I have elaborated on this in, 'Die USA und der Nahe Osten', *Internationale Politik* (Berlin), vol. 61, no. 9 (September 2006), pp. 91–97, and portions of the argument concerning the Israeli–Palestinian conflict are adapted from Robert J. Lieber, *The American Era: Power and Strategy for the 21st Century*, revised edition (New York: Cambridge University Press, 2007), Chapter 8, pp. 217–21.
5 Text of bin Laden Remarks in 'Hypocrisy Rears Its Ugly Head', as broadcast by Al-Jazeera television on 7 October 2001. *Washington Post*, 2 October 2001.
6 See especially Lewis, Bernard, *What Went Wrong? Western Impact and Middle Eastern Response* (New York: Oxford University Press, 2002), and Fouad Ajami, *The Foreigner's Gift: The Americans, the Arabs, and the Iraqis in Iraq* (New York: Oxford University Press, 2006).
7 Roy, Olivier, 'Why Do they Hate Us? Not Because of Iraq', *New York Times*, 22 July 2005.
8 Joffe, Josef, 'A World Without Israel', *Foreign Policy* (Jan/Feb 2005).
9 Lugar Survey on Nuclear Proliferation, June 2005; http://lugar.senate.gov/reports/NPSurvey.pdf.
10 Merton, Robert, *Sociological Ambivalence and other Essays,* New York: The Free Press, a division of Macmillan Publishing Co., Inc. 1976.
11 Pew Global Attitudes Project, 'The Great Divide: How Westerners and Muslims View Each Other', released 06.22.06; http://pewglobal.org/reports/pdf/253topline.pdf. Question38: 'On a different subject, do you believe that groups of Arabs carried out the attacks against the United States (the World Trade Center and the Pentagon) on September 11 (2001) or don't you believe this?' The six Muslim majority countries were Egypt, Jordan, Nigeria, Turkey, Indonesia, and Pakistan. Data cited by Pew for the latter three countries were from Gallup 2002.
12 Kagan, Robert, 'Power and Weakness' *Policy Review*, No.113, June–July 2002.
13 Roger, Philippe, *The American Enemy: The History of French Anti-Americanism* (Chicago, IL: University of Chicago Press, 2005).
14 See for example the concept of 'reactionary modernism' as identified by the historian Jeffery Herf. He analyses the way in which fascism and Nazism in the 1920s and 1930s embraced modern technology but otherwise rejected the values of Western liberalism and the Enlightenment, and he finds parallels in radical

Islamism. See *Reactionary Modernism: Technology, Culture, and Politics in Weimar and the Third Reich* (New York: Cambridge University Press, 1994); and 'Historic Transgressions: The Uses and Abuses of German History', *International Politik* (Berlin), Transatlantic Edition, vol. 7 (Spring 2006), 47–53, at 48–49.

15 Mandelbaum, Michael, *The Case for Goliath: How America Acts as the World's Government in the 21st Century* (New York: Public Affairs, 2005), p. 226.

16 Ferguson, Niall, 'A World Without Power', *Foreign Policy*, July/Aug 2004.

5 Perceptions, Misperceptions, and Transatlantic Relations

Past, Present, and Future(s)

Michael Smith

Transatlantic relations are simultaneously fertile and challenging ground for analysis of perceptions and misperceptions. They form one of the most densely institutionalized and strongly networked spaces in world politics and the global political economy, and they contain dynamic and growing exchanges and transactions in the diplomatic, economic, and security spheres. So it is to be expected that within this space, participants in diplomatic, economic, and security interactions will encounter problems arising from the framing, the maintenance, and the adaptation of perceptions, and that these perceptions will at many points run the risk of inaccuracy, error, and consequent recriminations. As with the most intimate of social relationships everywhere, the very intimacy of the relationships guarantees that misunderstandings, disputes, and recriminations will be as frequent as settled relations embodying trust and mutual dependency.

In this context, the systematic analysis of perceptions and misperceptions has an important role to play, both for analytical and for policy purposes. One reason for this is that transatlantic relations have a long and strong history, and that, therefore, they provide the raw material for the rigorous linking of history and theory that is characteristic of the work of Robert Jervis and others.[1] Another reason is that transatlantic relations demand of the analyst a methodical linking of several levels of analysis and of agents and structures in a way that is also characteristic of much work on perceptions and misperceptions. A third reason is that the current conjuncture – or that of the period since 2000 – in transatlantic relations raises questions of policy that directly respond to a concern with perceptions and misperceptions. How did the 'neoconservative' era reflect issues of perception and misperception? Were the disparities of perception that emerged during the early 2000s idiosyncratic, cyclical, or structural in character? What do the advances and reverses of the post-2000 period tell us about the changing nature of European perceptions in the transatlantic arena? Will there be a return to multilateralism in transatlantic relations (was there ever a decline in multilateralism), and how much does that depend upon issues of perception and misperception? Will the post-George W. Bush era consist of 'more of the same' with complex and messy relationships and concomitant problems of perception and misperception defeating the efforts of those who would advocate a new 'transatlantic bargain', or will it see the consolidation of American predominance – or maybe both at once?

This chapter attempts to explore these and other questions through a focus on perceptions and misperceptions, inspired by the work of Robert Jervis, and particularly by a number of specific insights that seem to me to bear closely on the past, present, and possible futures of the relationship. First, it can be observed that there is the possibility of misperception among even the closest of allies, such as those engaged in transatlantic relations. Second, this means that analysis of intentions and the formation of (accurate or flawed) images of others is central to the evolution of policy and process in transatlantic relations. Third, as a result, problems of perception and misperception that have on many occasions been analysed in adversarial contexts are central to transatlantic relations: among these are misperceptions of centralization, the tendency to play down the effects of one's own actions on partners, wishful thinking, cognitive dissonance, and the search for consistency.[2] These are well-established notions in the analysis of perceptions and misperceptions among competing actors, and it is my contention that they give us an important insight into the evolution of transatlantic relations. Just as in adversarial relationships, relations among allies can be characterized by key contextual challenges – the presence of competing values, of complexity and of ambiguous information – and these lend to transatlantic relations since their origins a specific atmosphere and set of policy problems.

The chapter proceeds by looking first at the 60-year perspective from 1946 to 2006 and beyond (using the 1976 publication of Jervis' key work on perception and misperception as the mid-point of this period), and asking what are the key components of continuity and change in the context for perception and misperception. It then proceeds to focus especially on the perception (and misperception) of the 'politics of limits' as a key component in transatlantic relations. This is then used as the basis for investigation of three approaches to perception and misperception in transatlantic relations: power and security; interdependence and integration; learning and forgetting. In broad terms, these correspond to Realist, Liberal, and Constructivist approaches, and thus they extend some elements of the 'classical' perception/misperception approach.[3] In the concluding section of the chapter, these approaches are extended through an analysis of possible futures for transatlantic relations, and the perceptions/misperceptions approach is reassessed.

From 1946 to 1976 to 2006 and Beyond: Then and Now

The period over which transatlantic relations have evolved, as noted above, lends importance to historical analysis, which seeks to identify trends and the coexistence of continuity and change. One such trend is that towards increased complexity and uncertainty in the context of transatlantic relations. Since 1946 – indeed, since 1976 – there has been a multiplication of new channels for communication across the Atlantic and within the broader global arena, which has vastly increased the range of information and services available to actors, but which at the same time has created dangers of information overload and saturation. At the same time, there has been a multiplication of risks and threats, especially but not only since the end of the Cold War in the late 1980s and early 1990s. These risks and threats have become not only more frequent, but also more difficult to pin down and often essentially fluid in their occurrence, creating a mobile mosaic of security and other concerns with which policy-makers are challenged to cope. Finally, and partly as a result of these two trends towards multiplication of channels of communication and risks/threats, there has been growing uncertainty about boundaries and rules in the global arena, which has transmitted itself also into transatlantic relations. The conventions of alliance relations, of crisis and conflict management, and of many forms of economic and social interaction have been challenged throughout the post-World War II period, and arguably much more widely and consistently since the end of the Cold War.[4]

These elements of change and uncertainty have gone alongside a second dimension: the change in system polarity. From the bipolarity of the 'high Cold War' we have seen episodes and trends more redolent of what might be called 'bi-multipolarity' and then (since the end of the Cold War) of essential unipolarity. These phases have not been clear-cut and have often intersected with or overlaid each other in conflicting ways. But they have given rise to a number of challenges for perception and misperception. One of these challenges is that of choice and necessity by actors within the system: to what extent do they see themselves constrained or empowered by the structure of transatlantic relations? There are implications here both for dominant and for subordinate actors. On the one hand, this is what might be termed the 'lonely superpower' problem, with US policy-makers simultaneously empowered, but also in subtle ways constrained, by their status since the end of the Cold War.[5] At the same time, though, it is a problem for subordinate actors (of whom there are many in the transatlantic system): how do they frame their responses to dominant power actions, can they form common perceptions of the dominant power, and what are the possibilities for them to enlarge their space for non-conformity or non-compliance? These are of course problems closely linked with the politics of alliance and issues of collective action and defection.[6] For the argument here, it is crucial to note that they raise key issues of perception and misperception.

A third dimension of long-term change in transatlantic relations is in what might be termed 'order'. There has been a secular – but uneven – trend from rigidity and predictability in the height of the Cold War towards confusion and chaos, which has raised key questions about the 'established order' of transatlantic relations, that is to say about the relationship between material power, institutions, and ideas or values. A core issue here is that of ownership: who has the right to define what transatlantic relations are about, the values around which they should revolve, and the institutions that can sustain common activities? It seems evident that there have been continuing disputes about ownership of the transatlantic order, but also that these have in some respects been exacerbated by the dominant position of the US since the end of the Cold War.[7] In terms of perception and misperception, this means that the search for regular and stable images of transatlantic order (and this also extends to broader international order) is encumbered by not only a shifting and unstable power structure, but also a contest for ownership of institutions and ideas. There has been a continuous assertion from policymakers and other analysts of the need for stable and reliable images, but on the one hand this encounters the systemic conditions noted above, and on the other hand it can in itself become part of an attempt to appropriate and manipulate images of transatlantic relations themselves.

These systemic features have been accompanied by another important dimension of transatlantic relations, which directly reflects both their long standing and evolution. This is what might be termed the generational issue. Throughout transatlantic relations there has been concern more or less openly expressed about the 'successor generation' and about how policy elites and the broader public will respond to shifts in power and prosperity within the transatlantic system. In the immediate post war years, this was largely bound up with the formation of democratic political cultures in Germany and other defeated countries. By the 1970s, the concern was with the attitudes and expectations of those who would come to power without having experienced the war itself or the post war acculturation process. Sixty years on, the issue is that of the views and political trajectories of those who are effectively not post-World War II, but post-Vietnam. This is important in terms of perceptions and misperceptions since we know that the historical experiences of policy elites are a key factor shaping in their images of world politics and policy processes.[8] This in turn has implications for the choices that they see as possible or appropriate and for the values that they pursue.

My argument is thus that in considering the role of perceptions and misperceptions in transatlantic relations, we need to consider history in the several dimensions set out above: the growth of complexity and uncertainty, the shifts in system structure, the rigidity and polarity of the transatlantic order, and the issues created by generational change. These are not givens so much as they are questions that must be asked. And each of them affects the context for perception and misperception in transatlantic relations by affecting the information available, the structural constraints that operate, the conventions and rules that are seen as significant, and the experiences and expectations of those who are making policy. It is through this route that we arrive at the possibility of what Jervis terms 'compound misperception', which is arguably more likely and dangerous between close allies than between known adversaries (see Chapter 2 in this volume). To paraphrase Donald Rumsfeld, whereas it might be felt that transatlantic allies would fall into the category of 'known knowns', they actually often fall into the realm of 'known unknowns' and sometimes into the area of 'unknown unknowns'. In terms of transatlantic relations during the past few years, this means that it is vital not to get hung up on the distinctiveness of the George W. Bush era: the problem of context and its role in shaping perceptions and misperceptions in transatlantic relations is far broader than that.

The 'Politics of Limits' and Beyond

The discussion so far has focused on broad historical and related patterns in transatlantic relations. At that level, it can account for a number of continuing trends and features, and for the ways in which successive generations of policy-makers on both sides of the ocean have promoted, resisted, or accommodated the demands of allies. The discussion now moves on to focus more closely on the ways in which the past few years have been distinctive and to tease out some of the implications of this distinctiveness for transatlantic relations. My argument is that the George W. Bush Administration has posed distinctive demands, and has created specific problems of perception and misperception, but that in order for these to be fully understood they need also to be put into the context of historical development previously outlined. The distinctiveness can be seen in terms of what I would call the politics of limits.[9]

What, then, is distinctive about the past seven or eight years? The first striking feature has been mentioned already: that the US since the end of the Cold War – and specifically since the collapse of the Soviet Union in 1991 – has found itself in a world without rivals. My concern is not so much with this well-covered phenomenon, but rather with its implications for perceptions and misperceptions. And my cue comes from Robert Jervis, in two guises. First, in his classic work on perception and misperception, Jervis focuses on what might happen if such a situation occurred:

> In some cases scholars, and, less frequently, decision-makers want to know what a state would do in the absence of internal constraints. For example, if the US found itself in a situation where none would oppose it, would it leave other states completely alone, take their territory, exploit their natural resources, or change their domestic political systems?[10]

The important point here is that such questions, and the ways in which policy-makers answer them, respond not only to the absence of external constraints, but also to the absence of internal constraints, thus allowing policy-makers to pursue what Jervis describes as their 'utopian intentions'.[11] Seen in this light, the George W. Bush Administration – or at least those parts of it that captured the policy initiative in the early days, and especially after the events of 11 September 2001 – is a collection of 'utopian radicals'[12] rejecting the politics of limits and espousing policy aims that could be seen as revolutionary in tenor.

This rejection of the politics of limits is of course partly a problem for US policy-making, as successive occupants of the State Department in particular have discovered since 2000. But it is also – and especially, in terms of this chapter – a source of challenges for transatlantic relations. Most particularly, it has been a challenge to the settled perceptions about US leadership and European followership that had been preserved even through the Reagan era and the early post-Cold War period. Policy-makers in Europe who had cherished the belief that US policies might respond to sustained lobbying by the allies, and who had seen this borne out at least partly by the Clinton years, found that this was by no means the case under George W. Bush and his 'vulcan' colleagues. The problem is that this did not lead to uniform perceptions and policy responses on the part of the Europeans; instead, it created a situation of divide and rule in which the oft-quoted but curiously elusive distinction between 'old' and 'new' Europe came to symbolize the fragmentation and lack of collective capacity-building. In this context, the inability of the European allies to contain US policy has been a striking feature of the past six years;[13] when this is added to the global situation of 'major power peace'[14] and to the permissive atmosphere of US domestic politics after 9/11, it can be seen that the restraints on US policies have been at a historically low point.

Why have the Europeans been incapable of containing US policy? The argument is not simply one about material power, although that is important. Rather it has to take into account the nature not only of the US, but also of the Europeans, and the ways in which this affects perceptions and misperceptions. The European Union plays a key role in this area: it has been described as the world's first 'multi-perspectival polity'[15] and as a zone in which 'mutual interference' between EU Member States has become a way of (postmodern) life.[16] When this zone is invaded by a dominant and disruptive force that cannot be contained other than by collective action of all members (and even this is doubtful), then the potential for disparities of perceptions is evident. I will return to this shortly, but it is important here to register that the debate about 'Mars and Venus' in transatlantic relations[17] is not just one about attitudes to power and purposes; it is also about the capacity to form collective perceptions of challenges and to foster a unified image of transatlantic relations. Seen in this light, issues of European values and identity, and the perception that in some way 'normal international politics' have been suspended between EU Member States, are as important in explaining transatlantic differences as the rationalization of European weakness through a focus on 'soft power'.

Drawing on these elements of difference between the US and the EU, which have been accentuated, but not created, by the end of the Cold War, it is possible not only to identify disparities between European and American responses to specific challenges, but also to tease out fundamental differences on some of the key issues of global politics. Europeans and Americans differ on the meanings of sovereignty;[18] they have profoundly different perceptions of the nature of security and of the possibility of achieving security; they are at odds on the potential and uses of 'hard power' and 'soft power', and not least of what has been termed 'normative power';[19] and they occupy very different positions on the potential for multilateral action as opposed to unilateral. These differences were at their height in the middle years of the George W. Bush era, and especially over the invasion of Iraq, but I would argue that they are persistent, despite the variations between US administrations and between EU Member States.[20] This means that the frames of reference within which US and European policy-makers view global issues and their own mutual relations are always contrasting and at times radically divergent.

What are the implications of this for transatlantic relations? Jervis[21] sees the troubles of the early 2000s as arising from both the US and their allies 'doing what comes naturally' and responding to (on the one hand) the perception of empowerment and choice and (on the other) to the need for resistance and containment. I think that this captures core elements of the issue, but I would add to it some more intangible factors which go beyond the rather materialist and structuralist interpretation offered by Jervis. First, I think the events of the early 2000s raise (not for the first time) the issue of legitimacy in transatlantic relations. This has been a persistent factor in the policy-making of European governments especially, from the Gaullist reaction of the early 1960s to the issues created by the Vietnam war to the problems of nuclear armaments in the 1980s. Second, and connected to this, there is the problem of reciprocity. This is a key element of multilateralism,[22] and expresses not only an exchange relationship, but also a perception of mutual need. Finally, there is the problem of trust – which in a sense expresses perceptions of legitimacy and reciprocity, and which goes to the nature of transatlantic relations as not only relations of power and alliance, but also forms of social interactions and understandings.

My conclusion from this discussion is that attitudes to and perceptions of the politics of limits are a litmus test for the sustainability of transatlantic relations in the post-Cold War period. The test can be seen as one based almost entirely on material power and its distribution, but I would wish to add non-material considerations to this formulation – specifically, issues of legitimacy, reciprocity, and trust. The next section of the chapter explores three perspectives on perceptions, misperceptions, and transatlantic relations as a means of adding flesh to the bones of this argument.

Perceptions, Misperceptions, and Transatlantic Relations: Three Perspectives

In this section, I present three contrasting perspectives on transatlantic relations and explore their implications for a focus on perceptions and misperceptions. I do not argue that any one of these gives the 'master interpretation': each has its own power and its own limitations. In order fully to understand the problem of perceptions and misperceptions in transatlantic relations, all three are needed, but in combinations that take account of the specific issues under consideration. The three perspectives are: power and security; interdependence and integration; and learning and forgetting.

Power and Security

To see transatlantic relations as the politics of power and security means to cast them in terms of material power and its distribution (see above). Depending upon the distribution of material power, these relations could be seen as a form of balance, as a form of hegemony and subordination, or as a form of collective defence against an external threat. In many situations, as was the case during many phases of the Cold War, transatlantic relations have contained elements of all three forms. This means that the management of power – and the formation of accurate perceptions about both its distribution and its management – is a core element in transatlantic relations and in the policy-making of those engaged within the transatlantic system.[23]

Central to the formation of accurate perceptions, and to the minimizing of misperceptions in this context, is the assessment of threats and opportunities, costs and risks. This is of course in many respects the argument set out by Jervis[24] , and it is a powerful one. Jervis rightly points to the ways in which this links to the process of choice, based either in necessity or in preferences that can be relatively freely exercised. The link to US foreign policy under the George W. Bush Administration needs scarcely to be underlined, but it must also be pointed out that there is a transatlantic dimension here. To put it simply, the freedom to choose is unevenly distributed within the transatlantic system generally, and in terms of particular choices its unevenness can be extreme. Jervis also points out that choices are always related to costs, and that ability to predict and willingness to pay the costs of specific choices affects perceptions in powerful ways. Not surprisingly, this can be projected onto the policies of the US Administration since 2000, revealing that its capacity to predict the costs has often been found wanting and that this in turn has had implications for the willingness both of policy-makers and of the broader US public to bear the costs[25]. But here too there is a transatlantic dimension since the European members of the system have arguably shown a greater propensity to emphasize costs than the US administration, but also an uneven willingness to bear them, depending on whether they are 'hard' military costs or the 'softer' costs of reconstruction and redevelopment.

This brings us to another key element of the politics of power and security in transatlantic relations. Although there is much to be said about material power, preferences, costs and capacity or willingness to pay them, there is also a powerful role for estimates of intentions and images. Within the transatlantic system, these function in at least two directions. First, there are US estimates of Europe. These suffer from a certain schizophrenia: on the one hand, American policy-makers claim to be looking for a Europe to relate to, and on the other, they cultivate special relationships and bilateral links that can serve to undermine the very collective Europe they claim to desire. In power and security terms, this is not unduly surprising since the dominant power might be expected to reserve the right to define its prota- gonists as it wishes, and since Europe is unquestionably divided in terms of material capacity and commitments, reflecting the relatively 'thin' institutio- nalization of its foreign and defence policies. On the other side lie European perceptions of the US. These have tended to be divided (although not always as divided as might be expected), reflecting the incomplete nature of the European polity and of European identity, which is particularly marked in areas of power and security. They have also tended at times to suffer from one of the problems identified by Jervis and mentioned at the beginning of this chapter: overestimating or underestimating the centralization and pur- posefulness of the protagonist. The net result is that whilst Americans have tended to underestimate the potential for European collective action, Eur- opeans have tended to underestimate the divisions and potential for confu- sion in US foreign policy. For both sides, the problem of forming stable images is central to the difficulties they have faced in transatlantic relations.

From the perspective of power and security, therefore, the recent history of perceptions and misperceptions in transatlantic relations is one of uncer- tainty and instability. The core problems of forming stable images and reli- able expectations based on an appraisal of power and preferences have been difficult to address, let alone solve. What George W. Bush might have termed the 'misunderestimation' of intentions and positions has been a frequent occurrence, reflecting the fact that the management of US power has been a challenge for all those engaged in the system. As a result, there have been uncertain responses to the structural imperatives of the post-Cold War era, and frequent pressures on the pursuit of multilateralism and restraint within the system. In consequence, we may now be at a point where we *have* come up against the politics of limits – a situation in which the US needs allies because its resources have been stretched too far, but in which the politics of (mis)perceptions are sticky and the perceived costs too high for the allies to want to pay.

Interdependence and Integration

When we move from a focus on the politics of power and security to a focus on the politics of interdependence and integration, this does not mean that we remove our concern with the three key elements that were identified in the previous section: legitimacy, reciprocity, and trust. As is to be expected, though, they emerge in different ways and have different implications within this perspective. The politics of complex interdependence, as advanced since the 1970s by Robert Keohane and Joseph Nye[26], depend upon a number of material considerations, but these are in many respects profoundly at odds with those of the power and security approach. For state power, hierarchy, and the competitive search for security, the interdependence and integration approach substitutes a mixed actor system in which processes of communication and exchange are central and in which 'hard power' is given a relatively restricted place. This in turn means that there is a key role for institutions and processes of governance, both in their own right and as means of managing the relations between increasingly interdependent national authorities.

In terms of transatlantic relations, there is ample empirical evidence of the growth of interdependence and of integration. As early as 1968, Richard Cooper pointed out the ways in which this linked with assumptions about legitimacy, trust, and reciprocity:

> These countries are closely and increasingly linked by ties of trade, technology and capital. Knowledge of each others' institutions and practices has increased enormously, and the level of confidence in national economic policies has risen to the point of greatly reducing psychological barriers to the movements of capital and the location of production. In short, the major industrial countries are becoming moreclosely 'integrated'.[27]

Given the subsequent growth in intensity of exchanges and in the density of transatlantic institutions, it is now possible to argue that not only are the societies of the Euro-American system interdependent, but that in a variety of ways they form an integrated economic, political, and security space that is increasingly served by institutions and by expanding areas of international governance.[28] The 'mutual interference' between countries on both sides of the Atlantic has grown, linkages and networks between them are at a historically high level, there is a well-established and expanding transatlantic elite, predominantly in commercial activity, but significantly also in matters of diplomacy and security. This means that interactions across the Atlantic have generated a large and increasing number of stakeholders whose concerns are relatively immune to changes of government or of international conditions. Seen from this perspective, a 'multi-stakeholder' system has come into being within which perceptions and misperceptions have a changed significance.[29]

What is this changed significance? One element in an answer to this question lies in information and its uses. Transatlantic relations conceived as interdependence and integration constitute an information-rich environment in which the danger is of saturation with the everyday and neglect of the strategic, but in which there is also the promise of increasing mutual sensitivity based on the open exchange of goods, services, data, and ideas. In terms of interdependence thinking, a key question generated by this information-rich context is that of vulnerability[30]: to what extent do perceptions of loss of control and of risk crowd out those of mutual sensitivity aided by comprehensive and open interchange of information ? This in turn merges into a further question: does the rapid increase in amount and speed of information flows undermine existing institutional structures, including those of the states engaged in transatlantic relations? It is no surprise in the circumstances that the management of information and challenges to authority over the gathering and release of information have been key to relations in the transatlantic system during the past decade, underlined by the 'war on terror' and its links to issues of data security.

If information plays a key role in shaping perceptions and misperceptions within the contemporary transatlantic system, it is clear that this is only one of several areas in which transactions, institutions, and networks can play a key role. The accuracy of perceptions, and thus the perceptual base for policy-making, is as important within an interdependence and integration perspective as it is within a power and security perspective, but in different ways. We should be aware that the frequency and intimacy of transactions, amounting to exceptional transactional density within the transatlantic area, has significant implications for the generation of legitimacy, reciprocity, and trust. But it is not a simple or a linear process: more does not necessarily mean better in this area. Sheer volume of transactions in trade, monetary relations, environmental politics, or security politics, for example, cannot simply be translated into better understanding and reliability of perceptions. It can, of course, lead to an escalation of disputes, to perceptions of vulnerability by governments or other groups, and to a reduction of practices of reciprocity and levels of trust because of the range of public and private interests involved. In this context, information and its manipulation can confer power and give the potential for misperceptions of the possibilities of 'private management' of the system. Institutions thus become doubly important, as a means, on the one hand, of managing information and establishing the reliability of perceptions, and, on the other hand, of establishing regulatory principles and structures to reduce the consequences of disputes and recriminations.

Another process that seems to be important in the context of interdependence and integration is that of lesson-drawing. As noted earlier in the chapter, there is an extensive history to transatlantic relations, and more specifically an extensive and well-documented history of cooperation and competition. In this situation of 'competitive cooperation',[31] where rules and institutions themselves can become part of the game alongside substantive differences of policy and preferences, the capacity and inclination of the protagonists can be critical to outcomes. This capacity and inclination are shaped by (among other factors) the lessons drawn from previous episodes of competition and cooperation, which become endogenous to the game itself. So relations between the EU and the US, or between member states within NATO, or between the US and individual European governments are to be seen here as reflecting the lessons drawn from history. As we know from theories of perception and misperception, these lessons may not be accurate, or may not be properly learned by those involved. The implications can be seen from transatlantic interactions in trade, monetary relations, environmental politics, or the increasing history in judicial competition and cooperation, for example in respect of the International Criminal Court.[32] They can also be discerned in areas of 'hard security', where a history of failure – or apparent failure – by the EU during the 1990s has conditioned not only EU policy responses, but also US expectations. One factor that should be noted here is that the level of integration – as opposed to interdependence – between those engaged is in principle likely to have a major influence on the achievement of accurate mutual perceptions by changing the situation from one of 'us and them' to one of competing 'us-es' (an inelegant term but one that conveys the change from 'other' to 'we' that has been unevenly emerging in transatlantic relations).

The key problems that emerge from this brief exploration of an interdependence and integration perspective on perceptions and misperceptions in transatlantic relations are threefold. First, the increasing density and complexity of interactions and flows within the system poses a major problem for the creation of accurate perceptions in both public and private spheres. Second, within this context, there is little room for strategies based on competitive bargaining, which can be self-defeating and can lead to errors and risks because of the lack of comprehensive information or lack of processing capacity. Management based on problem-solving and negotiation, often within mixed public/private networks, is both a more prevalent and a more appropriate approach, emphasizing as it does the exchange relationships and institutional contacts that can lay the foundations for legitimacy, reciprocity, and trust. Finally, issues of perception and misperception can be addressed – if not with inevitable success – through 'early warning' devices, the use of anticipatory adjustment, and the adaptation of regulatory structures to maximize the likelihood of accuracy and sensitivity. But this model of transatlantic relations demands of those involved a complex and sensitive view of motivations and alternatives, shared relatively evenly between those engaged. It might be suggested that neither the US nor its European allies have developed such a sense: the US because of the demands of domestic politics and the incapacity of political elites to develop a consistent view of the outside world based on interdependence and integration, and the Europeans because of the competing and coexisting institutional and political forms to which they are subject within Europe itself, which combine with the inconsistencies of US policy to create major obstacles to consistency or adaptation.

Learning and Forgetting

A third perspective on transatlantic relations, and one that offers a rather different approach to perceptions and misperceptions, can be framed in terms of learning and forgetting. We have encountered this in both of the other perspectives, where it has pointed to key issues of history and its uses, and the ways in which policy choices can be influenced by perceptions of past successes or failures. Jervis' approach to perception and misperception explicitly incorporates attention to 'how decision-makers learn from history'.[33] The approach can be taken much further, though, by linking it to processes of 'social learning' and to ideas put forward most consistently by social constructivists. Here, the psychological aspects explored by Jervis can be allied to awareness of transatlantic relations as a social process in which social learning is a key outcome from the kinds of long-term and intense interactions that have become characteristic of the system. To the importance of decision-makers' psychology, and the ways in which they remember or mis-remember historical episodes, can be added the ways in which elite discourses in transatlantic relations endogenize the views of policy elites in all parts of the system, and in which (at least according to constructivist views) structural factors retreat into the background.

Such an approach can readily be criticized, and indeed has been criticized by Jervis himself, as being empty of content and as adding very little to established perspectives such as those based on power and security or interdependence and integration.[34] I think it can be argued, however, that ideas of social learning and the construction of what (following John Ruggie) might be termed a partial 'multi-perspectival polity' in transatlantic relations can suggest at least an additional dimension to what established approaches can give us. We have confirmed already in this chapter that there is an enduring significance for power and security considerations in transatlantic relations, and that this must be seen in relation to the rapid growth of interdependence and integration within the system: now we can add a recognition of the fact that processes of more or less effective social learning have been taking place in transatlantic relations for more than half a century.

What issues does this alert us to? First, it underlines the process, noted above, by which the participants in transatlantic relations have been engaged in formation, projection, or protection of their own identities over a long period.[35] There is an inherent ambiguity here since the process is uneven, multi-layered, and often decidedly contradictory. From the early Cold War Years in which it might have been thought that reaction to a mutually perceived 'other' (the USSR) would lead to a reinforcement of values and ideas in the transatlantic community – but in which there was a very uneven conversion to this way of thinking – we have moved through phases in which both American and European identities were sought partly through a process of mutual 'othering', but never to such an extent that 'we-perceptions' were thrown out of the window. Indeed, empirically, as we have seen, it is sometimes difficult on the basis of transactions or institutions to recognize 'who is us' within transatlantic relations and, by extension, to recognize 'who is them'.

It has of course been argued that this empirical or transactional context cannot overcome profound and widening differences of norms and values, in which the US can be cast as a 'warrior state' and Europe as a 'civilian power', 'normative power', or 'trading state'.[36] This is what was earlier described as the Mars/Venus argument, implying that there is a genuine transatlantic gulf in terms of the ways in which power is perceived, used, and evaluated. In my view, it is more realistic to see this problem in terms of a rather fluid spectrum rather than a dichotomy, and the events of recent years in transatlantic relations would appear to bear this out.[37] Whilst the fragmentation of Europe in the face of the war in Iraq demonstrates the lack of a Europe when it comes to matters of hard security and the use of force, as well as a strong differentiation of norms and values, the same might also be said of fragmentation in the US political spectrum and US government in the wake of the 'neo-conservative moment'. But this is only part of the story in which social interaction at many levels has constructed more than one transatlantic system, and more than one set of identities and norms. It is no surprise in this context that images are used strategically, and that normative appeals have followed many of the same lines in a kind of market for identities over recent years. Such strategic considerations are well recognized by Jervis,[38] but I think it is important to supplement them with attention to the emergence and negotiation of norms as a key part of the transatlantic system itself. Maybe unsurprisingly, this has not been a major focus of scholarship in recent years, but it certainly merits exploration.

In such an exploration, I would suggest that three dimensions are central. The first is mutual entanglement. Both empirically and discursively, the members of the transatlantic system are entangled with each other and encounter each other in a qualitatively different way in the 2000s than the way in which they were entangled during the 1950s. This means that the process of identity formation, through discrimination and differentiation, but also through incorporation, has far more to draw on than it did in the days of restricted elite contacts and limited transactions. Not surprisingly, therefore, a second dimension of the issue is that identity formation and reformation itself has become a more prominent aspect of transatlantic relations. This does not mean that it has never been prominent before: the evidence of the 1960s and the 1980s argues against such a conclusion.[39] Rather, identity formation and reformation has become a central part of the system – part of the way the system works. The result is not a clear-cut redefinition of identities: rather it often is normative confusion accompanied by the intermingling of identities. Nor is it a clear-cut judgement in favour of one shape of identity or another: the case for 'normative power Europe'[40] is accompanied by many qualifications, as is the 'case for Goliath' (Mandelbaum 2005).[41] This leads to a final feature of the issue, that of understanding and misunderstanding. As noted earlier in this chapter, Jervis has argued persuasively that 'compound misperception' is one possible outcome of alliance relations within a turbulent context, and such a notion is by no means irrelevant to this enquiry. I would argue that the search for bases of understanding and misunderstanding goes further than Jervis suggests since the social processes of transatlantic relations produce types of learning and forgetting that are inherent to the system itself. To put it crudely, this is one of the things that transatlantic relations do.

The result of this discussion is a set of half-formed questions about transatlantic relations in the first part of the twenty-first century. One relates to the 'who is us?' problem: how far can transatlantic relations generate a consensus on norms and identities that resolves some of the problems of legitimacy, reciprocity, and trust noted throughout this chapter? A second question relates to the relationship between this perspective and those explored earlier in the chapter: to what extent can considerations of norms, values, and identities be explored independently of the structures of power and interdependence which are not only persistent but also pervasive in transatlantic relations? Finally, and in line with Jervis' work, how can arguments about norms, values, and identities be considered in relation to problems of wishful thinking, not only about but also within the transatlantic system? We need to explore the capacity of those involved in transatlantic relations to learn and forget both at the social level and at the psychological level – to generate norms, values, and identities that themselves become part of the system – but without neglecting the more material elements of the context that generate constraints and incentives within it. In other words, we need to consider the kinds of 'realist constructivism' or 'liberal constructivism' that can reconcile and add value to an ideational approach.

Conclusion

There are many stories to be told about transatlantic relations, and about the ways in which perceptions and misperceptions both enter into and are generated by the system. At one level, transatlantic relations are a story of crisis and change spread over more than half a century. At the same time, they are a story of world order (or competing world orders) encapsulating competing conceptions of the 'good world' and how it might be achieved. Alongside this, they are a story of intensifying and deepening exchanges and interactions in a multi-level system. Equally, they are a story of images and ideas in which the idea of transatlantic relations itself is part of a continuing contest for 'voice' and identity. This in itself is not surprising given the persistence, centrality, and complexity of the system. As we have seen in this chapter, the different 'stories' can be seen through different conceptual lenses, but this does not mean that they exist in separate compartments. Rather, the use of different perspectives is vital to the understanding of the system.

Whichever conceptual lens is used, there are strong arguments for incorporating attention to perceptions and misperceptions as a means of throwing light on transatlantic relations. As we have seen, the role of perceptions and misperceptions is central, complex, and contested. But such a focus provides a powerful means of relating policy across levels and across time, and asking what has changed and what has stayed the same. It also provides cautionary tales about the need for legitimacy, reciprocity, and trust in transatlantic relations, causing us to question the permanence of multilateralism and restraint in the system, but also drawing attention to the ways in which perceptions and misperceptions are not only observable within the system but also embedded within it as one of its 'products' and one of its conditioning factors. Above all, sensitivity to perceptions and misperceptions helps us to focus on questions about the present and future of the relationship: are the issues of the past few years conjunctural or structural, or are they just part of the way the system has been developed and is working?

Such questions are central to our appreciation of possible futures for the transatlantic relationship. Whether the future is seen as 'divorce', 'differentiation', 'deepening', or 'drift', the system will continue to throw up evidence for the persistence and vitality of perceptual factors, and power to help us to focus on key policy issues and their outcomes. As noted in the introduction to the chapter, the very intimacy of the relationships involved guarantees the continuation of internal ambiguities and contradictions alongside continuing increases in the density of transactions, information, and institutions. In such a context, sensitivity to the ways things are seen by participants, as well as the ways they present themselves to the analyst, is an essential part of enquiry.

Notes

1 Jervis, R. W., *Perception and Misperception in World Politics*, Princeton: Princeton University Press, 1976; 'Realism in the Study of World Politics', *International Organization*, 52(4), Autumn 1998, pp. 971–91; *American Foreign Policy in a new Era*, London: Routledge, 2005.
2 Jervis, *Perception and Misperception*, Introduction.
3 Jervis, 'Realism'.
4 Andrews, D. M., (ed.) *The Atlantic Alliance under Stress: US-European Relations after Iraq*, Cambridge: Cambridge University Press, 2005; Gann, L.H. and Duignan, P., *Contemporary Europe and the Atlantic Alliance*, Oxford : Blackwell, 1998; Sloan, S.R., *NATO, the European Union, and the Atlantic Community: The Transatlantic Bargain Challenged*, 2nd edition, Lanham, MD: Rowman and Littlefield, 2005.
5 Halper, S. and Clarke, J., *America Alone: The Neo-Conservatives and the Global Order*, Cambridge: Cambridge University Press, 2004; Held, D. and Koenig-Archibugi, M., (eds) *American Power in the 21st Century*, Cambridge: Polity 2004; Ikenberry, G. J., (ed.) *America Unrivalled: The Future of the Balance of Power*, Ithaca, NY: Cornell University Press, 2002.
6 Jervis, *American Foreign Policy*; Risse, T. 'US Power in a Liberal Security Community' in Ikenberry, G. J. (ed.) *America Unrivalled: The Future of the Balance of Power*, Ithaca, NY: Cornell University Press 2002, pp. 260–83; Smith, M. 'Taming the Elephant? The European Union and the Management of American Power', *Perspectives on European Politics and Society*, 6(1), 2005, pp. 129–54.
7 Smith, M., 'Between Two Worlds? The European Union, the United States and World Order', *International Politics*, 41(1), 2004, pp. 96–117.

8 Jervis, *Perception and Misperception*, p. 239.

9 Smith, 'Between Two Worlds?'

10 Jervis, *Perception and Misperception*, p. 49.

11 Jervis, *Perception and Misperception*, p. 49.

12 Jervis, *American Foreign Policy*, 2006.

13 Smith, 'Taming the Elephant?'.

14 Jervis, *American Foreign Policy*.

15 Ruggie, J. G., 'Territoriality and Beyond: Problematizing Modernity in International Relations', *International Organization*, 46(1), 1993, pp. 139–74; and *Constructing the World Polity: Essays on International Institutionalization*, London: Routledge, 1998, chapter 7.

16 Cooper, R., *The Breaking of Nations: Order and Chaos in the Twenty-First Century*, New York: Atlantic Monthly Press, 2003, chapter 2.

17 Kagan, R., *Of Paradise and Power: America and Europe in the New World Order*, New York: Knopf, 2003; Lindberg, T., (ed.) *Beyond Paradise and Power: Europe, America, and the Future of a Troubled Partnership*, London: Routledge, 2005.

18 Keohane, R. O., 'Ironies of Sovereignty: The EU and the US', in Weiler, J. H. H., Begg, I. and Peterson, J. (eds) *Integration in an Expanding European Union: Reassessing the Fundamentals*, Oxford: Blackwell, 2003, pp. 307–30.

19 Manners, I., 'Normative Power Europe: A Contradiction in Terms?', *Journal of Common Market Studies*, 40(2), 2002, pp. 235–58.

20 Smith, 'Between Two Worlds?'.

21 Jervis, *American Foreign Policy*, pp. 97–98, and see Chapter 2 in this volume.

22 Ruggie, J. G., 'Multilateralism: The Anatomy of an Institution', in Ruggie, J. G. (ed.) *Multilateralism Matters: The Theory and Praxis of an Organizational Form*, New York: Columbia University Press, 1993, pp. 3–47.

23 Smith, 'Taming the Elephant'.

24 See especially *Perception and Misperception*.

25 Jervis, *American Foreign Policy*; see also Daalder, I. and Lindsay, J. M., *America Unbound: The Bush Revolution in Foreign Policy*, Washington, DC: Brookings Institution, 2003; Halper and Clarke, *America Alone*; Lieven, A., *America Right or Wrong: An Anatomy of American Nationalism*, Oxford: Oxford University Press, 2004.

26 Keohane, R. O. and Nye, J.S., *Power and Interdependence: World Politics in Transition*, 3rd edn, Boston, MA: Little, Brown, 2001.

27 Cooper, R.N., *The Economics of Interdependence: Economic Policy in the Atlantic Community*, New York: Columbia University Press for the Council on Foreign Relations, 1968, p. 8.

28 Hamilton, D. S. and Quinlan, J. P., *Partners in Prosperity: The Changing Geography of the Transatlantic Economy*, Washington, DC: Centre for Transatlantic Relations, Johns Hopkins University, 2004; Pollack, M. and Shaffer, G. (eds), *Transatlantic Governance in the Global Economy*, Lanham, MD: Rowman and Littlefield, 2001; Steffenson, R., *Managing EU-US Relations: Actors, Institutions and the New Transatlantic Agenda*, Manchester: Manchester University Press, 2005.

29 Pollack and Shaffer, *Transatlantic Governance*, Chapter 1.

30 Keohane and Nye, *Power and Interdependence*.

31 Smith, M., 'Competitive Cooperation in EU–US Relations: Can the EU be a Strategic Partner for the US in the World Political Economy', *Journal of European Public Policy,* 5(4), 1998, pp. 561–77.

32 Peterson, J. and Pollack, M. (eds), *Europe, America, Bush: Transatlantic Relations in the Twenty-First Century*, London: Routledge, 2003; Pollack and Shaffer, *Transatlantic Governance*.

33 Jervis, *Perception and Misperception*, Chapter 6.

34 Jervis, 'Realism'.
35 Nicolaidis, K., 'The Power of the Superpowerless' in Lindberg, *Beyond Paradise and Power*, pp. 136–48; Smith, M., 'European Integration and American Power: Reflex, Resistance and Reconfiguration', in Slater, D. and Taylor, P. (eds), *The American Century: Consensus and Coercion in the Projection of American Power*, Oxford: Blackwell, pp. 136–48.
36 Smith, 'Between Two Worlds'.
37 Smith, M., 'European Foreign Policy in Crisis? EU Responses to the George W. Bush Administration', *European Political Science*, 5(1), 2006, pp. 41–51.
38 Jervis, *Perception and Misperception*, chapter 6.
39 Smith, 'European Integration and American Power'.
40 Manners, 'Normative Power Europe'; and 'Normative Power Europe Reconsidered: Beyond the Crossroads', *Journal of European Public Policy*, 13(2), 2006, pp. 182–99.
41 Mandelbaum, M., *The Case for Goliath: How America Acts as the World's Government in the 21st Century*, New York: Public Affairs Press, 2005.

6 How Transatlantic Relations can Reinforce the EU's Role as an International Actor

Natividad Fernández Sola

It is possible to analyse transatlantic relations from a variety of theoretical perspectives. Commonly, scholars pick up factual elements, relevant to some understanding or misunderstanding on both sides of the Atlantic and, from this point of view, they sketch a diagnosis in which there is an implicit normative value. By contrast, an analysis based on actors' perceptions and misperceptions has an explanatory value that aims at a better understanding of partners' attitudes currently and in the future. The immediate result of this kind of analysis should be to clarify the essential nature of both parties and consequently to arrive at a better conceptualization of the EU as international actor and a more accurate understanding of US reasons for acting as a hegemonic power. Since a well-functioning transatlantic relationship is a source of EU empowerment, as we will try to demonstrate, and thus an invigorating factor for the EU's international presence, our conclusions will contain some normative influences too.

After describing the main elements acting to change the parameters sustaining the transatlantic relationship, this chapter will explore the current conceptualization of the EU as an international actor, which is an evolutionary role that inevitably affects the transatlantic relationship. The different international roles and perspectives of the US can explain differences in perceptions about similar interests and so about each other. To ground our reasoning we need to distinguish between what role the EU plays currently and what kind of actor it aspires to become in the future. How such a role will develop in the future will depend not only on developments in the EU, but also on world events, as well as internal changes, both at the EU level and at that of its Member States. Transatlantic relations are thus a crucial factor for the development of the EU's Common Foreign and Security Policy (CFSP). At the same time, the US also needs allies to cope with new security challenges and to maintain its primacy in a slightly different normative framework than the previous one.

The explanation of the reasons why any strengthening of transatlantic relations will imply an improvement in the international role of the EU leads us to the conclusion that common needs, common interests, and common strategies can reinforce international influence and even help to forge a separate identity for the EU, an identity that is based on the results and efficiency of the EU's actions in the international arena and that reflects its ability to spread its governance model and its own values according to European methods or, at least, methods agreed by Member States through a deliberative process.

The Changing Parameters of Transatlantic Relations

Until nearly the end of the twentieth century, the international system was bipolar. The transatlantic community lived under the Soviet threat, which led the allies to move progressively closer because of their fear of the adversary. US pre-eminence was accepted by the European allies as a consequence of the Americans' undisputed military superiority and political primacy. A network of economic relations, shared values, and common institutions completed the normative framework within which transatlantic relations developed. The US was the main liberating power that allowed Europe to recover its freedom after Nazism and to counter the Communist threat. Both elements legitimated US hegemony.

In the early 2000s, the general framework of transatlantic relations had changed. If in the early nineties, the change of situation could be anticipated, the progressive transition towards a new international order did not throw it into sharp relief. The successive crises in the Balkans established the necessity of reaffirming transatlantic cooperation. The New Transatlantic Agenda was agreed in 1995, but only after the 9/11 attacks were the substantial changes in the international system that affected the transatlantic relationship evident. International terrorism became the main threat and the US has acted unilaterally, in a world where it has no major state rivals, to confront it. From the economic point of view, the world has seen the rise of a global economy. Transatlantic partners discovered that the means to spread democracy and manage conflicts were not the same according to Americans and Europeans, which implied a questioning of the normative pre-eminence of the US.[1] There were different understandings of the meaning of democracy and human rights. 9/11 was thus a major conjuncture in a series of events that have shifted the global structure of power and risk.[2]

The 2003 Iraq war had a negative effect on transatlantic relations revealing a rift in values and interests, but it also represented a disaster for EU foreign policy cohesion.[3] However, building on a traditional claim in the European integration literature that the whole process of integration is based on overcoming crises, it is argued that this war pushed the EU a few steps further in elevating its role to that of a global actor and that this was partly possible because the Iraq crisis accelerated the development of the European Security and Defence Policy (ESDP).[4]

If current transatlantic relations are not as acrimonious as in 2003, there are still fundamental tensions – political and structural – that can be a continuous source of friction. One of them is the unilateralist tendency of the

US; a tendency that was revealed in 2001 by the refusal to ratify the Kyoto Protocol or the International Criminal Court Statute. This unilateralist tendency, supported by neoconservative thought, prevailed just after a period of benign hegemony, which was represented by President Clinton whose foreign policy promoted an assertive multilateralism where regional actors were able to contain non-strategic threats in their geographical areas.[5]

The US will to act in a unilateral way goes together with an apparent immunity to pressures and criticism from other international actors. Moreover, American society assumes that its values and practices are universally acceptable and its political positions are the most suitable in moral terms. Its position in international fora is determined by domestic factors, sometimes with the aim of ensuring that national regulations prevail over international responsibilities and agreements. This is the result of the general conviction among US politicians and legislators that, in order to satisfy national interests, acting through multilateral institutions is only an option, not a duty.[6]

Even if transatlantic relations during the Cold War evolved in a continuous crisis framework (from Suez to Euro-missiles), 'At that time' (during the Cold War) the difficulties were surmounted because of the continuing parameters that sustained the Alliance. The change in the international system brought about by the end of the Cold War pushed the states to work mainly in favour of their particular interests: in the case of the US, the achievement of primacy;[7] in the case of the EU, the creation of a distinctive identity different from the US. As underlined by Berenskoetter, the US preference is clear: 'building up a greater foreign and defence identity within the EU are welcomed as long as this takes place within a NATO framework'.[8] In this changing environment, Europe no longer represents the priority for US foreign policy.

Together with changes in US foreign policy, there has been a different evolution in EU and US societies, as well as changes in the international system structure as a consequence of the end of the Soviet threat and the consolidation of European integration. As a result, because of the hegemonic unilateralism of President Bush, the perception of the need for an autonomous EU security and defence policy has grown. The main developments in the EU's establishment of a CFSP and an ESDP have been produced within this framework, starting with the implementation of the first EU military operations in the world.[9] The parallel processes of enlargement, constitutionalization, and militarization had an impact on Common Foreign and Defence Policy. Enlargement might have a negative impact on CFSP and ESDP decision-making processes as all the new Member States bring new perspectives on the world arena that are closer to those of the US and thus different from those of other 'traditional' Member States. But a progressive convergence on all these issues is equally possible through the socialization effect of the 'Brussels corridors'. As Elfriede Regelsberger has shown, there has been a regular alignment of the new members on the CFSP *acquis* which started in the mid-1990s and which consolidated itself in the early 2000s.[10]

On the other hand, the Constitutional Treaty, today succeeded by the similar Treaty of Lisbon,[11] states explicitly its respect for Member States' rights and duties arising from NATO, and thus we can clearly appreciate its respect for the transatlantic relationship (Article 27.2). The guidelines established in both treaties for EU external action, the single international legal personality, the new Presidency system for the Council, and the creation of what the Constitutional Treaty called a Ministry of Foreign Affairs, are bound to affect the EU's relationship with the US. All these innovations (preserved in the Lisbon Treaty) tend to clarify the EU's ability to speak on international issues and attribute to it more political weight and stability.[12]

The enumeration and clarification of the tasks of the ESDP have special importance in this context. The European Constitution, as well as the Lisbon Treaty, update the so-called 'Petersberg tasks' to include conflict prevention, joint actions on disarmament, stabilization missions, and military assistance, and enlarge EU functions to collective defence and assistance in situations of conflict or humanitarian crises,[13] whilst respecting NATO commitments. The updating of the Petersberg tasks could lead to a division of labour between NATO and the EU that would appeal to many US political groupings because the most demanding missions would be preserved for NATO.[14] However, the inclusion in the Treaty of collective defence missions and the solidarity clause[15] places the EU in the same orbit as NATO and could give rise to suspicions on the part of NATO and the US. The rules included in the European Constitution as well as in the Lisbon Treaty tend to shape an autonomous European Security and Defence Policy whilst avoiding the generation of suspicions among some European allies, as they respect the specific defence policies of some Member States, including NATO member engagements. This is important as for the majority of Member States, their defence is better ensured by NATO than by the EU.

No EU constitutive treaty foresees the elaboration of a European Security Strategy (ESS) that allows appropriate planning of forces and future actions to be developed by the EU. This gap was covered by the ESS, 'A secure Europe in a better world', approved by the European Council in December 2003. The ESS bridges the gap of understanding between the EU and the US while reaffirming European principles and values, many of them not shared on the other side of the Atlantic. Even if the threat description is similar in the ESS and in the National Security Strategy Document (NSSD),[16] the strategic objectives show how distinctive the European answer is to those threats. Even the first of the strategic objectives has a clear European character as contributing to stability and good governance of neighbour Member States reflects the EU's role as a regional power, clearly different from that of the US as a global power. The consolidation of international order is the second EU strategic objective; this implies a multilateral system founded on law, whereas the US tends to understand international order as reflecting their interests and backing their global leadership. The EU emphasis on multilateralism, including the complementary character of relations with the US and NATO, is the only possible choice if Europe wants to have a leading role in international affairs. We can find similar statements in the EU and the US concerning the need for international rules to evolve and for democratic states to lead in this process. However both documents are inspired by different philosophies. The EU looks for new international norms for new situations and reflecting global institutional developments, and not for a reinterpretation of the existing ones in order to adapt them to its interests. Its recipe for the good governance of third states relies on the implementation of trade, development, and assistance policies and not on the aim of changing regimes or on direct action by force. Finally, the third EU strategic objective is the readiness for an early, quick and, if necessary, powerful intervention. Even if we associate these terms with US 'pre-emptive action', the consensus among European States (i.e. not just Member States) centres on conflict prevention and civil crisis management, acting before the conflict starts and using all the possible instruments (diplomatic, economic, military, and political).

However, and even though we can discern the beginnings of an EU militarization process, the EU lacks strategic credibility as there is no concrete determination of European global interests, there are no convergent vital national interests, there is a capabilities gap and a self-limitation of its periphery where there are divergent interests too. The ESS, conscious of the EU's need for credibility as international actor, states that 'there is no substitute for the transatlantic relationship' and so Europe continues to search for an efficient and balanced association with the US. Therefore this document sets up the guidelines for a future US–EU relationship in defence and security issues. It represents an effort to rebuild European collective action around shared values and also an approach to the American ally.

Following the Security Dilemma' reasoning, the dynamic pushing Americans and Europeans to prioritize their particular interests has an influence on the choice of cooperative or defection postures in bargaining processes within the transatlantic alliance, and produce fears about entrapment and abandonment.[17] However, the problem is not only the internal dynamic of the transatlantic relationship, but also how both sides perceive threats and adversaries. Hence, we have to keep in mind that, quite often, sets of political concepts dominate our perceptions and actions.[18]

The EU's Characteristics as an International Actor: Implications for Transatlantic Relations

One of the elements forcing a reappraisal of transatlantic relations is the changing nature of the EU. As a polity evolving towards an 'ever closer union', the European Community developed into the EU and it appears as a new type of actor in international relations. If previously the US had economic relations with the EC, but political ones with each Member State, today Europe is trying to speak internationally with one single voice, an intention expressed both in the Constitutional Treaty and in the 2007 Treaty of Lisbon. This new self-perception on the part of the EU has given rise to contradictory feelings in the US, from fear to satisfaction, from distrust to full support.[19]

When speaking about the EU as international actor and trying to classify it into a category in this scenario, it is necessary to underline differences and similarities with other international actors. According to the result of that analysis, we can discover whether there is a distinctive European way of facing new challenges to international peace and security. Three events characterize the EU's development in recent years and are the origin of its current international physiognomy as they impact on the EU's role in the world: its historic 2004/07 enlargement, its constitutionalization, and its militarization.

Does this mean that the concepts traditionally used to describe the EU's international role, such as economic bloc, regional power, or civilian power, and even super-power in the making,[20] are still useful, or do we instead need to use new ones such as the EU as a military actor or even as a civilizing power? If we enter this debate it is because, as Wessels has said, narratives about the historical and desirable position of Europe in the world are based on explicit or implicit theoretical assumptions and logics.[21] After the original debate in the early 1970s,[22] which considered the EEC as a half-baked international actor,[23] a range of approaches has developed; these can be placed broadly into four categories, each of which has different implications for the transatlantic relationship.

First of all, the EU has been conceptualized as a civilian power and *soft power*: a useful concept that was first used in relation to the EEC in the early 1970s[24] and which has dominated the intellectual and academic agenda for many years.[25] Once the Cold War finally ended the debate rekindled with two contradictory arguments: the dominant one considers that the militarization of the EU means the *de facto* end of the utility of the concept of a European civilian power because it contradicts the very nature of the non-military means of integration.[26] Others, starting with Hans Maull in his analysis of post-Cold War German foreign policy,[27] consider instead that the new international order will allow for the full use of civilian power instruments, including their military dimension, as was the case in the 1999 Kosovo War.[28]

Others have argued that the EU is not only a civilian power, but also a *civilian superpower*.[29] From a constructivist point of view, Larsen considers that the EU was clearly a civilian power until the 1990s, but that it still is one taking into account the EU's reaction to post-September 11th developments.[30] This approach is partly linked to the *soft power* concept, as coined by Joseph Nye in 1990 and later developed in a number of his works.[31] Although he is particularly interested in reproaching the US for lacking soft power, or the power of persuasion, which can in some cases be more effective than traditional hard power (military means), the point for comparison in his reasoning is the EU.[32] But some are critical of the concept because it is seen as a weak approach to world affairs, especially after the end of the Cold War, the war in the Balkans in the 1990s, and the events of 11 September 2001.[33] What has been often missed until now in the literature is the need to take into consideration not only the means, but also the objectives, of any international actor. Since 'military capabilities could also protect civilian populations from terrorist attacks',[34] a global actor needs both soft and hard power.

Finally, as Giegerich and Wallace have argued,[35] whilst the EU might have been described as a soft power in the past, recent developments tend to demonstrate the contrary. Thus, in peacekeeping operations, so many EU Member States are now acting together in one way or another, and within the past decade the governments of EU Member States have doubled the number of troops deployed abroad. They also stress how important gendarmerie and police force deployments have been. In the same vein, since the end of the 1990s, according to discourse analysis in external relations, the EU has shown itself to be more than a mere civilian power because of its own decision to develop itself in the long term into a political actor with a global role.[36]

What role can the EU play in transatlantic relations if it is defined as an international civilian actor? In this case the European role would also be subordinate and complementary given the limits of its capabilities to face up to challenges to transatlantic security. The relationship would be based on a division of labour where the US would use its hard power capabilities, leaving the EU to tackle the soft power tasks, usually after a conflict ('doing the dishes') without any real power to influence decisions taken during the conflict on how to solve the conflict. This situation is characterized by its clarity: it does not create suspicions, and it respects the hegemonic power. But it gives the EU no international role corresponding to its economic weight, and it perpetuates unilateralism. It has been said that the importance of this task will be appreciated more in the light of American 'doing the dishes' in Iraq.[37] Even if it is effective in itself, EU soft power is dwarfed wherever and whenever the US is strongly involved. A different conclusion would arise if we consider the EU as a civilian actor in terms of the priorities or the objectives it protects. In this case, the EU role in transatlantic relations will be complementary to the US one, but both would be necessary in a different way.

Another category when considering the EU's international role is that of *global actor*. It is argued that, first, the war in Iraq has pushed the EU 'a few steps further in elevating its role to one of a global actor'.[38] When using this concept the real point is not so much whether or not the EU is an important actor in the international system,[39] as it appears that today this point is beyond doubt; what matters is how much real influence the EU does have. But if we use a geographical approach, it is not easy to affirm the global nature of the EU. Some scholars consider the EU as a regional actor and 'not a global actor'[40] because it is active and important in Europe, NATO, and Central and Eastern Europe, but not elsewhere. Nonetheless, from this geographical point of view and given both its interests and its capabilities, the EU would be a global actor according to its potential theatre of operations even if its priority is situated in its immediate periphery. If we accept this regional actor assessment, the EU can only have a complementary and subordinate role in transatlantic relations given the geographical limits of its field of activity and/or its limited impact on international issues. Even if the US encounters the EU as a global strategic actor in several fields, including security and defence, the US has permanent doubts about the ability of European institutions to bear the burden of defence.[41]

A third category is that of *military power* or *emerging military superpower*. As early as 1973, Johan Galtung put forward a case for a military Europe as a possible alternative to the then existing superpowers.[42] After the seminal changes to the international system in 1989–91, there is renewed interest in the EU as a potential military power, or even as a superpower[43] based on the process of EU militarization since the 1998 Franco-British summit,[44] even if it continues to be more effective in the civilian part of the spectrum. Developments since 11 September 2001 and the subsequent terrorist attacks have led to the use of the already existing SITCEN (EU Situation Centre) in the EU planning cell in Brussels to address internal security threats, as well as to analyse terrorist threats abroad. Similarly, the EU–NATO December 2002 agreement to use NATO capabilities where necessary for EU operations (i.e. without direct US participation)[45] is undoubtedly a way for the EU to improve its security actor role, but it stresses the use of non-exclusive EU means through NATO. This limited autonomy is the main reason for disagreement between Paris and London about the interpretation of the EU as a security/military actor. The apparent position adopted by some Member States (France, Germany, Luxembourg and Belgium) is that of the EU as a 'counterweight' to the American *hyper-puissance*.[46] In the short term (and from an economic perspective), this position is not incompatible with that which sees the EU as a complement of US power, as it implies that we avoid an unnecessary duplication of NATO assets and capabilities. In the long term however it becomes a crucial point of disagreement,[47] especially now that the Western European Union's (WEU) role as a 'cushion' between an EU option and a NATO alternative has been removed.[48]

'Perception' is also very important in this discussion. The question of 'how and if' the EU is perceived as a military power by third parties needs to be addressed. For instance, since the launch of the ESDP, defence ministries of EU Member States (usually those holding the EU Council Presidency) have organized information seminars with their counterparts from the southern shores of the Mediterranean under the framework of the Barcelona Process. When the EU strengthens its military capabilities and gives its policy an explicit security dimension, this will increase its ability to influence international affairs. In turn, this will raise a number of normative dilemmas.[49] The European Security Strategy is in our view a positive answer to the question 'is the idea of a militarized EU defensible from a normative point of view?' because it establishes implicit and explicit limits to the use of military force by the EU and makes the EU a civilizing civil and a military actor. So, we can agree with NATO General Secretary Jaap de Hoop Scheeffer when he concluded that the EU is finding its own distinct role as a security actor.[50] He was stressing the link between NATO and the EU, but the idea can be also applied to outline the EU's specific normative role in international affairs.

It remains clear that the question of the militarizing of the EU and the development of an ESDP/CSDP is part of a wider question of political unification in Europe. The European Security Strategy tends to cover this shortfall in part by making explicit a number of specific threats to EU security and by defining the objectives and instruments of this policy. The *non-nato* Constitutional Treaty and the 2007 Reform Treaty also contribute to this aim by designing a common umbrella for the CFSP (and ESDP/CSDP) and the EU's external relations and by establishing principles and objectives of EU external action in general. Any assessment of the question needs to bear this fundamental dimension in mind.[51] Otherwise, it would be unfortunate, but fair, to say that the CFSP amounts only to *des illusions vérbales* and that the ESDP might well end up as only being *des mots surréalistes.*[52]

Accepting the EU as a military actor implies an answer to the question whether the EU can be a counterweight or complement to the superpower US. The first alternative – counterweight – is not realistic and risks a loss of EU legitimacy. The second seems to us to be more correct, but it depends upon the achievement of perfect interoperability, allied to clear communication and information between both actors.

So, it remains unclear if all these changes in the EU's constitutional framework will allow for the emergence of a military (super)power, at least in the short to medium term. National and EU budgets on defence do not seem to predict any serious development in that particular direction, although a better rationalization of existing budgets could be useful. Similarly, the lack of clarity over existing and proposed arrangements between NATO HQs and EU HQs,[53] as well as the role of non-NATO EU states, leads to further doubts about the feasibility of a military power role for the EU. The developments in this sense are the basis for a capabilities-expectations gap that influences the state of the relationship, as viewed on both sides of the Atlantic, by exaggerating expectations on the one hand and leading to corresponding disappointments on the other.[54] The question of burden-sharing between the US and Europe is a crucial issue in transatlantic relations. Even if there is a general feeling in the US that the Europeans should take on a larger share of the burden to uphold global stability, it is uncertain whether independent European action would be welcomed. As the US is apparently aware of, and wishes to preserve, its own primary world role it often prefers not to ask for European contributions.

More recently and from a normative point of view, the EU has been considered as a *civilizing power*, entering in this way into the European identity debate. The 'identity' debate can be traced back to the setting up of the EU in the early 1990s with the Maastricht Treaty.[55] Even without a conventional *demos*, there appears to be now some emerging consensus, at least in the constructivist mode, that the EU's international identity is a 'collective, post-national and liberal identity'.[56] A European identity can and must coexist with national ones. Instead of mere feelings of 'natural' belonging, this new identity accepts common values and principles and is an expression of 'rational thinking'. The implications of this debate for European defence relate to the question of strategy and common culture (or lack of it). Here the impact of the 2004/07 enlargement might be crucial because of the different strategic cultures of most of the new Member States as mentioned above.

The EU as a civilizing power represents a more recent academic debate[57] which contains a similar vein of argument. It only partly builds on that of civilian power Europe (CIDEL 2004). This new concept also builds on the debate about what has been called 'normative power Europe'[58] as the EU tends to spread its values and concepts. The argument that is being made is that what really matters is the power to impose norms on other actors in the international system.[59] Although Manners' study uses the case of the abolition of the death penalty, his overall assessment is that one needs to go beyond traditional conceptions of the EU's international role, and include in any such assessment its particular normative power.

According to this approach, the very meaning of the term 'civilising power' lies in the fact that the EU uses norms, which it has elaborated in a communicative process. This process involves autonomous sources of motivation owing their validity to their impartial justification.[60] So instead of intending to impose norms and values by the use of military force, the EU develops a strategy for persuasion which combines both soft and hard (military) power. It is likely to do so even more in the future. We do not enter here into the wider debate about the validity of this approach in general or in particular about why the EU is necessarily acting in a rational and argumentative way thanks to deliberative theories. We simply mention it as an increasingly important dimension in the literature. As for 'civilian power' and 'soft power' Europe, but also its 'normative dimension' more generally speaking and its 'civilizing power' approach in particular, it seems that the definition of clear principles and values in both the Constitutional and the reform treaties and the ESS would further reinforce these elements.

The new Reform Treaty, agreed in Lisbon in autumn 2007, introduces a series of developments in the CFSP and the ESDP with the potential to modulate the existing conceptualizations of the international role of the EU, as did the Constitutional Treaty. Summarizing the way that the new Treaty will alter the existing foreign policy, and security/defence arrangements, we note the following reforms: first of all, it recognizes a single international legal personality for the EU[61]. The non-existence of a single international legal personality has always been presented as a serious drawback for EU cohesion and coherence. Therefore a strengthening of the EU's international role under international law may have a positive effect on its 'global actor-ness'. In that respect, it is also possible that other developments will strengthen further the possibility of a future European identity in the world. Given their special significance in foreign and security policy, it is important to mention the new Presidency for the European Council which will have a role in the EU's foreign representation, the new configuration of the High Representative for Foreign Policy, the inclusion of solidarity and mutual defence clauses, the extension of the so-called Petersberg tasks, the strengthening of military capabilities, including rapid reaction forces, the way these forces are financed, and how to deploy them faster, the introduction of flexibility in defence issues mainly through the concept of 'permanent structured cooperation', the developments towards specific military headquarters for the ESDP (even if at this stage the new Treaty still only refers to a planning cell), the setting up of a new rapid deployment force or the actual use of EU forces in peacekeeping operations in the world. Other innovations anticipated by the Constitutional Treaty, such as the creation of a European Armaments, Research and Military Capabilities Agency in order to progress towards a common defence procurement market, an area previously explicitly excluded from open competition (Article 296.1 of the Treaty of Rome), became reality with the creation in 2004 of the European Defence Agency (EDA).

In short, at present the EU can be considered as a global actor, geo-graphically speaking, because its possible theatre of operations is worldwide and not limited to the European continent and its immediate neighbour-hood, even if it does give priority to these areas according to its current interests and limited military capabilities. Normatively speaking, the EU is a civilizing actor as it tends to expand its own values and principles. This is close to the civilian power Europe approach in many ways, although, as mentioned above, this would only continue to be valid under an 'objective-led' reading of the concept of a civilian power Europe – and not a 'means-led' reading. Finally, it is also a military actor, at least in terms of potential means at its disposal, i.e. NATO and other national Member States.

As noted above, the international EU role is evolving, so the time factor is extremely important in any assessment, let alone prediction. Referring briefly to Hill's celebrated notion of capabilities-expectations gap(s),[62] the recent and forthcoming enlargement, the Constitutional and Lisbon Treaties, and the emerging ESDP have increased both expectations and capabilities. But the gap(s) might have also been increased with the addition of new members with Atlanticist views, a reluctance to increase defence budgets (although a rationalization of expenditure via the new EDA might alleviate part of the problem), and a deep division among the EU 27 about how to deal with US foreign and defence policy in the future. The flexible decision-making pro-cedures that the Constitutional Treaty and the 2007 Reform Treaty adopt might be able to help in that respect, but the issues involved are so significant that only flexibility is not enough. In spite of criticism on the multi-speed result that flexibility produces, a more issue-specific analysis shows different levels of integration in different policy areas.

These constitutional changes will probably affect our reading of existing concepts, but it is unclear in what particular direction. What we consider as more important however is the fact that all these institutional and constitutional alterations cannot (and should not) obscure the fact that at the end of the day what matters is coherence and credibility in foreign policy. If Europe shows itself as divided over an issue, as it did on Iraq in 2003, the image and subsequent perception of the EU as a single actor disappears completely.

All these 'constitutional' changes are made in order to facilitate the emergence of a single EU voice in the world. They have direct implications for the concept of the EU as a 'global actor' and for the enhancement of policy efficiency. What kind of international actor the EU is or will be in the future will not solely depend on academic characterizations or on institutional developments, whether or not the latter are accompanied by military capabilities. The key issue will remain that of the existence (or lack of) a common foreign policy allowing the EU to speak with one voice in the international arena. We will now illustrate why we argue that what is really missing in order for the EU to be a truly important international actor is coherence and cohesion at the foreign policy level, that is to say in the CFSP. In other words, the EU 'cannot be a global actor because it has no common foreign and security policy'.[63]

The need for consistency in EU foreign policy is also a requirement for the emergence of a common EU stance on world affairs.[64] There is still a long way to go before we reach that stage. The EU's deep divisions over Iraq are a reflection of this lack of unity among EU Member States, but divergences between EU members pre-date Iraq. Iraq has only put them into sharper relief.[65] Enlargement in 2004 and 2007 to include Member States whose governments overall supported the US line over Iraq has simply strengthened this important cleavage between the Franco-German axis and a group led by the UK. There are also important divergences over how to respond to the US plan for a 'Greater Middle East', where Germany appears to agree with the plan[66] in spite of the existence since 1995 of the EU sponsored Euro-Mediterranean Partnership (which excludes the US). A similar argument can be made about EU cohesion at the UN, even if some progress has been achieved over the years. A recent study shows that there is still a long way to go, and that factors other than the development of a 'European foreign policy' may explain any convergence better, such as a decrease in the number of resolutions adopted by vote, or a shift from East–West, and decolonization issues, as well as more socio-economic themes.[67]

Thus, on foreign policy and international affairs there is a clear divergence of views between the French, the British, and the Germans over what kind of Europe we want (a superpower, a civilian power, etc.) and what kind of world is desirable, let alone feasible (a multipolar one or a multilateral one or a world dominated by the only hyper-power). This in turn implies a divergence about how to define clear CFSP objectives. The Europeanization of foreign policy, let alone defence, remains problematic. As a result, the need for 'more Europe' in the ESDP cannot replace the need for 'more Europe' in the CFSP. As Lawrence Freedman has correctly noted:

> European governments have not yet developed a very successful EU foreign policy. And such a foreign policy is a pre-condition for EU success in the military sphere. No European soldiers will be deployed on EU missions if the Union's governments cannot agree on their political objectives.[68]

Thus, between the inconsistencies and paradoxes that characterize Europe's foreign policy:

> there is a striking gap between the Union's normative power of attraction and its weak empirical power to shape the international environment in any instrumental fashion; this is due not to the lack of adequate instruments, but to the inability to establish collective goals and set into motion any collective action in pursuit of these goals.[69]

Explaining Differences by Dissimilar Perceptions and Similar Interests

The perceptions of recent world changes and domestic ones in the EU and in the US are not exactly the same on both sides of the Atlantic, but are either nuanced or even sharply opposed depending on the approaches and perspectives of those involved. First in this part of the chapter we explore the interests and the risk perceptions on both sides. On this basis we then expose the ways in which this might be managed and link this to the discussion about the existence of different systems of values within transatlantic relations. The argument will also take into account 'the perception of third party states' of the evolution of US and EU foreign policies, and will explore the ways in which perceptions are derived from all these factors.

As already noted, it is easy to conclude that the US National Security Strategies of 2002 and 2006 and the European Security Strategy of 2003 focus on the same threats to the security of both continents: international terrorism, weapons of mass destruction, rogue states, etc. However, it is also possible to discern differences concerning the implied interests in both powers' strategic documents. While the US reveals itself as a global actor with global interests that give it its hegemonic position, Europeans are more concerned with their immediate environment, and with the periphery from which most of the recent threats to their security have emerged. Apart from the Balkans, the political situations in Ukraine, South Caucasus, and

Maghreb have direct implications in Europe through their propensity to generate migration flows, organized criminality, and problems of energy supply. The Europeans also promote a different way to cope with security threats; whereas for the US the most important instrument seems to be the use of military force, even pre-emptively, for the EU the focus is on the prevention of conflicts, even by using force as a last resort. The US attitude has led them to emphasize homeland security, and to develop the concept of societal security in a distinctive way, while the EU's emphasis on soft power instruments has led it to develop the concept of human security.

This difference of approach reflects different perceptions and interests in the international arena on the part of both actors, and this in turn can be related to their different historical experiences. The US had the power to bring World War II to a conclusion through its military power, and to assure the European security from the Soviet threat over four decades. Meanwhile, Europe was able to reach a durable peace through dialogue, mutual understanding, and institutionalized cooperation, and through processes of bargaining, and sometimes deliberative reasoning, typical of a continental 'multiperspectival polity'. Consequently, Americans see security as an output of their political, economic, and military power while Europeans see it as only possible through perpetual dialogue.

It has been said that both Americans and Europeans have always used values to mask the pursuit of interests, and the level of ambition of what is possible in the international environment shapes how interests and values are perceived on both sides of the Atlantic. As already noted, transatlantic consensus on democratic peace[70] as legitimating framework for the use of power has been questioned from a theoretical point of view. The constructivist approach to international relations tends to question the basis of the neo-liberal institutionalist approach, according to which institutions and international regimes can change national interests and so transform identities, thus helping to create order and security[71] in conditions of international anarchy. Although the approaches share the final aim, the neo-liberal institutionalist approach is based on a hierarchical system where a hegemonic state establishes a liberal international order, while the constructivist approach to international order is more deliberative and the consequent end-state is a democratic security community. So the normative framework that legitimates the action of international actors can be seen in very different ways. This new theoretical approach has been adopted by some EU Member States and reflected in some EU positions, with the consequence that the US perceives the EU as a revisionist actor in the international system, questioning US hegemony. In practice, this leads to the idea that, whilst Americans tend to use values as a cover for the pursuit of narrow interests and the application of power, Europeans use values as a means of avoiding responsibilities, even when their longer-term interests are at stake.[72]

The explanation of the European approach is clear. Europe wants to share with the US the responsibility to shape the international order according to a series of common values. The constructivist approach provides a basis for the search for intersubjective meanings, instead of a unilateral definition of them. However, the model fails when extended to global order as the very nature of the international system is determined by states with asymmetric capabilities and legal, cultural, and moral differences that lead to very different values.

Currently, in general terms, interests are not so contradictory between the US and the EU and we can find good examples of common ones, such as perspectives on the impact of new economic powers, new concerns about democracy and market reforms in Latin America and Africa, the threat of international terrorism and its links to the proliferation of weapons of mass destruction (WMD), the growing instability in the Middle East, the competition for energy resources, and the desire for strong international institutions promoting shared Atlantic values.[73] Hence, it appears that a strategic dichotomy is no longer sustainable. With common interests only different images about the situation and the other's attitude towards it form an obstacle to a durable understanding.

The problematic issues in transatlantic relations are related to two main categories: the war against terror and the attitude towards international institutions and agreements. One of the main concerns is about the nature of international terrorism. We will try to explain these differences by reference to the perceptions generated by the attitude and conduct of the parties in the international arena. First of all, the reactions of US policy-makers to the St Malo Declaration, the starting point of the European Security and Defence Policy, were strong as they perceived it as a big challenge to NATO's dominance in transatlantic security. Moreover, after the experience in Kosovo in 1999, they were sceptical of the Europeans' ability to provide hard security on their own when required to do so. After 11 September, the US became a more defensive actor, realizing that even although it was the only superpower, and in a period of sustained domestic economic growth, it was vulnerable to the turbulence in the world outside. According to Niblett: 'US reactions to terrorist attacks was to rush to seal America's borders through the creation of a new Department of Homeland Security and to take the fight to the enemy beyond its shores'; a 'sense of external threat, combined with continuing domestic normality'. The feeling on the western side of the Atlantic was that while the US was fighting for freedom and helping every country (victim of a foreign attack, genocide, etc.), the EU only wanted to be present and take the benefits of involvement without any risk and any effort. In general, European societies do not support the use of force without an explicit Security Council mandate and they prefer joint (multilateral) actions.[74] This idea, however, tends to ignore the Kosovo war where the consensus among allies was arrived at with no Security Council resolution.

One of the main reasons for the different US and EU perceptions can be found in the different backgrounds to concerns about homeland security and the way to assure its protection. Whereas the US has a military approach to homeland security as the threat comes from outside national borders,[75] the EU has a civilian one as most of the time the threat of terrorism emerges at home, and that approach also takes natural catastrophes into consideration. If Americans focus on reducing their country's vulnerability to terrorism, Europeans tend to adopt a comprehensive concept of security that encompasses naturally occurring dangers as well as the threat of terrorism. If the Bush Administration in its proclaimed war on terror has taken extraordinary actions beyond the jurisdiction of domestic or international law, many European countries have adopted laws to confront domestic terrorism, whilst yet preserving civil liberties. This has led to American criticism of European complacency,[76] while Europeans accuse Americans of extremism. Today, however, it is clear that individual national efforts must be aligned with more effective transatlantic cooperation.[77] In order to fight efficiently against international terrorism, the US has, since 2002, promoted law enforcement cooperation with Europe.[78] Mutual legal assistance and extradition agreements have been signed between the US and the EU, intelligence sharing has been improved, and both parties share airline passenger data.

The prospect of greater integration of European foreign policy generated high expectations for transatlantic relations. Even if the US conservatives have always feared this process, the internationalists hope this will convert the EU into a more powerful and credible partner. The failure of the Constitutional Treaty, even if substituted by a very similar treaty, is perceived by American officials as another sign of the lack of credibility of Europe as strategic partner and as an obstacle to the development of a shared strategic vision. As few Americans share the extremely unilateral approach of the Bush Administration, a new era of more consensual international diplomacy is expected after the 2008 US election – an era that started with the 2006 Congressional elections that created a Democratic majority in Congress. Although all potential candidates for the US presidential elections have adopted a strong approach to national defence as a consequence of the expanding US perception of the geographical spread and size of the threat,[79] change may well be afoot. According to media opinion,[80] after Iraq, America has lost confidence in its capacity for international leadership, it feels more isolated from friends and allies, and it may pursue more self-interested policies.

On the European side, there is a feeling that such developments might constitute an *emancipation trap*. Although European countries want to be more autonomous from the American ally,[81] wars in the Balkans, Afghanistan, and Iraq showed that US interests are currently far from those of Europe and that the EU is not yet able to chart and steer its own course without American guidance.[82] The European dilemma is between freedom and entrapment. Bewildered by the ambiguous behaviour of Europeans, Americans are more likely to choose a unilateral direction in international affairs or deal with individual European countries, perhaps to the point of forcing change in UK foreign policy in order to take into consideration and promote EU collective positions and interests, and thus promoting European solidarity.

As we have seen, supranational integration in Europe tends to raise question marks on both sides of the Atlantic. The US is predominantly interested in the way that Europe can contribute to international security, its technological progress, and its credibility as a sharer of the burden of global political responsibility. The EU experiences this pressure at the moment when, with 12 new Member States, it is trying to gain coherence in its foreign policy by a difficult constitutional process, and when European public opinion is against US unilateralism, but hopefully in favour of a Common Foreign and Security Policy. After the 2004 and 2007 enlargements and the failure of the Constitutional Treaty, there is little confidence that transferring further control to the EU's supranational decision-making institutions will imply more European capability in whatever fields. The inclusion of new Member States in the process of defining EU foreign policy imposes new limits on the EU's ability to develop coherent common positions, for example towards Iraq or Russia. The most recent and biggest enlargement has pushed the EU's borders up against more unstable neighbours who can undermine the EU's internal security. As countries well beyond the European neighbourhood are looking to the EU as a potential partner (not only economic), the EU perceives that it can no longer live with the ambition of being a regional security power and a global civilian power. In this context the EU has to take into account the US transformation from a benign hegemon to a unilateral interventionist power acting for its own interests (mainly economic and supremacy). Public opinion is generally against this kind of attitude, even if many new Member States prefer a US defence guarantee to one from an EU that depends on France and Germany. There is a certain feeling that Europe is still not central to the global process, even if it has the will to be an international actor with its own voice.

Even though this discussion underlines a certain lack of interest and of efficacy from the EU when dealing with security issues, there is a strong desire among European countries to export the 'European model'. In terms of security, this means an emphasis on devolving parts of national sovereignty to international organizations and support for efforts to invigorate international institutions and promote multilateral agreements as a way to solve most of the current security changes (Kyoto protocol, International Criminal Court, negotiations with China or Iran to solve the challenge to our collective security that they represent, etc.). But when we talk about a European model of security and defence, the first question that appears is a fundamental one: what is the content of the 'European model'? In our opinion, it centres on a twofold concept. First, one of the main features of the EU as an international actor is, as we previously saw, its normative approach to international relations due, in part, to concrete limitations on military capabilities but also, and most importantly, to its multicentred and multilateral structure. As the approaches of Member States to international issues are different, even divergent, the only way to arrive at a common position is consensus. Internal deliberation is permanent and based in reasoning that leads, when agreed, to common intersubjective meanings. This is most obviously true in internal community policies; for example, in CFSP there is also a place for bargaining according to the relative power of each Member State, even though common EU positions are based on common understanding obtained through a deliberative process. Accustomed to working this way internally, the EU tends to extend it to international relations, conceived as an arena with similar characteristics to the EU polity: in particular, EU perceptions would emphasize the plurality of sovereign states, divergences of national interest, and a trend to chaos if there is no political power able to coordinate them and even impose its moral or/and legal authority. So, the normative approach is part of the European political strategy to improve EU legitimacy. The EU tends to set up normative frameworks with the rest of the world, for example at the World Trade Organization (WTO) where it looks for normative positions, but also for a mechanism able to legitimate EU policies.[83] As it wants to introduce European constitutive rules into international relations, the EU can be considered a co-optive power, to use Nye's expression.

Second, and this is a more substantive aspect of our concept, but linked to the normative one, human security has been characterized as the European way of security.[84] Democracy, rule of law, respect of human rights, equality, solidarity, and respect for international law according to the principles of the United Nations are the guidelines for the EU relations with the world. If the three first postulates are, at least in principle, shared values in the transatlantic community, equality and solidarity as well as the respect for international law are principles only expressly set out in the Treaty that establishes a Constitution for Europe and in the Lisbon Treaty. As a result, they represent a clear contrast to US foreign policy, the main trait of which is the instrumental use of *ius gentium* rules and the UN principles or simply indifference to them when national interests are better protected in other ways. This explicit setting out of foreign affairs principles could present some EU Member States with difficulties when they try to reconcile them with some key dimensions of foreign policy as practised by the George W. Bush Administration, for example the use of preventive attacks. The priority accorded to sustainable development, the abolition of all restrictions to international trade, and the promotion of an international system based on multilateral cooperation and global good governance[85] embodies principles apparently different from the ones guiding the US foreign policy; they tend to imprint a distinctive European way and European priorities, and in doing so they shape the European identity

Exploring our concept further, we can say that human security is about the basic needs of individuals and communities in times of peril – an idea that recognizes that 'freedom from fear' and 'freedom from want' are both essential to people's sense of well-being and their willingness to live in peace. According to a human security approach, civilian and military initiatives should prioritize the protection of civilians over the defeat of an enemy, as protection of human rights is the main challenge. A second principle is that any outside intervention must provide the conditions for a political process through which a legitimate political authority can be built. Intensive consultations with local people are required. Human security implies effective multilateralism, which means a commitment to work within the framework of international law, alongside other international and regional agencies, individual states and non-state actors; it also requires an integrated regional approach. Finally, EU external interventions, according to a human security approach, need a clear and transparent strategic direction.

According to Kaldor, human security is a distinctive European approach to security, different both from the war on terror and from territorial security.[86] One of the best examples would be the EU mission in Aceh.[87] Thus, its content is not the same as that of the notion of 'societal security', as developed by Brimmer, and centred especially on one's own national population rather than on the partner's or enemy's population. Meanwhile, the aim of EU military operations is not defeat of the enemy, but containment in order to help civilian populations.

We can also discern this European approach in the EU's strategic approach to questions of energy security. According to a neo-realist approach, the US tends to project its power into supplier regions and create strategic alliances with axial countries in the world energy system. In this way, US policies generate reactions that can become stronger and breed resistance to US aims. However, closer to a neo-liberal approach, the EU priority is developing markets and crisis management in the framework of multilateral or supranational institutions, thus creating areas for cooperation and shared welfare through trade and the promotion of liberal values.[88] Moreover, the adoption of a human security concept has the potential to promote homogeneity inside the EU as its principles are shared by all Member States. In the same way, good transatlantic relations can be another factor in promoting internal EU consensus, as all EU governments agree on the need to improve relations with US even if they have differences over the way to manage the international arena. Close links with the US is one channel through which to show the benefits of a distinctive European approach to security that is shared by 27 Member States.

Even if these conceptual differences are real, it appears that with the continuing violence in Iraq, the metastasizing of the terrorist threat beyond Afghanistan, Pakistan, and Iraq, and America's reputation for positive leadership in decline across the world, the US presidential candidates are determined to usher in a new era of more consensual international diplomacy, and to lead internationally by example, rather than by brute force. Thus the issues discussed here show the interdependence between both sides of the Atlantic, which in turn promotes a wide range of shared interests.

Even if we accept that interdependence by itself is not enough to create cooperation, it can be argued that the reasoning between allies ought to be that both parties obtain benefits from interdependence as both increase their power towards other actors whose values are different, thus leading to a win-win situation for both parties. This supports the idea that common interests are promoted by interdependence and thus they are partly determined by the network of transatlantic relations. Systems of shared ideas, beliefs, and values can inform interest and, in turn, actions.[89]

The Need to Maintain the Transatlantic Link – But on a New Basis

There have been changes in the EU and in the US that seem to demand a search for a new model or new basis for the transatlantic relationship. In Europe, the main innovations concern the development of CFSP and ESDP and the agreement on the Lisbon Treaty after the failure of Constitutional Treaty. However, the EU has not achieved a coherent or effective approach to external actions due to the frequent lack of common interests among Member States and its deficit in military capabilities – a deficit that implies the need for NATO assistance for the most demanding missions. On the other hand, there is a certain crisis of legitimacy in US, a lack of credibility and post-conflict efficiency

The European Constitution and Lisbon Treaty, as well as the European Security Strategy, establish guidelines to clarify what the EU is looking for in security and defence matters. These normative instruments create the potential for cooperation and complementarity of EU activities with those taken by NATO and the US. The main questions to be answered here are, first, whether the Europeans have the political will to cooperate and why; and second, whether the US as a hegemonic power is interested in redirecting its foreign policy in this way or whether it will prefer to continue the path of unilateralism or multiple selective bilateralism, outside international institutions, as more suitable for their national interests.

Even from a realist point of view it has been pointed out that there are risks for the US in maintaining a foreign policy based on a forward presence, and using force in a preventive manner. Obviously, the country has enough capabilities to act this way and to satisfy, at least in the short term, its national interests centred on the war on terror, but this strategy threatens to throw into question the US international reputation and its capacity to exert world leadership.[90] To our mind, there is a theoretical model capable of explaining the need for US to reset its security strategy and to reshape the basis of transatlantic relations. This explanation could spring from Luhmann and Hayek's systemic conception of social reality, and be completed with Habermas' critical comments on that concept and his concept of 'communicative action'.[91] We will explain briefly the key components of this model.

One trait of international relations, as a rational organization of individual and collective interests, is the tendency to order. However, the emergence of a rational systemic order does not imply the removal of a natural systemic order centred on human beings. Both coexist. Political authority has effective power as it is able to provide a sense of unity to a set of interests and arrange them in such a way as to achieve a certain aim. Together with this effective power, which operates in the institutional framework of social order, there is an emotive power, which works within a civil framework or at social levels where individuals show themselves. The notion of emotive power implies identifications with an idea able to provide common understanding as the basis for social interaction. That is to say, emotive power refers to the evocative capability of a sign to identify itself with the representative bodies of a rational way of life and prepare them for action.

There is a rational tension between both of these concepts that shows that social dislocation is sustainable as long as emotive power legitimates a social system and effective power provides a sense of unity allowing material sustenance of the community, thus preserving it. However, a social system can be in crisis when one power – or both – are in crisis or divergent. According to Habermas' fourfold categorization of social crisis – of economic, of rationality, of legitimacy, of motivation – the reason for a legitimacy crisis is the lack of identity between the system and the unity of social sense. A motivation crisis implies a loss of values that previously supported the unity of the system.[92] If we apply this thinking to international relations, we can see that usually political systems have exerted a certain external influence. Domination is the most aggressive of possible state behaviours – a behaviour that implies the unilateral use of state authority to coerce other actors into accepting the state's objectives rather than a search for mutual understanding. In this situation, states can resort to all kinds of coercive measures. Dominant states act according to notions of strategic action since their decisions are based on beliefs that they consider to be true even if they do not try to give them validity through intersubjective recognition. Only when their attitude towards other states is based in solidarity or utility will they try to achieve mutual understanding through the use of communicative actions.[93]

In international relations – as well as in national social systems – power can be exercised effectively where there is the capability to do so. US power and its effectiveness are clear. However, when disconnected from the emotive power expressed in international public opinion, it produces a legitimacy crisis as effective power does not correspond with emotive power. This is the risk that would be run if the US tried to rebuild its relationship with Europe on the basis of its domination over the European states or through more aggressive use of NATO. In fact, this is one of the main reasons for the NATO crisis: here is an organization that would subsist with common will among all parties, but that will cannot be maintained if one member can exert dominium over its partners individually, and if it does not allow the allies a more egalitarian relationship and more influence over decision-making.

If the US wants to exert its power effectively and maintain its international leadership, a change of attitude is necessary: from the pursuit of relationships of domination to the pursuit of a relationship based on solidarity and cooperation, or based on mutual utility. In Habermas' terms, the US has to move from the use of strategic action to the use of communicative action. The search for mutual understanding could envisage a degree of convergence, more or less important depending on the existence of an underlying community of values or the lack of it. This is a problematic issue, even if it has been frequently stated that NATO is and has been more than a strategic alliance, and that it is a community of values.[94] Within this institutional framework, the new Transatlantic Agenda and Action Plan in 1995 pointed to a form of transatlantic co-leadership inspired by mutual coordination in pursuit of international order and security; the vision was that the combination of complementary capabilities of the EU and the US would multiply their influence over other international actors and make it easier to pursue world governance. The inspiring philosophy of the Transatlantic Agenda has to be reinvigorated.

Only an open attitude and sustained dialogue between both parties can underpin the transatlantic relationship. From the point of view of political liberalism, the processes of communication on which the relationship is founded should be based more in declaration than in conjecture; this can be achieved if the actors are conscious that values that they promote are not fully shared, but that they are firmly decided that this will not be an obstacle to their future relationship, or to a society whose members subordinate their power to reasonable aims.[95]

The aftermath of the war in Iraq has demonstrated US inability to control a situation where civilian and police capabilities – soft power instruments successfully deployed by the EU – are more important than hard military ones. Equally it has demonstrated US inability to consolidate world moral leadership, which has been put in question both by the choice of means and by their negative results. One of the implications is for the positions of other international actors since the Bush strategic doctrine promotes the spread of a permissive normative order where norms of self-restraint, law, and international institutions are ignored, even though they may be the only way to consolidate the actual power of a country that has dominant material power.[96]

In the EU, instead of a rationalist model of state security centred in national interest, there prevails a broader conception of security, centred more on individual citizens' rights than on national sovereignty. This model can be seen as the framework for the EU as a communicative rational international actor.[97] The adoption of this model by the EU has a simple explanation. As the EU is not a homogeneous entity, its security and defence policy must be based in a deliberative democratic system that allows it to justify its actions on the basis of intersubjective valid norms. In other words, as national defence interests are not similar, they cannot be the theoretical basis for integration in this field. The basis for integration in the field of foreign policy and defence must therefore be values that all Member States consider equitable. The perception that European values are different from those of the US makes it easier to conceptualize the EU as an international actor and to legitimate its foreign policy. This normative dimension does not disappear with progressive EU militarization; thus the EU can preserve its self-image as a civilizing actor.

The first problem that is encountered in an effort to translate this model to transatlantic relations is the hegemonic character of one of the actors, whose foreign policy is based on its national interests and who is able to impose them. As already noted, there are theoretical reasons for a change in this approach. On the other hand, the EU needs the relationship with the US as European military capabilities do not match the EU's security and defence ambitions, and European security cannot be autonomously guaranteed. In developing this relationship, the NATO way is better than the bilateral one in which every Member State has a 'special relationship' with the US. NATO is the only organization able to organize and develop international military missions in order to fulfil most of the stabilization tasks that have emerged in the world arena. Channelling transatlantic relations primarily through NATO links the US to common consultation and cooperation procedures; it also allows and forces the EU to present itself as a unit and to try to defend a common interest that is different from the national ones prevailing when transatlantic relations work bilaterally with individual European countries. It is not realistic to think about an isolated ESDP, which is completely autonomous, for reasons already discussed. In addition, such an ESDP would fly in the face of the perception and preference – particularly among new EU Member States – to be defended by the US rather than by the EU led by France or by Germany. Hence Europeans also have an interest in finding a new basis for transatlantic relations, keeping in mind that the basis would not restrict ESDP development and its progressive autonomy.

Today the US and the EU are confronted by global threats even more important than eight or ten years ago: for example, the situation with nuclear missiles in North Korea, the need to mount counter-insurgency forces in Iraq and Afghanistan, and the crisis over Iranian nuclear intentions. For this reason, and after one of the coolest periods in transatlantic relations, there have been attempts at rapprochement, even with France, in order to reach an agreement on alliance participation in the stabilization of Iraq, which was earlier rejected due to French and German opposition.[98] Apart from such concrete problems that reveal common interests on both sides of the Atlantic, the US has to respond to the structural change implied by the EU's growing international presence, by the side of or replacing EU Member States. In its turn, the EU has to accept the US as the only superpower with truly global interests.

In sum, the deep-seated changes on both sides of the Atlantic have changed US and EU attitudes – an evolution that has implied the need to adjust perceptions of each other. The only way to avoid misperceptions about the other in such a situation is to understand the fundamental reasons explaining the policies and the ways in which the other acts and reacts. Such knowledge can lead to a better mutual comprehension, or at least it can eliminate the misperception about the true motives of the ally's behaviour.

How the EU's International Role can be Developed Through the Strengthening of Transatlantic Relations

To measure the way in which the EU functions as international actor in transatlantic relations there has been proposed a multiple approach that considers its international *actorness*, its character of civilian power, the expectations-capability gap, and the consistency between national foreign policies and CFSP.[99] Only a Europe able to speak with one voice on the international economic stage will be able to preserve its influence and help to shape the process of economic globalization by making its values the principles of increasingly necessary global economic governance;[100] the same applies to global political governance since the world lacks political institutions with sufficient authority to provide it. Clear evidence of this is the 2006 failure to reform the UN system.

The EU is a solid, influential, and respectable power in world trade. However, emergent economies will reduce the proportion of world production that the EU represents, and this will imply a subsequent decrease of the economic and political influence of EU Member States in international relations. Europe cannot avoid the structural change in the international system that this will imply, even if it manages to fulfil the major structural reforms proposed by the Lisbon strategy, and the situation would lead to a gradual decline of Europe. If these are the threats to EU economic power despite its unity and coherence, the problem in relation to CFSP, immigration, or energy issues is even more pronounced since the EU's internal conflicts weaken its international position and negotiating power – something that other states take advantage of. So it is clear that to gain the fullest impact from its principles in the international arena, and to help to reshape transatlantic relations, the EU needs to improve its coherence and coordination between Member States.

Even if it is true that differences between the two sides of the Atlantic often reflect existing differences among Europeans, the current US pre-eminence in the world and the foreign policy choices of the Bush administration make the emergence of a truly autonomous EU foreign and defence policy all the more difficult. It is however correct to point out that the Europeans should get their act together if they do not want the Americans to exploit these divergences. Reinforcing CFSP coherence would make Washington's leadership in Europe more difficult as the Americans would find a united front instead of a group of states who usually look for the leader's (i.e. the US') individual favour.[101] In considering this problem, it is important to note the changing atmosphere of European integration itself. Recent constitutional changes in the EU show how 'masters of the Treaty' look for modes of governance which will strengthen the EU as an actor without really transferring sovereignty.[102] Thus, a reinforcement of transatlantic relations on a new basis has to invigorate the EU's international role, but this can happen only if Europe is able to frame a coherent transatlantic policy.

Moreover, we have to add that some EU initiatives, such as the creation of a European Arrest Warrant and a common judicial space (Eurojust), and the setting up of joint criminal investigations teams, have been accompanied by intense US pressure. The signature of US–EU mutual extradition and legal assistance treaties has made the US gradually accept the EU as a bilateral partner in issues of societal protection. In this sense, transatlantic efforts have helped to advance deeper European integration. Taking the example of homeland security, and according to Hamilton, its effective transformation is not just about building the right structures, but cultivating the right culture for networked cooperation. Effective homeland security may begin at home, but in an age of catastrophic terrorism no nation is home alone. If Europeans and Americans are to be safer than they are today, individual national efforts must be aligned with more effective transatlantic cooperation.[103] This transatlantic challenge implies that EU Member States need to consider what is their concept of homeland security, what is its content, and what resources they are prepared to dedicate to it. This exercise of internal coordination will help the EU to project its priorities in the world arena, or at least in the transatlantic community.

Most current international challenges, such as the one posed by Iran's continued pursuit of nuclear capabilities, can only be handled by a unified international response. The maintenance of a united front depends on a core consensus between the transatlantic allies. Disappointment and disunity over the Iraq war has not been reproduced in the Iran crisis, although EU–US solidarity has not yet produced the desired results with Iran due to Russian and Chinese opposition to the imposition of penalties. However, it is time for the two sides of the Atlantic to confront several difficult questions as to how great a risk from Iran they are willing to tolerate or what tools they are willing to employ to prevent the emergence of a nuclear Iran. In order to reinforce the transatlantic relationship, Europe and the US have to move from an introspective approach to an objective analysis of external threats, and of global challenges. Progressively, Europeans and Americans seem to be rediscovering their mutual need. The US has military power that the EU lacks, but US international action needs also the support of an ally with normative power to legitimate it.

After reviewing a series of different gaps between US and Europe we conclude that there is the need to continue our strategic alliance for security reasons, as well as in order to provide a means to achieve our goals and to apply and extend our values. The US National Security Strategy Document of 2006 develops this very idea after recognizing disagreements with 'some of our oldest and closest friends' over US policy in Iraq. The strategic document states that US strength is not founded on force of arms alone, but also on strong alliances, friendships, and international institutions which will enable the US to promote freedom, prosperity, and peace in common purpose with others. In this vein, the US declares itself to be prepared to act alone if necessary but, immediately, recognizes that 'there is little of lasting consequence that we can accomplish in the world without the sustained cooperation of our allies and partners'.[104] The US assessment contained in these sentences should be followed by EU recognition that the stability of the current international system is important for its own success as an international actor. Viewed in terms of hegemonic stability theory, there is a perception of the loss of hegemonic power that encourages the establishment of alliances. As the EU participates in the current power system, it has to promote some elements that give stability to it as a whole system.

Conclusions

The US and the EU have different traits as international actors. Their conceptions of security and their roles in the world arena are different. On the one hand we find a hegemonic superpower that, even though it has some characteristics of a global empire, acts as a nation-state with foreign policy centred around its national interests, and which has sufficient military capacity to impose its world leadership. On the other hand, there is a new kind of international actor with a comprehensive conception of security. Usually described as a civilian actor, it wants to develop a military capacity so as to implement its own security and defence policy, even if at the moment it depends on US for the full implementation of some of its missions. The positions of both are clearly complementary since on the one hand the EU has to resort to the US to make up for its military deficiencies, and on the other hand the superpower needs the EU, for example for post-conflict reconstruction. More importantly, the US needs support from the EU to legitimate its actions and to underpin its world leadership in the face of increasing criticism about its foreign policy and its neglect of international law and institutions.

One of the conclusions arising from this chapter is that the US and the EU have experienced a change in their identities that has led to an evolution of their values or, at least, of the way in which they are interpreted.[105] Change in the US identity has occurred as a consequence of the changed strategic international environment in the post-Cold War era in which the US has become the only superpower, but in which it has also been challenged by new threats. Change in the EU's international identity has occurred because of its multifaceted evolution associated with processes of enlarging, constitutionalizing, and militarizing. In these circumstances the main unknown factor to be clarified is whether there is still a transatlantic community.

According to the theory of world leadership cycles,[106] and for the afore-mentioned reasons, it is possible to explain why a paradigm shift such as the one represented by US unipolar dominance should lead to rejection of its inter-national strategy and challenges to its legitimacy. At this point the EU and the model it represents could be considered as an alternative, founded on general recognition on the basis of shared values, clear affirmation of multilateralism and international law as the basis for international relations and support for the UN as world forum for the resolution of international conflicts.[107]

However, the above hypothesis faces two main objections. The first one is the current EU lack of capabilities. It is not possible in the medium term to see the EU coping by itself with all security challenges; thus the transatlantic relationship is needed. Even if EU autonomy were a reality, the established principles of EU external action would lead it to maintain the relationship so that collective security could be based on cooperation, multilateralism and consent. At the same time, the EU can no longer be a civilian power with military capabilities. It has to have the complete range of capabilities. Hard power and soft power are required in a global world with global security threats as there are multidimensional vulnerabilities concerning geographical areas, political, economic, social, environmental, and humanitarian issues. This implies the use of military resources to support, in some cases, dissua-sion missions or coactive diplomacy. Moreover, as Lawrence Freedman has correctly pointed out, the ESDP should not fall into the same trap as Eur-opean Political Cooperation (EPC) and CFSP did earlier, that is developing 'procedure as a substitute for policy',[108] a phrase coined by Wallace and Forster that they later refined into 'procedures without policy, activity with-out output'.[109] Freedman also stresses that 'the key innovations in EU defence policy tend to be about setting up new institutions in Brussels, rather than defence ministries buying new equipment'.[110] Finally, the single most important element is the will to act and to overcome divergences of interest and strategy between Member States.

The second objection is that the EU and the US are part of the same international system – a system dominated by values advocated by both. A loss of US hegemony would imply a shift in the dominant paradigm in international relations and bring other states into hegemonic positions, probably with different values and guidelines for conducting international affairs. In this light it is in the EU's interest to keep the current system, although modifying some aspects of its operation. As preserving the Euro-Atlantic link is necessary in order to face common interests and concerns that cannot be solved by one side acting alone, a redefinition of transatlantic security is required; this is a difficult task as there are divergences on con-crete issues and on the values sustaining the EU and the US. The former is looking for greater political autonomy within NATO, whilst the US is doing its utmost to preserve its hegemony and thus European military dependency even if there is some evidence of the will to improve relations, as for example in Afghanistan or in Kosovo.

So any proposal for reconstructing transatlantic relations would require mutual agreement on a new transatlantic agenda; and in the agenda there should be a clear statement of common values, arising from a clear understanding of the fears and interests of others. The EU has to have a greater and more effective international role that promotes its collaboration with NATO since without NATO support European efficiency in the implementation of a wide range of missions is not achievable. In turn, the ESDP will only gain popular support through its efficient implementation of such missions. If such efficiency can be achieved it will be possible for European citizens to identify this policy as one projecting European values in the world, as well as one promoting a distinctively European approach to leadership in international relations. Moreover, a new transatlantic agenda, formal or informal, has to facilitate the consolidation of American leadership, not only through the use of force but through relations with allies that legitimize the international position of the US and who support it. Thus, showing not only their *potestas*, but also their *auctoritas*,[111] will provide greater strength for the bargaining position of the US and will give them a greater moral authority, preventing any attack on its position as a dominant power. In this way mutual understanding based on a deliberative relationship between the two sides of the Atlantic can facilitate a US approach to international order based on effective power, and ensure that world public opinion recognizes values and guidelines that, in the medium term, are the only ones that can provide the hegemon with a power accepted and supported because of its positive consequences.

Wallace's words in 2001 are completely valid today as he asked for a mutual adaptation of interests between transatlantic partners: 'Europe and US were too essential to each other to refuse to adjust to the new reality of an EU that wanted and deserved more decision-making authority.'[112] The EU position is clearly reflected in the European Security Strategy that states: 'our aim has to be an efficient and balanced partnership with the US.' This willingness to be present in the international arena and to participate in shared leadership can provide the necessary strength to negotiate the end of entrenched conflicts,[113] conflicts that can have devastating local effects and that also threaten international peace and security. At the same time, the US position is visible in the National Security Strategy Document (NSSD) where the superpower outlines the will to reform existing international institutions or create new ones with its partners and proposes that NATO deepen working relationships between and across institutions, as it is doing with the EU.

Notes

1 See García Cantalapiedra, David, Chapter 7 in this book ('Perceptions on US Policy, Transatlantic Relations, and the Alliance Security Dilemma'), for a realist approach to these changes.
2 Smith, Michael, 'The Shock of the real? Trends in European Foreign and Security Policy since September 2001', in *Studia Diplomática,* vol. LIX, No. 1, December 2006, pp. 27–44.

3 Bertram, C, in Lindstrom, Gustav and Schmitt, Burkard, eds, *One Year On: Lessons from Iraq*, Chaillot Paper No. 68 (Paris: Institute for Security Studies, 2004), p.16; Bildt, C., ibid., p. 23; Dassu, M., ibid., p. 34; Daadler, I. H., 'The End of Atlantism', *Survival*, 2004, vol. 45, no. 2, pp. 147–66; Barbé, E., ed., *Existe una brecha transatlántica? Estados Unidos y la Unión Europea tras la crisis de Irak* (Madrid: Catarata, 2005), pp. 23–47, where the author demonstrates the similarities between the Iraq crisis and earlier transatlantic crises of confidence.

4 Sedivy, J., in Lindstrom, Gustav and Schmitt, Burkard, eds, *One Year On: Lessons from Iraq*, Chaillot Paper No. 68 (Paris: Institute for Security Studies, 2004), p.107; de Wijk, R., ibid., p. 47; Everts, S. and Keohane, D., 'The European Convention and EU Foreign Policy: Learning from Failure', *Survival*, 2003, vol. 45, no. 3, pp. 167–86

5 Brzezinski, Z., *El gran tablero mundial* (Barcelona: Paidós, 1998), p. 36.

6 Luck, E.C., 'American Exceptionalism and International Organization: Lessons from the 1990s', in Foot, R., Macfarlane, S. N. and Mastanduno, M., eds, *US Hegemony and International Organizations* (Oxford: Oxford University Press, 2003), p. 27.

7 NSS 2002 set up a strategy for primacy to safeguard the new world order on the basis of spreading democracy and avoiding the emergence of any competitor; http://www.whitehouse.gov/nsc/nss.html . Some of the threats to US security are international terrorism and weapons of mass destruction. According to this document, there is a break with international law in force concerning the use of force and a perception of other actors as potential opponents in an attitude of competition not easily understandable coming from the superpower.

8 Berenskoetter, F. S., 'Mapping the Mind Gap: A Comparison of US and EU Security Strategies', *FORNET Working Paper*, 2004, no. 3, pp. 17–18; http://www.fornet.info.

9 Respectively in the Former Yugoslav Republic of Macedonia (FYROM) and Congo during 2003, and in Bosnia since December 2004.

10 She shows that within seven years the percentage of such alignment with CFSP positions rose from 25.5 per cent in 1995 to 71.8 per cent in 2002. (Regelsberger, Elfriede 2004), *Are the problems arising from enlargement and the Draft Treaty leading to paralysis instead of synergy?* 23 April 2004 as printed on 9 February 2005: www.fornet.info) Smith, Michael (2003), 'The framing of a European foreign and security policy: towards a post-modern framework?', *Journal of European Public Policy*, vol. 10, vo. 4, August, pp. 556–75). Lebas, Colomban (2004), *Enjeux, réalisations et perspectives pour l'Europe de la Défense*, Synthèse No. 138, Fondation Robert-Schuman, June: www.robert-schuman.org.

11 Constitutional Treaty approved at Brussels Summit (17–18 June 2004), CONV 850/03, 18.7.2003, *OJ* n° C , 18.7.2003, Approved by European Council in Brussels on 18.6.2004 (*OJ* n° C 310, 16.12.2004). Title V of the third part, Chapter II, section 2 of the European Constitutions contained ESDP rules.

12 Articles I-22 and III-296, Treaty establishing a Constitution for Europe, contain the setting of a new European Foreign Affairs Ministry. See Cowe, B., 'The Significance of the New European Foreign Minister', *Fornet, CFSP Forum*, vol. 2, issue 4, 2004, pp. 1–4. We have to keep in mind the possible appointment of Special Representatives by the Council according to a proposal of the Foreign Affairs Minister (Article III-302); according to the Treaty currently in force and to the Lisbon Treaty, this function attributed to the High Representative.

13 The enlargement of the Petersberg missions is a formal question as, quite often in practice, humanitarian missions become conflict prevention, joint actions on disarmament, or stabilization missions, and military assistance is common in EU practice too Constitutional and Lisbon Treaties. See Article III-309 of the Constitutional Treaty, and Article 28 TEU (Treaty of the European Union) according to the Lisbon Treaty.

14 Peterson, J., 'The US and the EU in the Balkans: America Fights the Wars, Europe Does the Dishes', paper presented to the 7th biennial International Conference of ECSA, Madison, 2001; and Wallace, W., 'Europe, the Necessary Partner', *Foreign Affairs*, vol. 80, no. 3, 2001, pp.16–34.

15 Articles I-41.7, I-43, and III-329, respectively.

16 US National Security Strategy Document (NSSD), 17 September 2002; http://www.whitehouse.org .

17 About the Security Dilemma, see Glenn Snyder. 'The Security Dilemma in Alliance Politics'. *World Politics*, vol. 36, no. 4. July 1984. pp. 461–62 and D. García Cantalapiedra 'Perceptions in US Policy, Transatlantic Relations and the Alliance Security Dilemma' in Chapter 7 of this book.

18 Wessels, W., 'Theoretical Perspectives. CFSP Beyond the Supranational and Intergovernmental Dichotomy', in Mahncke, D., Ambos, A. and Reynolds, C., eds, *European Foreign Policy. From Rhetoric to Reality?* (College of Europe Studies, n.1, Brussels: P.I.E.-Peter Lang, 2006), p. 63.

19 Brimmer, E., *Seeing Blue: American Visions of the European Union*, Chaillot Paper, no.105 (Paris: Institute for Security Studies, 2007).

20 Sjursen, H., 'Changes to European Security in a Communicative Perspective', *Cooperation and Conflict*, vol. 39, no. 2, 2004, pp. 108–9.

21 Wessels, W., p. 63

22 EPC stands for European Political Cooperation. See de Schoutheete, P., *La coopération politique européenne*, 2nd edition, (Brussels: Labor, 1986); and Nuttall, S., *European Political Cooperation* (Oxford: Clarendon Press, 1992).

23 Sjostedt, G., *The External Role of the European Community* (Farnborough: Saxon House, 1977).

24 Duchêne, F., 'Europe in World Peace', in Mayne, Richard, ed., *Europe Tomorrow* (London: Fontana/Collins, 1972), pp. 32–49 and Duchêne 'The EC and the Uncertainties of Interdependence', in Kohnstamm, M. and Hager, W., eds, *A Nation Writ Large* (London: Macmillan, 1973), pp. 1–21.

25 In the debate, some argued that such a concept was a 'contradiction in terms' (Bull, H., 'Civilian Power Europe: A Contradiction in Terms', in Tsoukalis, Loukas, ed., *The European Community – Past, Present and Future* (Oxford: Blackwell, 1983), pp. 150–70), that it reflected the limitations of cooperation and integration Rummell, R., 'Speaking with One Voice – and Beyond', in Pijpers, A., Regelsberger, E. and Wessels, W., eds, *European Political Cooperation in the 1980s – A Common Foreign Policy for Western Europe?* (Dordrecht: Martinus Nijhoff, 1988), pp. 118–42, that it highlighted the limitations of 'crude military power' as a foreign policy instrument (Hill, C., 'European Foreign Policy: Power Bloc, Civilian Model – or Flop?', in Rummel, R., ed., *The Evolution of an International Actor – Western Europe's New Assertiveness* (Boulder, CO: Westview Press, 1990), pp. 31–55), and that the EU was *not* a strategic actor, but something more like a *civilian* one (Bertram, p. 16).

26 Smith, K., 'The End of Civilian Power Europe. A Welcome Demise or a Cause for Concern?', *The International Spectator*, vol. 35, no. 2, 2000, pp. 11–28.

27 Maull, H., 'Germany and the Use of Force: Still a "Civilian Power"?', *Survival*, vol. 42, no. 2, 2000, pp. 56–80.

28 Stavridis, S., 'Militarizing the EU: the Concept of Civilian Power Europe Revisited', *The International Spectator*, vol. 36, no. 4, 2001, pp. 43–50, and Smith, M., 'Trends in European Foreign and Security Policy since September 2001', p. 19

29 Hill, C., 'The Future of the European Union in World Politics', in Tsoukalis, Loukas, ed., *Globalisation and Regionalism – A Double Challenge for Greece* (Athens: ELIAMEP, 2001), pp. 97–107, and Working Paper 2002/3. The Common Foreign and Security Policy of the European Union: Conventions, Constitutions and Consequentiality, EFPU Working Paper no. 2003/1 (London: European Foreign Policy Unit, 2002); www.lse.ac.uk.

30 Larsen, H., 'The EU: A Global Military Actor?', *Cooperation and Conflict*, vol. 37, no. 3, 2002, pp. 283–302.
31 Nye, J., *Soft Power: The Means to Success in World Politics* (New York: Public Affairs Press, 2004).
32 Nye, J., ibid., p. 77
33 See Heisbourg, F., 'The "European Security Strategy" is Not a Security Strategy', in Heisbourg, *A European Way of War* (London: Centre for European Reform, 2004), pp. 27–39, Grant, C. in Lindstrom, Gustav and Schmitt, Burkard, eds, *One Year On: Lessons from Iraq* 70.
34 Smith, K., *European Union Foreign Policy in a Changing World* (Cambridge: Polity, 2003).
35 Giegerich, B. and Wallace, W., 'Not Such a Soft Power: The External Deployment of European Forces', *Survival*, vol. 46, no. 2, 2004, pp. 163–82.
36 Larsen, H., op.cit., pp. 283–302.
37 Mahncke, D., 'Transatlantic Relations', in Mahncke, D., Ambos, A. and Reynolds, C. eds, *European Foreign Policy. From Rhetoric to Reality?* p. 204.
38 Sedivy, J., Chaillot Paper, no. 68, p. 107.
39 See previous debate from Sjöstedt and its notions of 'international actorness', and Allen and Smith's notions of 'international presence' (Allen, D. and Smith, M., 'Western Europe's Presence in the Contemporary International Arena', *Review of International Studies*, vol. 16, 1990, pp. 19–37), to 'Sjursen's notion of unorthodox international actor' (Sjursen, H., *Outline of Core Theme and Research Questions*, workshop on 'From Civilian to Military Power: The European Union at a Crossroads?', Project *Citizenship and Democratic Legitimacy in the EU* (CIDEL) (2004), Workshop on 'From civilian to military power: the European Union at a crossroads? www.arena.uio.no/cidel, published as 'What Kind of Power? European Foreign Policy in Perspective', Helene Sjursen, ed., Special Issue of the *Journal of European Public Policy*, vol.13, no.2, 2006; www.arena.uio.no/cidel, p. 1, or even the notion of 'unique actor' due to the combination of means in its hands (Larsen, p. 292). Here, we use the term 'global' in a non-specifically geographic manner; that is to say that we refer to intentions, means, and capabilities. For this 'global' approach, see Ginsberg, R. H., *Foreign Policy Actions of the European Community: The Politics of Scale* (Boulder, CO: Lynne Rienner, 1989), Smith, Hazel, *European Union Foreign Policy – What it is and What it Does* (London: Pluto, 2002), and Smith, Karen, *European Union Foreign Policy in a Changing World*; and against this approach, Hassner, Pierre, in Lindstrom, Gustav and Schmitt, Burkard, eds, *One Year On: Lessons from Iraq*, p. 81.
40 Lejins, A., in Lindstrom, Gustav and Schmitt, Burkard, eds, *One Year On: Lessons from Iraq*, p. 90
41 Brimmer, E., *Seeing Blue*, p. 9.
42 Galtung, J., *The European Community: A Superpower in the Making* (London: George Allen & Unwin, 1973), pp. 117–49.
43 In a certain degree it includes an implicit criticism on the subordination or otherwise of the EU to the US, as discussed above and will not be repeated here.
44 Salmon, T. and Shepherd, A., *Toward a European Army? A Military Power in the Making?* (Boulder, CO and London: Lynne Rienner, 2003).
45 Berlin-Plus agreements; letter exchange between NATO Secretary General and EU High Representative, 17.3.2003; *Nota general informativa del Cuartel General del Estado Mayor de la Defensa*, 21.3.2003.
46 A 'Gaullist' view of the world; see Duke, S., *The Convention, the Draft Constitution and External Relations: Effects and Implications for the EU and its International Role*, European Institute of Public Administration Working Paper No. 2003/W/2 (Maastricht: European Institute of Public Administration, November 2003); www.eipa.nl, p. 7.

47 Stavridis, S., 'European Security and Defence After Nice', *The European Union Review*, vol. 6, no. 3, 2001, pp. 97–118.
48 'A shock absorber' in Deighton's own words (Deighton, Anne, 'The European Security and Defence Policy', *Journal of Common Market Studies*, vol. 40, no. 4, 2002, p. 731). Deighton also mentions Ojanen's suggestion that an EU-NATO fusion might eventually take place (p. 733). This is the (trans) Atlantic community approach favoured by many Americans and many pro-US Europeans (Streit, C. K., *Union Now. A Proposal for a Federal Union of the Democracies of the North Atlantic* (New York: Harper & Brothers, 1938); Gompert, D., 'America as Partner', in Gompert, David and Larrabee, F. S., eds, *America and Europe. A Partnership for a New Era* (Cambridge: Cambridge University Press, 1997), pp. 143–65); Goodby, J., Buwalda, P. and Trenin, D., *A Strategy for Stable Peace: Towards a Euroatlantic Security Community* (Washington, DC: USIP, 2002).
49 Sjursen, H., op. cit., 2004, pp. 107–28; Smith, M., *Trends in European Foreign Policy*, pp. 16–18.
50 Speech by the NATO General Secretary, New Defence Agenda, Brussels, 17 May 2004.
51 See Stavridis, S., 'European Security and Defence After Nice'; Lindley-French, J., 'In the Shade of Locarno? Why European Defence is Failing', *International Affairs*, vol. 78, no. 4, 2002, pp. 789–811.
52 Comments made by R. Barre and C. F. Nothomb during the *Colloque* on '*L'élargissement de l'Union européenne et le dialogue euro-méditerranéen: impact et stratégie de réponse*', Centre d'Etudes Européennes, Université de Lyon-3, Lyon, 10 May 2004.
53 On the eventual setting up of specific EU military headquarters for the ESDP, see Pérez, García, 'La PESD en el proyecto de tratado constitucional', in Pueyo, Jorge, ed., *Constitución y ampliación de la Unión Europea. Crisis y Nuevos retos* (Santiago de Compostela:Tórculo, 2003), pp. 316–17; de Wijk, p. 46. See also Keeler, J., 'Transatlantic Relations and European Security and Defense', *EUSA Review*, vol. 17, no. 2, p. 5.
54 C. Hill first developed the concept in 'The Capabilities Expectations Gap, or Conceptualizing Europe's International Role', *Journal of Common Market Studies*, vol. 31, no. 3, 1993, pp. 305–28. Mahncke, D., 'Transatlantic Relation', p. 197.
55 See García, S., ed., *European Identity and the Search for Legitimacy* (London: Pinter, 1993).
56 Schimmelfennig, Frank, 'Liberal Identity and Post-Nationalist Inclusion: The Eastern Enlargement of the European Union', in Cederman, L. E., ed., *Constructing Europe's Identity: The External Dimension* (Boulder, CO: Lynne Reiner, 2001), p. 182; Cederman, L. E., 'Political Boundaries and Identity Trade-Offs', in Cederman, L. E., ed., *Constructing Europe's Identity: The External Dimension* (Boulder, CO: Lynne Reiner, 2001), pp. 1–32; Neumann, I., 'European Identity, EU Expansion, and the Integration/Exclusion Nexus', ibid., pp. 141–64; Smith, M., 'The Framing of a European Foreign and Security Policy: Towards a Postmodern Framework?', *Journal of European Public Policy*, vol. 10, no. 4, 2003, pp. 556–75.
57 Debate mainly centred round the ARENA-CIDEL project in Oslo; http://www.arena.uio.no.
58 Manners, I., 'Normative Power Europe: A Contradiction in Terms?', *Journal of Common Market Studies*, vol. 40, no. 2, 2002, pp. 235–58; Aggestam, L., 'A Common Foreign and Security Policy: Role Conceptions and the Politics of Identity in the EU', in Aggestam, Lisbeth and Hyde-Price, Adrian, eds, *Security and Identity in Europe: Exploring the New Agenda* (London, Macmillan, 2000), pp. 86–115; Sjursen, Helene (2004), 'Changes to European Security in a Communicative Perspective', *Cooperation and Conflict*, vol. 39, no. 2, pp. 107–28.

59 See Youngs, 2001, pp. 191–206; see also Smith, K., *European Union Foreign Policy in as Chnaging World.*

60 Sjursen, H., op. cit., 2004, pp. 107–28.

61 Fernández Sola, Natividad, 'La subjetividad internacional de la Unión Europea', *Revista de Derecho Comunitario Europeo*, vol. 11, 2002: 85–112.

62 Hill, C., 'The Capabilities Expectations Gap, or Conceptualizing Europe's International Role'; and Hill, C., 'Closing the Capabilities-Expectations Gap?', in Peterson, John and Sjursen, Helene, eds, *A Common Foreign Policy for Europe? Competing Visions of the CFSP* (Londlon: Routledge, 1998), pp. 18–39.

63 Lejins, A., Chaillot Paper, no. 68, p. 90.

64 See Nuttall, S., *'Consistency' and the CFSP: A Categorization and its Consequences*, EFPU Working Paper no. 2001/3, LSE European Foreign Policy Unit; http://www.lse.ac.uk; and Medina, Manuel, *The Coherence of European Foreign Policy: a Real Barrier of an Academic Term?*, IUEE Obs Working Paper No. 27, September 2002; http://www.uab.es/iuee.

65 Duke, S., p. 4.

66 Vinocur, John, Schroder gives support to Bush's Mideast plan, February 27, 2004; U.S.-German reasons to reconcile Schroder and Bush find mutual interest, March 1, 2004, *International Herald Tribune.*

67 Johansson-Nogués, E., *The Voting Practice of the Fifteen in the UN General Assembly: Convergence and Divergence*, IUEE Observatory of European Foreign Policy, UAB Barcelona, Working Paper No.54, January; http://www.uab.es; see also Stavridis, Stelios and Pruett, Duncan (1996), *European Political Cooperation at the United Nations: A critical assessment 1970–1992*, Reading Papers in Politics no. 20 (Reading: University of Reading, Department of Politics, 1996); cfr. Monteleone, Carla, Chapter 8 in this book, 'The End of the Euro-Atlantic Pluralistic Security Community? The New Agenda of Transatlantic Security Relations in the Global Political System'.

68 Freedman, Lawrence, 'Can the EU Develop an Effective Military Doctrine?', in Steven Everts, Lawrence Freedman, Charles Grant, François Heisbourg, Daniel Keohane and Michael O'Hanlon *A European Way of War* (London: Centre for European Reform, 2004), p. 15. B. Crowe rightly refers to some key elements in diplomacy, such as perception by other/third other/third-party actors actors or players and by selected states within and without the EU, and the 'light' input from Brussels, i.e. the continued dominance of national governments in EU foreign policy ('A Common European Foreign Policy After Iraq?', *International Affairs*, vol. 79, No. 3, 2003, pp. 533–46).

69 Zielonka, J., 'Transatlantic Relations Beyond the CFSP', *The International Spectator*, vol. 35, no. 4, 2000, p. 28; and Zielonka, J., 'Constraints, Opportunities and Choices in European Foreign Policy', *Paradoxes of European Foreign Policy. Policies Without Strategy. The EU's Record in Eastern Europe*, EUI WP, no. 97/66, 1997, pp. 10–11.

70 Democratic peace as a model to spread implies representative government, rule of law, respect for political and civil rights, and a free market. These elements would be able to transform international anarchy and provide citizens with economic well-being in a democratic framework. See García Cantalapiedra, D., "La PESD versus la política de seguridad nacional de los estados miembros". *Cuadernos Constitucionales de la Cátedra Fadrique Furió Ceriol nº 49 (2004)*. Monográfico. Universidad de Valencia: 2006: pp. 227–41..

71 See Russett, B. and Antholis, W., 'Do Democracies Fight Each Other? Evidence from the Peloponnesian War', *Journal of Peace Research*, no. 4, 1992.

72 Lindley-French, Julian, 'Two Roads to the Same Place? The Diverging Pursuit of Values and Interests in the Transatlantic Relationship', in Hochleitner, E., ed., *Europa und Amerika-eine Beziehung in Wandel* (Lindley-French J. (2002) "Two Roads to the Same Place?", Vienna: OIES, 2003, pp. 69–70). Cantalapiedra, ibid.;

Lott, Anthony D., *Creating Insecurity. Realism, Constructivism, and US Security Policy* (Burlington: Ashgate, 2004), pp. 128–36.

73 Niblett, R., 'Choosing Between America and Europe: A New Context for British Foreign Policy', *International Affairs*, 83, 4, vol. 83, no. 4, Ch. 6, 2007, p. 634.

74 Ibid., pp. 627–41.

75 National Strategy for Homeland Security (Washington DC, Office of Homeland Security, July 2003) defined it as 'a concerted national effort to prevent terrorist attacks within the US, reduce America's vulnerability to terrorism, and minimize the damage and recover from attacks that do occur'; however, as Hamilton Daniel points out, Hurricane Katrina in 2005 demonstrated that not all homeland security challenges stem from terrorism ('Introduction: Transforming Homeland Security: A Road Map for the Transatlantic Alliance', in Brimmer, E., ed., *Transforming Homeland Security. U.S. and European Approaches* (Washington, DC: Center for Transatlantic Relations, The Johns Hopkins University, 2006), p. x.

76 Apart from EU gaps in intelligence-sharing and in interoperability between police, judicial, and intelligence services due to the exclusive competence of the national security and intelligence services for operational work, even if the analysis of information belongs to the centre for intelligence in the Council Secretariat (SitCen).

77 Hamilton, D., 'Introduction: Transforming Homeland Security: A Road Map for the Transatlantic Alliance', pp. ix, xiii.

78 According to E. Brimmer, transatlantic relations under the Bush Administration has gone through four phases: (1) ignoring the EU's political-strategic aspects; (2) heralding anti-terrorist law enforcement cooperation; (3) engaging the EU through a charm offensive in 2005; and (4) focusing on pragmatic political actions, after the failure of the Constitutional Treaty; *Seeing Blue: American Visions of the European Union*, p. 65.

79 Niblett, p. 630.

80 Brooks, David, 'The Age of Skepticism', *The New York Times*, 1 December 2005.

81 Smith, M., 'The European Union and a Changing Europe: Establishing the Boundaries of Order', *Journal of Common Market Studies*, vol. 34, no. 1, 1996, pp. 5–28; Waever, O., 'European Security Identities', *Journal of Common Market Studies*, vol. 34, no. 1, 1996, pp. 103–32.

82 Weidenfeld, W., *Partners at Odds. The Future of Transatlantic Relations. Options for a New Beginning* (Brussels: Verlag Bertelsmann Stiftung, 2006), p. 43.

83 García Cantalapiedra, D., *Hacia una nueva relación transatlántica*, UNISCI Papers, Mai 2005. http://www.ucm.es/info/unisci, 2005; Morth, Ulrika, 'The EU as an Ethical Power in the WTO, paper given at CIDEL workshop, Oslo, 22–23 October 2004.

84 Kaldor, Mary. 'A Human Security Doctrine for Europe.' Centre for the Study of Global Governance, LSE. The Barcelona Report of the Study Group on Europe's Security Capabilities (2004), and Kaldor, M., *A European Way of Security* (Madrid: Madrid Report of the Human Security Study Group, 8 November 2007); see http://www.lse.ac.uk/depts/global/studygroup/studygroup.htm.

85 Article III-292 of the European Constitutional Treaty.

86 Kaldor, M., *A European Way of Security: The Madrid Report of the Human Security Study Group Seminar* (Madrid: CIDOB, The Centre for the Study of Global Governance, 8 November 2007).

87 Schulze, K. E., *Mission Not So Impossible: The AMM and the Transition from Conflict to Peace in Aceh, 2005–2006*, Case study for the Madrid Report of the Human Security Doctrine, 2007; http://www.lse.ac.uk/depts/global/studygroup/studygroup.htm.

88 Escribano, G., 'Geopolítica de la seguridad energética: concepto, escenarios e implicaciones para España y la UE, *Jornadas Energía e Infraestructura: la nueve*

agenda internacional de las regiones, F. Manuel Giménez Abad, Fiedrich Ebert Stiftung, Zaragoza, 24–25 October 2007.

89 Reus-Smit, C., 'Constructivisme', in Scott Burchill, Andrew Linklater, Richard Devetak, Jack Donnelly, Matthew Paterson, Christian Reus-Smit, Jacqui True, *Theories of International Relations*, 3rd edition revised and updated, Palgrave, 2005, pp. 196–97.

90 Kegley, C W. and Raymond, G. A., 'Global Terrorism and Military Preemption: Policy Problems and Normative Perils', *International Politics*, 41, 2004: 37–49.

91 Luhmann, N., *Teoría política en el Estado de bienestar* (Madrid: Alianza editorial, 1993); Hayek, F. A., *Droit, législation et liberté* (París: PUF, 1980). From these theories, F. Vigalondo (*La arquitectura de la seguridad en el proceso de integración europea: observaciones obtenidas a partir de un modelo interpretativo basado en fundamentos teóricos de J. Habermas* (unpublished: DEA Unión Europea, University of Zaragoza)) elaborated a theory applicable to EU external action and, as we understand, to analyse US foreign policy too.

92 Habermas, J., *Problemas de legitimación en el capitalismo tardío* (Madrid: Cátedra, 1973), p. 94.

93 Habermas, J., *Verdad y justificación* (Madrid: Trotta, 1999), pp. 117–22.

94 Hassner, P., *The United States. The Empire of Force or the Force of Empire?* Chaillot Paper, no. 54 Union Institute for Security Studies, (2002) pp. 20–25 http://www.iss.europa.eu; Heisbourg, F., 'US-European Relations: From Lapsed Alliance to New Partnership?', *International Politics*, 41, 2004, pp. 123–24. Joint declaration by former US officers assuming the existence of a community of values and interests between the US and the EU (*Joint Declaration Renewing the Transatlantic Partnership*, 14 May 2003).

95 Rawls, J., *Teoría de la justicia* y *Liberalismo político* and *El Derecho de Gentes y Una revisión de la idea de razón pública* (original 1999, Spanish translation, Barcelona:Paidós, 2001). According to Rawls, peace is not the result of an irrational war but of people's effort to develop a basic structure founding an equitable regime that makes possible a reasonable law (p. 145).

96 Kegley, C. W. and Raymond, G. A., 'Global Terrorism and Military Preemption: Policy Problems and Normative Perils', p. 45.

97 Sjursen, H., op. cit., 2004, pp. 112–15.

98 G. W. Bush proposal in Dromoland Castle Summit (Ireland, 26.6.2004) to contribute to Iraqi professional security forces training. Proposal approved by the NATO Istambul summit on 28.6.2004. About different interpretations from US and France, see Shishkin, P., 'NATO Agreement Sought', *The Wall Street Journal* Europe, 28 July 2004.

99 Mahncke, D., 'Transatlantic Relations', p. 197.

100 Steinberg, F., 'Europe's Place in Economic Globalisation', *Working Paper* 34, 2007, *Real Instituto Elcano*, 5 November 2007.

101 Zielonka, J., 'Constraints, Opportunities and Choices in European Foreign Policy'.

102 Wessels, W., 'Theoretical Perspectives. CFSP Beyond the Supranational and Intergovernmental Dichotomy', p. 96.

103 Hamilton, D., 'Introduction: Transforming Homeland Security: A Road Map for the Transatlantic Alliance', in Brimmer, E., ed., *Transforming Homeland Security. U.S. and European Approaches* (Washington, DC: Center for Transatlantic Relations, The Johns Hopkins University, 2006), p. xxix.

104 NSSD 2006 The National Security Strategy, March 2006, http://www.whitehouse. gov/nsc/nss/2006/, p. 42.

105 We use here E. Brimmer' expression; Brimmer, E., *Changing Identities and Evolving Values: Is There Still a Transatlantic Community?* (Washington, DC: Center for Transatlantic Relations, The Johns Hopkins University, 2006).

106 According to the world leadership cycles theory developed by G. Modelski (in 'Long Cycles in World Leadership', in Thompson, W. R., ed., *Contending Approaches to World System Analysis* (London: Sage, 1983), and followed by F. Attina (in 'Transatlantic Relations in Post-Iraq War Global Politics', Jean Monnet WP in Comparative and International Politics, JMWP no. 50, 2003, University of Catania; http://www.fscpo.unict.it/EuroMed/jmwp50.htm, p. 5), the power of the world leader is declining, and its strategy to control world problems with the consent of the other States finds opposition, new problems rise, coalitions change, new powers want to exert an influence in international relations. Two coalitions settle down with different world agendas and one of them triumphs over the other as it has more support. In this period there is a delegitimation of the agenda of the first coalition or power.

107 For that model of action, see Communication de la Commission au Conseil et au Parlement Européen, Union Européenne et Nations Unies: le choix du multi-latéralisme, COM *(2003) 526 final* de 10.9.2003.

108 William Wallace's and David Allen's famous phrase in the 1970s; see 'Political Cooperation: Procedure as Substitute for Policy', in Wallace, H., Wallace, W. and Webb, C., eds, *Policy Making in the European Community* (Chichester: John Wiley and Sons, 1977), pp. 227–48.

109 Forster, A. and Wallace, W., 'Common Foreign and Security Policy', 1996, p. 420.

110 Freedman, L., p. 21.

111 On the consolidation of US Leadership by permanent alliances supporting and legitimating their position, see Nye, J., *The Paradox of American Power: Why the World's Only Superpower Can't Go It Alone* (Oxford: Oxford University Press, 2002). About the necessity of moral authority together with their effective power, see García Cantalapiedra, D., *'Peace through primacy': la Administración Bush, la política exterior de EEUU y las bases de una Primacía Imperial*, UNISCI Paper no. 30 (Madrid, 2003), pp. 110–12. www.ucm.es/info/unisci.

112 Wallace, W., 'Europe: The Necessary Partner', *Foreign Affairs*, vol. 80, 2001, p. 25.

113 UN Security Council Resolution 1546, 8 June 2004, provides a good basis for a model upon which to found international relations and a future security guarantee; this model is one that counts on the contribution of the hegemonic power and the other states, as far as they can, to arrive at a common aim according to guidelines established by the United Nations'.

7 Perceptions on US Policy, Transatlantic Relations, and the Alliance Security Dilemma

David García Cantalapiedra

A monarchy that has lost its reputation, even if it has lost no territory, is a sky without light, a body without a soul.

Baltasar de Zuñiga, Counsellor of the King Philip IV of Spain

Introduction

US policy, strategies, and behaviour during the Bush Administration have been considered profoundly destabilizing for the foundations of the US–Europe Alliance and for transatlantic relations as a whole. The way in which the Bush Administration has been driving US Foreign Policy since the 9/11 attacks has produced a perception of disengagement in the US–Europe alliance. Nevertheless, at the same time, the behaviour of European allies has also created in the US government a perception of abandonment or, in certain circles, even defection related to issues such as the global war on terror (GWOT) or Iraq.

In this chapter, the work and writings of Robert Jervis and other academics in the Defensive Realism realm, such as Charles Glaser, Thomas Christensen and Glenn Snyder,[1] will be used first to identify the key perceptions underlying US policy, and second how those perceptions affect transatlantic relations and influence the alliance security dilemma in a mixed polarity system, which is a post-post-Cold War international system with features of unipolarity and multipolarity. According to structural realism, alliances are a general incentive created by an anarchic international system to address the security dilemma. Thus, the current alliance formed by the United States and the European allies should be shaped by the structure of this new international system, and it should not simply be a follow-up of the Cold War transatlantic alliance. Since the proposed alliance would not be a completely new one; it would have some features from the former and some *ex novo*. The analysis in this chapter will identify common and different positions on strategic and particular interests, and the assessment and response to the main threats and adversaries in the new international system from both sides of the Atlantic, and how these differences affect transatlantic relations and hinder the creation of transatlantic policies towards certain common threats and challenges.

The chapter will start by analysing US strategic policy from the end of the Cold War to the current Bush Administration, and will identify continuity and changes in US policy, including the existence of a primacy strategy and Bush doctrine. After this, the chapter will review the evolution of transatlantic relations and then, mainly using the alliance security dilemma model, it will find out the structural changes in the US–European alliance and differences in responses to adversaries, threats, and challenges. The main findings of the analysis are that transatlantic relations have changed according to the transformation and evolution of the international system and within the members of the alliance. Nevertheless, these changes have allowed the maintenance of the alliance, although in a different form than during the Cold War, which explains why the alliance survives, its new nature, and the character of the problems that it faces.

US Policy since the End of the Cold War: Change and Continuity.

The 2002 National Security Strategy (NSS) is the culmination of the drive to create a truly new US grand strategy after the Cold War. The 2002 National Security Strategy Document (NSSD) established new parameters, but maintained certain features from the approaches taken by the Bush Senior and Clinton administrations. In fact, some of these features were already included in the Cold War containment policy, although they were directed towards/to the Soviet threat and the global struggle between both superpowers.[2] The containment strategy and the Bush and Clinton projects contained a posture of primacy,[3] which included the following parameters:

- An international order open to US interests and values: this means international institutions, rule of law, democracy, and free markets. The US would be the centre of this system.
- Prevention of any hostile power from dominating a region the resources of which would, under consolidated control, be sufficient to generate global power. This would mean technological and military superiority.

The Truman Administration was the first US administratrion to establish a strategy of primacy using parameters of political predominance or preponderance:

> The US and the USSR are engaged in a struggle for preponderant power: To seek less than preponderant power would be topped for defeat. Preponderant power must be the object of US Policy.[4]

This posture created the Cold War grand strategy, which was the containment policy that included the coordinated use of every political, economic, military, and moral national resource to face the threat posed by the USSR.

Following this pattern, and in the aftermath of the end of the Cold War, the George H. W. Bush Administration maintained the primacy posture, although without a clear and existential threat such as had been presented by the Soviet Empire. The strategic reviews carried out during the end of the Cold War kept primacy as the core of US strategy. Thus, the Defence Planning Guidance 1992–99 asserted:

> Our first objective is to prevent the re-emergence of a new rival, either on the territory of the former Soviet Union or elsewhere that poses a threat on the order posed formerly by the Soviet Union. This ... requires that we endeavour to prevent any hostile power from dominating a region whose resources would, under consolidated control, be sufficient to generate global power. ... Our strategy must now refocus on precluding the emergence of any potential future global competitor. These regions include Western Europe, East Asia, the territory of the former Soviet Union and Southwest Asia.[5]

There are three additional aspects to this objective:

1. The US must show the leadership necessary to establish and protect a new order that holds the promise of convincing potential competitors that they need not aspire to a greater role or pursue a more aggressive posture to protect their legitimate interests.
2. In the non-defence areas, we must account sufficiently for the interests of the advanced industrial nations to discourage them from challenging our leadership or seeking to overturn the established political and economic order.
3. We must maintain the mechanism for deterring potential competitors from even aspiring to a larger regional or global order.

In 1990, President George H. W. Bush announced the creation of a new world order[6] which was centred on a democratic and stable international system anchored in American values under a UN system of peace and security; this was a set of principles issued to structure a US strategic vision for the post-Cold War world: a collective engagement approach and a democratic peace, enlarging the number of democratic states.[7] This approach was also followed and improved upon by the Clinton Administration as the core of its foreign policy: ' ... ultimately the best strategy to insure our security and build a durable peace is support for the advance of democracy elsewhere.'[8] This would mean a theoretical framework to develop its engagement and enlargement strategy:[9] 'the successor of a doctrine of Containment must be a strategy of enlargement, enlargement of the world's free community of market democracies.'[10]

All of the above principles were maintained after the Cold War. After the Soviet Union's demise, the primacy strategy focused on uncertainty about risks and threats to US national security instead of the Soviet threat, but stayed within the parameters of primacy as noted above: an 'open' international order and prevention of major challenges to US superiority.

Following 9/11, the GWOT took the place of uncertainty, and focused the mobilization of all the resources available to fight this threat, thus creating a truly new grand strategy.[11] The neoconservative influence on the Bush Administration promoted an ideological core for the new grand strategy, which was beyond Wilsonian concepts. In fact, this envisaged a posture *á la Reagan*. The neoconservatives from Congress had already been pushing during the Clinton Administration for a hard-headed foreign policy.[12] Thus, the three pillars that would support the new 2002 National Security Strategy were made public by President Bush at the 2002 Graduation Exercise of the United States Military Academy at West Point.[13] They are directly related to the three principles that constitute the US grand strategy:

- To 'defend the peace against threats from terrorists and tyrants': Global War on Terror, the first principle of the Grand Strategy.
- To 'preserve the peace': through preventing any hostile power from dominating a region whose resources would, under consolidated control, be sufficient to generate global power.
- To 'extend the peace by encouraging free and open societies on every continent': an international order according to US values.

According to those premises outlined above, this strategy establishes an approach to fight terror (weapons of mass destruction (WMD), terrorist and tyrants), thus re-creating the Reagan approach of 'peace through strength', and restoring the militarization of US foreign policy, including the rhetoric of the fight against 'evil' (evil empire, axis of evil) as its key ideological aspect. Thus, the GWOT is not only the fight against terrorism as most European countries understand it. It is not only a fight against 'well-known' terrorist organizations such as the Irish Republican Army (IRA), *Euzkadi ta Azkatasuna* (ETA), *Bader-Meinhoff*, Red Brigades, *Hamas*, *Jihad* Islamic o *Hezbollah*, but a fight against the following aspects of vulnerabilities:

- terrorist groups, organized crime;
- proliferation of WMD;
- aggressive regional behaviour;
- support of terrorism, including WMD proliferation by non-democratic states and so-called rogue states.

This grand strategy represents a renaissance of the Reagan doctrine, in the form of the so-called Bush doctrine. The Reagan doctrine identified, first, those that were the objective of the US counterterrorist policy – the so-called League of Terror. Later, the Clinton Administration called them 'rogue states' and the Bush Administration called them the Axis of Evil. They were the same countries: Iraq, Iran, Libya, Syria, and North Korea. The Reagan Administration[14] had also begun to consider a turn in anti-terrorist policies towards a more pre-emptive approach. On 4 July 1984, Secretary of State George Shultz made the following statement at the Jonathan Institute in Washington, DC:

> Can we as a country, can the community of free nations, stand in a purely defensive posture and absorb the blows dealt by terrorists? I think not. From a practical standpoint, a purely passive defence does not provide enough of a deterrent to terrorism and the states that sponsor it. It is time to think long, hard and seriously about more active means of defence-defence through appropriate preventive or pre-emptive actions against terrorist groups before they strike.[15]

This conviction would later help to create the Bush doctrine and an approach based on pre-emptive action. For Bush Administration neo-conservatives, the behaviour of these countries could be contained, but not always and not forever. In fact, this rogue behaviour is only the 'effect'; then, the goal should be to attack the origin of this conduct, and the origin of this conduct is the nature of the regime itself. Containment can not be indefinitely sustained because this could fail. Thus, pre-emptive action or even a regime change appear as the only solution. The Bush doctrine then would go beyond containment and deterrence, moving towards prevention and compellance.[16] Both the National Security Strategy 2002 and its later revision of 2006 focus on global terrorism and terrorists as non-state actors. The NSS 2002 states:

> We will not hesitate to act alone, if necessary, to exercise our right of self-defence by acting pre-emptively against such terrorists, to prevent them from doing harm against our people and our country ... Prevent attacks by terrorist networks before they occur. A government has no higher obligation than to protect the lives and livelihoods of its citizens. The hard core of the terrorists cannot be deterred or reformed; they must be tracked down, killed, or captured.[17]

Accordingly, the NSS 2006 establishes that the United States and its allies 'make no distinction between those who commit acts of terror and those who support and harbour them ... '[18]

> If necessary, however, under long-standing principles of self-defence, we do not rule out the use of force before attacks occur, even if uncertainty remains as to the time and place of the enemy's attack. When the consequences of an attack with WMD are potentially so devastating, we cannot afford to stand idly by as grave dangers materialize. This is *the logic of pre-emption*. (emphasis added)[19]

It is also important to expose the underlying assumptions of the NSS 2002 language: The last time that a state of war had been assumed by a national security strategy was during the Reagan Administrations. Then, the objectives of defending and expanding peace were also asserted. In Clinton's NSSs, there is a clear assumption of a state of peace and the goal was to reinforce this situation using a strategy of enlargement and engagement.[20] Moreover, the 2002 NSSD introduces a set of concepts that, although they do not appear clearly in the document, can be envisaged as core assumptions in the conduct of the US foreign policy and strategy. Thus, according to the parameters settled by the NSS 2002, the 'peace through strength' motto reaches its ultimate manifestation and become 'peace through primacy'. The US grand strategy would be an 'imperial primacy'. This approach, however, is not couched in terms of a relationship of dominance and subordination between a metropolis and its colonies, but rather in terms of the nature and implementation of power.[21] In this sense, this primacy would be sustained by military superiority dissuading possible competitors from challenging the US position in the international system and the order it promotes and defends.

> The foundation of a peaceful world for us and for our posterity rests on the ability of the US Armed Forces to maintain a substantial margin of national military advantage relative to others. The US uses this advantage not to dominate others, but through cooperation with its friends and allies around the world to dissuade new functional or geographic military competitions from emerging and to manage them if they do.
>
> The US is committed to expanding its network of friendships and alliances with the aim that eventually all of the world's great powers will willingly cooperate with it to safeguard freedom and preserve peace. The aim is to extend the conditions favourable to peace and the US geostrategic position far into the future.[22]

Perceptions and Transatlantic Relations after the End of the Cold War

Alongside strategic and particular interests, the impact of perceptions and misperceptions on intra-alliance relations and on how allies face adversaries (for instance, states or terrorist groups) and threats (WMD proliferation and terrorism) can be traced in every area of transatlantic relations throughout most of the last 60 years. Above all, it can be discerned in every transatlantic crisis since the 1956 Suez Crisis, France's abandonment of the NATO military structure in 1966, Indochina, the Yom Kippur War, the intermediate nuclear forces (INF) deployment and the strategic defence initiative (SDI), Bosnia, Kosovo, and Iran. However, even though the 2003 Iraq crisis has probably been the most significant rift in the alliance since the Suez Crisis, the alliance did not break, and the Iraq crisis only showed the current reality of a relationship that has been evolving since the end of the Cold War.[23]

Although the 9/11 attacks also changed some key parameters of the international system, those attacks were the first real general confirmation that the world had evolved since 1991and the key parameters that constituted the international system have changed. At the transatlantic level, the attacks were the first clear perception (maybe foreshadowed by the Kosovo crisis) of the change in the allies' relationship. But Iraq was surely the first real major crisis in the new transatlantic relations framework, and one that showed sharply the chain of changes produced within it since the end of the 1980s.

There are different perceptions about the international system that influence US and European policies and behaviour. For instance, one of the most debatable issues after the end of the Cold War and since the 9/11 attacks has been the use of force.[24] For the United States, the assumption of a more anarchical international system (including a lower confidence in the UN), the perception of vulnerability in the face of terrorist and unconventional attacks (whether or not using weapons of mass destruction),[25] and the experience of short and decisive operations in previous wars thanks to technological superiority (from the 1991 Gulf War to the 2001 Afghanistan invasion, for instance) fuelled the creation of the Bush doctrine and US National Security Strategy 2002.[26] Thus, there are structural incentives in the international system for the US position. However, European perceptions of terrorism and European experience of recent wars created a different result in terms of policy, although similar in certain ways to US policy: the European Security Strategy is a reflection of European interests and capabilities just as the Bush Doctrine and NSS 2002 are for the Bush Administration.

Even though the changes in the structure of the international system since the end of the Cold War had really modified the parameters of transatlantic relations, US behaviour in alliance politics has also created certain perceptions of US disengagement; for example, the US withdrawal from the anti-ballistic missile (ABM) treaty, the almost complete lack of real consultation over the Iraq issue (except with the UK), and the launch of the GWOT created an image of unilateral behaviour. In this sense, there are also some situations that reflect not so much the actions of the Bush Administration, but rather European positions and misperceptions when interpreting US behaviour and which have more to do with the new realities of the international system's structure and with a new transatlantic relationship. Thus, Europe, as even EU reports point out, must be conscious that 'Europe is at peace, but the world is not'.[27] From this point of view, the alliance between the US and Europe is suffering due to these changes in the international system, and because of the perceived threats and challenges both have to face. In this sense, the image and perception of Al Qaeda or Iran as adversaries also impact on alliance policies and behaviour. In sum, both sides of the Atlantic face structural changes and suffer from problems compounded by perceptions (perceptions of the other and perceptions of the adversary).

Structural changes have to do with the international system, transatlantic relations, and the allies themselves. Perceptions are related to how each side sees the other and sees the adversary/adversaries.

Transatlantic relations must face an international system different from that of the Cold War, a different distribution of power and capabilities at global and transatlantic level, and the changes produced within each part of the alliance. Taking into account these parameters, the tendency in transatlantic relations is that allies face problems on material capacities, incentives to cooperate, and convergence in interests and expectations (present and future), that is, they face uncertainty. This situation is also fed by: perceptions, misperceptions, images of the international system, the transatlantic alliance, and, very important, of the adversaries and challenges. Thus, these parameters create or help to create the identity, values, and political system that compose each side of the alliance, and the mechanisms used to choose alignments and to identify friends and foes. The problem of choosing alignments goes to the basis of traditional transatlantic relations: a (real and perceived) common threat, a strong economic relationship, and a common vision of democratic peace[28] and its meaning.

Post-1945 transatlantic relations were developed within the Cold War system, and based on certain core parameters:

- Political-military parameter: an existential security threat posed by the Soviet Union, with Europe protected by US extended deterrence.
- Economic parameter: a deep bilateral relationship since the Marshall Plan.
- Democratic peace parameter: common values such as democracy, rule of law, civil freedoms and human rights, and free market economy. Democratic states do not fight each other, so the spread of democracy will create 'perpetual peace'. In Karl Deutch's words, 'the creation of a Security Community'.[29]

Nevertheless, these relations were established within a situation of relative power that favoured US pre-eminence, and which was accepted by the European allies. The US enjoyed the three pre-eminences that denote primacy, or *in strictu sensu*, hegemony: political-military, economic, and normative. The last means an acceptance by European states of a situation of US primacy in the sense of the old Greek definition of hegemony, *Hegeisthai*: 'just and legitimate leadership, accepted by the others.'

With the end of the Cold War, changes in transatlantic relations began to be envisaged, although a certain Cold War inertia and relative stability of the framework for the relationship allowed the structure of transatlantic relations to be maintained, but with small and slow changes. However, the Cold War element of US extended deterrence policy progressively lost its rationale and US normative pre-eminence started to be challenged in discussion of a new normative framework; this was at a time when the US was the sole superpower and the European allies started to search for a common and separate identity through the consolidation of the European Union.

The International System, Transatlantic Relations and the Security Dilemma

From a theoretical point of view,[30] the structure of the international system after the end of the Cold War and the 9/11 attacks has clearly and significantly changed. First, there is an anarchic international system with different parameters than those of the Cold War.[31] Secondly, there is a different and asymmetrical distribution of power and capabilities at global and transatlantic level: clear US military superiority (pre-eminence), with a concert of great powers at the economic level (US, EU, Japan, China, some BRICs). And, as a result of certain US policies and behaviour, there is weakened acceptance of the US role as a benign hegemon (weakened normative pre-eminence): a mixed polarity international system, a kind of 'unipolarity-multipolarity complex' has finally arisen, and most clearly after the Iraq crisis.

Since the fall of the Berlin Wall, there were progressive changes in transatlantic relations, certainly since the middle of the 1990s. But the inertia and stability of the end of the Cold War allowed this structure to be maintained almost without changes during the early 1990s. The 'soft landing' after the Cold War and the evolution toward a new international system during the 1990s were not well recognized in spite of successive crises in the Balkans. Due to the inertia after the Cold War, the transatlantic link was maintained and reinforced by some gradual institutional changes. These changes were due, in part, to a thirst for the dividends of peace. The North Atlantic Treaty Organization (NATO) started a policy of enlargement in the east which instigated a change in the vision and mission of the Atlantic alliance. The 1999 NATO Strategic Concept represented the changes in the nature of the alliance. As Sir Andrew Burns put it after the fall of the Berlin Wall: 'We tired of the discipline of unity and the costs of eternal vigilance; we were seduced by the siren call of a peace dividend and by the new gods of globalization and interdependence.'[32]

However, changes in the international system and in the parameters of transatlantic relations were clear and progressive during the 1990s, producing a unipolar system where the US enjoyed a situation of global primacy.[33] But, at the same time, US extended deterrence in Europe lost its rationale after the end of the Soviet threat, and the role of transatlantic relations in US strategic policy then started to change:

- Europe was not the central priority of the US global policy although it was still a main element.
- Europe was not the centre of US strategic policy in geopolitical terms: there were other areas such as East Asia and the wider Middle East.

- Europe was not the main objective of US security policy, although the George H. W. Bush and Clinton administrations were focused on the Balkans problem, and now the global war on terror (GWOT) is the main objective.
- The main value of Europe/the EU as a partner and ally is for economic, moral, and practical support of US global policy.
- The progressive development of a Common Foreign and Security Policy (CFSP) and a European Security and Defence Policy (ESDP) creates alternative visions and strategies for the EU's general and particular interests.

From an economic point of view, the members of the original transatlantic market turned their attention increasingly to a globalized economy. The transatlantic market, although reinforced after successive initiatives and buttressed by the largest mutual foreign direct investment in the world, is not the only market for Europeans and Americans. The European integration process has been focused on a progressively enlarged common market, and both sides of the Atlantic have focused on the opportunities offered by Asian economic growth. The consensus about US normative pre-eminence has changed to a new normative framework. According to this, 'democratic peace' should be achieved, according to different needs of the US and Europe: there is a different understanding in the US and in Europe of the extent of democracy and human rights and the ways to promote them globally.

Finally, there have been changes within each part of the alliance. For instance, the idiosyncrasy of the European integration process, related to a growing assertiveness on security and defence issues, and certain economic and social divergences since the late 1980s. There had been economic and social convergence since the progressive European economic recovery after the Marshall Plan, where the European income per capita ratio improved from 54 per cent to more than 80 per cent of the US level in 1990. The fertility rate and population were similar until the mid-1980s. Nontheless this economic convergence between the economies of the US and Europe, although reflecting more liberal economic models during the Reagan–Thatcher years, maintained certain important differences. However, from 1990 on, Europe started to reverse this convergence with the United States in terms of fertility, population, economy and technological growth and innovation related to the United States.[34] In this sense, the allies face problems of different material capacities, incentives to cooperate, and divergent expectations of interests (present and future): as a result, they face uncertainty.

According to Robert Jervis, states suffer a security dilemma in international politics. Uncertainty regarding others' current and future motivations under the influence of anarchy feeds this security dilemma and it arises as states take measures to augment their security that other states perceive as being detrimental to theirs. This spawns reactive behaviour that ultimately undermines the security of all involved, and makes war more likely.[35] The security dilemma is one of the fundamental assumptions within defensive realism in the theory of international relations, alongside offence–defence theory, perception processes, and domestic policies. Nevertheless, the security dilemma is a common concept for all defensive realist approaches. This concept reflects the anarchic nature of the international system that produces uncertainty. States cannot be sure about present and future intentions of other states and thus they implement security-seeking policies. But these policies make others feel threatened and then they seek to increase their own security, thus reducing security for all.

Since the formation of alliances is a mechanism through which to address the security dilemma in international politics, alliances will suffer the problems of uncertainty, perception process, and, eventually, 'the self-defeating aspect of the quest for security in an anarchic system'. Thus, according to security dilemma theory, states may also face an alliance security dilemma[36] and this dilemma will be more severe in multipolar systems than in unipolar systems or in bipolar systems because multipolar systems are less stable.[37] The alliance game will deal with the 'interior' aspects of alliance formation, but it is the adversary game that considers the 'external' relations of alliances, that is, in the end, threat perception. The adversary game will be of extreme importance when analysing the behaviour of both sides of the current transatlantic alliance: the perception process about possible adversaries (global terrorism, Iraq, Iran) of each side, each side's position on adversaries as perceived by the other side of the alliance, and the impact of both previous perception processes on alliance behaviour.

The Alliance Security Dilemma and the New Transatlantic Relationship

The international system after the Cold War was marked by unipolarity, and after the 9/11 attacks, US policy and behaviour provoked reactions to balance this situation.[38] There were some in Washington who had envisaged this development: for instance, Peter M. Rodman, Assistant Secretary of Defence for International Security Affairs in the first Bush term, wrote in 1999:

> Most of the world's other major powers have made it into a central theme of their foreign policy to attempt to build counterweights to American power. This is in fact one of the main trends in international politics today.[39]

However, from an economic and normative point of view, this unipolarity does not appear to be so clear. Even if one considers the current international situation as an interregnum between unipolarity and multipolarity, an analysis using the alliance security dilemma model would assume a multipolar system rather than a unipolar one.

As noted above, due to the anarchy in the international system, the security dilemma arises as states take measures to augment their security and then other states may perceive these measures as being detrimental to theirs. This spawns reactive behaviour that ultimately undermines the security of all involved, and makes war more likely.[40] Jervis concedes that differences among states, especially in the priority given to security in relation to other domestic concerns and the degree of threat perceived, will have an impact upon the severity of the security dilemma by shaping the costs associated with the 'sucker's payoff'. Geography, commitment to particular beliefs, and technology also markedly affect the degree to which the security dilemma prevails. Specifically, the offence–defence balance and the ability to differentiate between offensive and defensive strategies alter the likelihood of spiralling security-related behaviour. According to Glenn Snyder, the alliance security dilemma is a sub-game of this self-defeating aspect of the quest for security in the anarchic international system.[41]

The alliance game explains one of the ways that states accumulate power to face the security dilemma (others would be armaments and territorial expansion: the armament game and the adversary game).[42] The alliance game has two phases: the game of alliance formation, or primary alliance security dilemma, and the alliance bargaining process, or secondary alliance security dilemma. As alliance creation is a general incentive generated by the structure of the international system, states will search for allies or abstain from alliances, and since there are asymmetries in capabilities and different security interests, alliance formation will mean gains and costs. The main goals in creating alliances are to achieve membership in the most powerful one and to maximize this membership, but there are other major interests in the bargaining process of creating the alliance: general interests and particular interests, which predispose states to align with certain other states.

General or strategic interests are related to the international system and the geographic position of each states'. These interests do not involve conflicts over specific issues with specific other states, but will be defended against all comers. From this point of view, as already noted, US extended deterrence in Europe lost its *raison d'etre* after the end of the Soviet threat, and Europe is not the centre of the US strategic policy: there are other areas such as East Asia and the wider Middle East that command greater attention. But the European Security Strategy 2003 and the National Security Strategy (NSS) 2002 and 2006 identified a more anarchic international system and common threats such as terrorism, weapons of mass destruction (WMD), and rogue states.

Particular interests create conflict or affinity with other states, establishing a tacit pattern of alignment prior to alliance negotiations. Thus, features such as power content, ideology, prestige, and economy can create a set of affinities, giving states expectations that they will be supported by those with whom they share interests: for instance, the US expects the support of Europe/the EU in its fight against terrorism because of NATO's military support during the Cold War, a shared ideology based on liberal democracy, economic interdependence, and general normative agreement on international rules. Moreover, the internal political configuration of states, apart from general ideological preferences, is also important in alliance creation. Even though during Cold War and post-Cold War years there were competing parties, such as Gaullists/socialists, Conservative/Labour, and German Social-Democratic Party (SPD)/Christian Democratic Union (CDU) in the main European allies and Republicans/Democrats in the US, the alliance was maintained in spite of different positions in some crises. These alignments created a core of precedents and relationships which conditioned the process of alliance bargaining, predisposing the system toward certain alliances and against others. In this case, the experience of US/European alliance during the Cold War created a predisposition to maintain the alliance. But, as Snyder points out, conflicts and affinities reduce, but do not eliminate indeterminacy in choosing allies or adversaries due to underestimation by allies of conflicts with third parties. For instance, the perception and assessment of terrorism (and Iraq) was seen differently by the US and European states.[43]

Once formed, alliances move towards the so-called secondary alliance dilemma, that is, how allies move between cooperation and defection. Jervis analyses this process using other terms such as firmness and accommodation, pointing out that the choice between them depends on one's estimate of the ultimate aims of the adversary, in this case of the ally.[44] In this sense, it is necessary to analyse how allies deal with adversaries and interact with the so-called adversary game because both games proceed at the same time and complement each other.[45] Cooperation means a strong general commitment and full support in specific adversary conflicts. The strategies of strong commitment will deter the adversary, enhance a reputation of resolve, but reduce the bargaining leverage over the ally. For instance, NATO European allies promoted the use of Article V of the North Atlantic Treaty after 9/11; most European countries, especially the UK, Spain, and Italy, supported the US invasion of Iraq. Strong commitment makes the ally less influential: the GWOT and Enduring Freedom Operation in Afghanistan were launched with European full support and commitment. These strategies also reduce options of realignment with other states (Russia or China, for instance) and, at the same time, reinforce the probability that adversary alliances may be consolidated, as for example the current Syria–Iran alliance in the Middle East.

A defection or abandonment posture means weak commitment and no support in specific adversary conflicts. There are different variants of this position: for instance, realignment, de-alignment, failure on explicit commitments, and failure to provide support in contingencies where it is expected. In the current situation of the US–European alliance, the failure on explicit commitments and failure to provide support in contingencies will be the only ones to be considered because the alliance remains, although expectations of support are weakened. A strategy of weak commitment reduces the risk of entrapment and enhances bargaining leverage, and reduces tension; there is

EU support at anti-terrorist level, but ambiguous European military commitment on the GWOT in spite of NATO's military strategy to fight terrorism.[46] Besides, some groups within the US government evaluate the European position on anti-terrorist policy negatively. For example:

> Indeed, it is passing strange that European leaders are here today to complain about very successful and security-enhancing US Government counterterrorism operations, when their European Union presides over the earth's single largest terrorist safe heaven, and has done so far for a quarter century. The EU's policy of easily attainable political asylum and its prohibition against deporting wanted or convicted terrorists to countries with the death penalty have made Europe a major, consistent, and invulnerable source of terrorist threat to the United States.[47]

Charles Glaser[48] introduces into the analysis the possibility that each state's perception of other states' motives affects the security dilemma. In this sense, how the US and European states perceive the motives of each other influences the process by which the adversary game is resolved. Different US administrations had argued unsuccessfully since the end of the Cold War that the main threats to the transatlantic alliance were terrorism and WMD. The lack of European interest in these issues was one of the parameters that contributed to the US tendency towards unilateral solutions to global problems. Even the effects of 9/11 and the Iraq war on European threat perceptions have been ambiguous.[49] This ambiguity also enhances the risk of abandonment, that is, some allies try to avoid alignment and burden-sharing in the face of a rising threat, expecting not to bear unnecessary costs and/or to improve their relative position vis-à-vis their allies in the future. In terms of Iraq, Iran, or the military aspects of the GWOT, European states see the costs of intervention as being high and pass them to the US; they believe that, due to the commitment to fighting these countries and US military superiority, this buck-passing and partial abandonment (in the case of the GWOT) will not mean a dangerous reduction in either US security or European security. But it increases the risk of abandonment, reduces their reputation for resolve, and encourages the adversary to stand firm.[50] A US strategy of deterrence (threat of force) is opposed by some European states that are unwilling to use force, in an attempt to restrain US behaviour; for instance, France and Germany's position against the Iraq invasion or withdrawal of Spanish and other countries' troops from Iraq. A European/EU strategy of conciliation could produce an entrapment effect. For instance, Iran is appeased by the EU-3/EU, emboldening and reinforcing Iran's bargaining position on its nuclear programme. As a result, the US may become more intransigent and aggressive if the EU supports US policy later.

Moreover, the progressive development of an EU security and defence policy creates alternative visions and strategies for EU general and particular interests; since the end of the Cold War, Europe is not the priority of US global policy – although it is still a main element – but the vision of military superiority might create a tendency in the EU 'to pass the buck' to the US.[51] Thus, the Central Intelligence Agency (CIA) rendition programme, created in 1995, did not create problems with the European allies until 2005, and in 2002 the CIA and French Intelligence established a joint intelligence/counterterrorist centre in Paris called Alliance Base. At the same time, while President Chirac of France publicly opposed the US invasion of Iraq, 200 French Special Operation Forces were fighting under US command in Afghanistan.[52] Although the allies committed themselves to fight against terrorism, and undertook a number of common actions, they continued to maintain quite different views of how important the threat was, as well as how to combat it. This perception certainly matches poll data that found that 55 per cent of Europeans think that US policies contributed to 9/11.[53]

Alliance bargaining considerations tend to favour a strategy of weak or ambiguous commitment. Bargaining power over allies is reinforced by weak, ambiguous commitment, but the incentives or disincentives to choice are also affected by some key determinants: the relative dependence of the partners on the alliance, the degree of strategic interest in defending each other, how explicit the alliance agreement is, the degree to which allies' interests in conflict with the adversary are shared, and recent historical behaviour.[54] The US, while it led the transatlantic alliance throughout the Cold War, maintains different attitudes towards EU security policy[55] and, in some cases, remains suspicious of its allies because of fear that 'alliance obligations might force America to act in circumstances not of its choosing',[56] for instance, in situations such as Kosovo.[57] The Kosovo crisis came shortly after the 1998 St Malo decision to agree to an autonomous EU military force, thus reversing 50 years of British policy. The UK was better positioned to exert leadership within the EU on military rather than on fiscal or monetary affairs, but also thought that the development of an EU force would improve transatlantic relations as it would encourage Member States to increase military spending. Nevertheless, a collective European military force gives the EU more options, allowing Europeans to be less bound to follow the US lead in NATO, particularly if that involves operations such as Iraq. However, there is a growing technological gap between US and European military forces, and there also is a change in the American security concerns, focusing mainly on global security rather than on European security. The establishment of US bases on the periphery of Europe – in Rumania (Kogalniceaunu and Fetesti), Bulgaria, (Bezmer and Novo Selo) and Azerbaijan, near Baku – to address extra-European threats will only sharpen this trend. On the other hand, NATO is trying to narrow the military gap through the NATO Reaction Force and various capabilities initiatives, including new organizational and operative doctrine, such as effects based on operations (EBAO), in which both Europeans and Americans would participate.

However, in the adversary game, firm commitments tend to strengthen bargaining power vis-à-vis the opponent, that is, leverage over the adversary is strengthened by a firm, explicit commitment. In this sense, explicit agreements, a high degree of shared interests in conflict with the adversary, and recent common historical behaviour would support a strategy of strong commitment in the alliance. From this point of view, there is a large number of US–European agreements identifying and creating common policies on terrorism and WMD, from as early as 1990. The 1990 Transatlantic Declaration stated that 'the United States of America and the European Community and its Member States will fulfil their responsibility to address trans-national challenges ... combating and preventing terrorism ... and preventing the proliferation of nuclear armaments, chemical and biological weapons, and missile technology'. The New Transatlantic Agenda of 1995 and its Joint Action Plan also set out the intention to respond to the same challenges.[58] Even NATO Military Committee (MC) 472 implicitly supports pre-emptive strikes in a similar way to that established in the National Security Strategy 2002:

> NATO's actions should work on the assumption that it is preferable to deter terrorist attacks or to prevent their occurrence rather than deal with their consequences. Counter-terrorism is offensive military action designed to reduce terrorists' capabilities. Allied nations agree that terrorists should not be allowed to base, train, plan, and stage and execute terrorist actions and that the threat may be severe enough to justify acting against these terrorists and those who harbour them, as and where required.[59]

Thus, the European Security Strategy 2003 and the NSS 2002 and 2006 identified common threats in terrorism and WMD, and the US and the EU/European states have reinforced this posture through several agreements. Since the 2002 US–EU Summit in Washington, DC, a wide range of accords and partnerships on anti-terrorist policy have been signed in various areas;[60] for example, the Proliferation Security Initiative, the Container Security Initiative, the Bio-terrorism Act, the Europol–US Agreement to collaborate on police matters, the EC–US Customs Experts Group, and the 2004 US–EU Passenger Name Record (PNR) Agreement. Thus, in the adversary game, the EU or US commitment against opponents may foreclose compromise settlement options. Strengthening EU commitment to the US tends to foreclose any alternative alliance options for the EU, and the EU hastened to publicly reject Osama bin Laden's reported offer of a 'separate peace'. Since Al Qaeda has expansionist goals, a policy of firmness will enhance the reputation for resolve, but a strategy of conciliation would produce a falling domino effect: Al Qaeda or Iran might interpret EU overtures as weakness and thus push harder on both present and future issues.

Conclusions

Once the international system has changed or is in process of change towards greater multipolarity, there is a general incentive for creating alliances, and certain states will ally with other states, according to the logic of the security dilemma. However, the alignments result from a process that is indeterminate. This indeterminacy can be reduced, but not eliminated, by general and particular interests. From this point of view, the US–European alliance is undergoing a process of structural adjustment. The current alliance would, however, not be a completely new one and, as we saw above, there would persist some features from the former Cold War alliance, such as those reflecting certain general and particular interests which predispose the US and European states to align with each other. US extended deterrence in Europe is no longer necessary; there is no potential insecurity spiral and Europe is no longer at the centre of US strategic policy. But the European Security Strategy 2003 and the NSS 2002 and 2006 identified a more anarchic international system and common global threats, such as terrorism, WMD, and rogue states, which provide a general incentive to form (or maintain) an alliance. Furthermore, there is a core of precedents and relationships (democratic ideology and political systems, NATO support, common values) that condition the process of alliance bargaining, predisposing towards certain alliances and against others.

During Cold War bipolarity, the Western allies were under Soviet threat; this created an insecurity spiral that in turn produced an integrative spiral in which allies moved progressively closer because of fear of the adversary, thus reducing the risk of abandonment among the allies. This sort of existential threat does not exist anymore or, at least, there is no common perception of a threat as severe as that emanating from the Soviet Union during the Cold War. In fact, there are perceptions and assessments of rogue states and/or terrorists with WMD that offer different evaluations of their importance as key threats. Thus, it seems that there is no incentive to sustain the integrative spiral and strategies of strong commitment that existed during the Cold War. The main problem within the US–European alliance now rests upon a disagreement about how to deal with the adversary game within the security dilemma, and how this affects alliance bargaining (secondary alliance dilemma). Each side tends to adopt different approaches to deal with terrorism: the US is more prone to a strategy of confrontation, using pre-emptive actions and a military counterterrorist posture, while Europeans prefer a strategy of moderation and perceive excessive US bellicosity.

These strategies directly affect the alliance game. The United States and the European allies have divergent images of the motives and intentions of the adversary. At the same time, Europeans tend to see more danger in the dynamics of the conflict than in the adversary. The US places less emphasis on moderation after the spread of terrorist networks, and the proliferation of bombings not only in certain Third World regions, but also in Europe.

However, there was a common vision on terrorism during the 1990s (including US–EU summits and the 1999 NATO Strategic Concept), and Europeans shared the vision that terrorism and WMD were serious threats and that international law would have to be revised to take care of these new concerns. In this regard, and using a strategy of strong commitment in order to maintain solidarity with the US after 9/11, the EU did not fight the US position on the proposed verification protocol to the Biological Weapons Convention. Prior to 9/11, the EU had overwhelmingly rejected this position. Moreover, the 2003 European Security Strategy is an acknowledgement in principle that Europe shares US fears about terrorism and WMD, as can be seen in the range of agreements between both sides of the Atlantic on counterterrorism measures signed following the 9/11 attacks. Besides, EU law enforcement and intelligence officials clearly agree with the US threat assessment and this is reflected in the substantial counterterrorism cooperation that has emerged among the EU Member States since 9/11. Sadly, this EU policy of cooperation did not exist until after the events of 9/11.

Nevertheless, there are European perceptions of a declining credibility in the US commitment to alliance interests. The US focuses on global, rather than European, security concerns: for instance, the US Global Posture Review, the plans for troop withdrawals in Europe even before the Bush Administration took office, the establishment of US bases at the periphery of Europe to address extra-European threats, and the wider Middle East strategic vision.[61] All these procesess would reinforce an alliance game's prediction about European fears about entrapment, of being dragged into a conflict over an US interest that they do not share or share only partially. In this sense, European allies value preservation of the alliance more than the cost of supporting the US in Iraq or military support of the GWOT. Moreover, they see possibilities of extra-regional entrapment: for instance, a further NATO enlargement (to Ukraine and Georgia), an entanglement in Afghanistan or supporting NATO global partners.

Europeans thus try to escape or minimize risks of entrapment without any serious risk of US abandonment, although accepting partial abandonment in the form of troop withdrawals, priority for the wider Middle East, and unilateralism. Even NATO European allies even accepted a US ballistic missile defence system (BMD) in Europe related to threats coming from the wider Middle East. However, there has been no troop withdrawal in Europe,[62] the future deployment of a BMD system is under negotiation within NATO, the EU also gives a priority to the Middle East, and the lessons learned from the campaigns in Afghanistan, Iraq, and the GWOT have driven a remarkable change in US policy towards a more multilateral approach during George W. Bush's second administration. Secretary of Defence Donald Rumsfeld envisaged this new posture after the 'Long War' statement in February 2006.[63] There was an implicit acknowledgement by the Bush Administration that it was necessary to de-emphasize unilateral solutions and coalitions of the willing, and to accept other powers' interests, and to seek partnership with regional powers in order to face problems and crises. In this sense, this means a better understanding in Washington of the limitations of military power and a greater appreciation of the European contribution. Unfortunately, the controversy over Iraq has tended to obscure these positive trends in US–European cooperation.

European states debate the balance between cooperation and defection in alliance bargaining mainly because of the influence of certain aspects of the structure of the international system (for instance, the absence of a perceived existential threat that would create an integrative spiral within the alliance), a perceived reduction in US commitment and, above all, the influence of the adversary game on the secondary alliance dilemma (reflecting different threat perceptions). Since the end of the Cold War, with clear unipolarity, prospective or actual peace dividends, and the absence of perceived major threats, there were no clear perceptions of changes and needs for adjustment, but inevitably the alliance dilemma is more severe in a potentially multipolar international system. Members of the US–European alliance currently respond differently to the adversary game depending on threat perception, and this makes for different results in the alliance game.

According to Snyder's model and the results of the analysis above, there is a mutual fear of abandonment in the case of fighting terrorism and WMD, which promotes convergence of policies in terms of mutual support and firmness towards adversaries and, thus, although there is a tendency towards weak commitment in the alliance game, fear of abandonment outweighs fear of entrapment. However, in such cases as the invasion of Iraq, there are different threat perceptions and structural pressures, making abandonment more possible because allies may adopt opposing policies. But in terms of the existence of the alliance, this will not produce its breakdown because, after adjustment, it is already a reflection of the current international system, there are certain interests that predispose the US and European states to align with each other, and, even in the case of European buck-passing and partial abandonment, US military unipolarity means that there will not be a dangerous reduction in European security.

Notes

1 In this sense, see the seminal works of Jervis, Robert, *Perception and Misperception in International Politics* (Princeton, NJ: Princeton University Press, 1976), and 'Cooperation under the Security Dilemma', *World Politics*, vol. 30, no. 2 (January 1978), pp. 168–214; also the work of Glaser, Charles L., 'The Security Dilemma Revisited', in *World Politics*, vol. 50, no. 1 (October 1997), pp. 171–201; Snyder, Glenn, 'The Security Dilemma in Alliance Politics', *World Politics*, vol. 36, no. 4 (July 1984), and Christensen, T. and Snyder, J., 'Chain Gangs and Passed Bucks: Predicting Alliance Patterns in Multipolarity', *International Organization*, vol. 44, no. 2, Spring 1990, pp. 137–69.

2 See García Cantalapiedra, David, *Una Estrategia de Primacía: la Administración Bush, las relaciones transatlánticas y la construcción de un Nuevo Orden Mundial 1989–1992*, UNISCI Papers, no. 23–24, Madrid, 2002. For a wider review, see

García Cantalapiedra, David, *EEUU y la construcción de un Nuevo Orden Mundial: la Administración Bush, las relaciones transatlánticas y la seguridad europea 1989–92*, PhD dissertation, Department of International Studies, Faculty of Political Sciences, Universidad Complutense de Madrid, Madrid, 2001, pp. 148–69.

3 García Cantalapiedra, *Una Estrategia de Primacía,* pp. 11–12.

4 Policy Planning Staff. 'Basis Issues raised by Draft NSC', Reappraisal of US Objectives and Strategy for National Security, *Foreign Relations of the United States.* 1952–54, no. 2, Washington DC, Department of State, 1985, pp. 64–65.

5 President Ronald Reagan, *National Security Strategy of the United States 1988*, Washington, DC: The White House, 1988. p. 1; President George Bush, *National Security Strategy of the United States August 1991*, Washington, DC: The White House, 1991. pp. 4, 7; President William Clinton, *National Security of Engagement and Enlargement, February 1996*, p. 2; President William Clinton, *National Security for a New Century*, 1998, Washington, DC: The White House, p. 5.

6 President George H.W. Bush, Remarks at the Aspen Institute Symposium in Aspen, Colorado. *Public Papers of the President George Bush*, Washington DC National Archives. August 2, 1990, pp. 1190–94; President George Bush. *Toward a New World Order.* Address before a Joint Session of the Congress. Washington DC, US Department of State Current policy no. 1298. September 11, 1990.

7 The concept of enlargement and democratic peace responds to the Kantian concept of 'permanent federation in a permanent enlargement'.

8 President Clinton's State of Nation Message, *New York Times*, 26 January 1994. p. A17. Also Owen, John, 'How Liberalism Produces Democratic Peace', *International Security*, vol. 19, no. 2, Fall 1994, pp. 87–125.

9 President William Clinton, *National Security Strategy of Engagement and Enlargement*, Washington, DC: The White House, July 1994.

10 Lake, Anthony, "From Containment to Enlargement". Washington DC. US Department of State, vol. 4, no. 39, 27 September 1993.

11 García Cantalapiedra, David, 'Irak, la política exterior de EEUU y las elecciones de noviembre', *UNISCI Discussion Papers,* no. 6, October 2004, in http://www. ucm.es/info/unisci. Also see Gaddis, John Lewis, 'Grand Strategy in the Second Term', *Foreign Affairs,* vol. 84, no. 1, 2005, p. 5.

12 'Kristol, W. and Kagan, Robert, 'Toward a Neo-Reaganite Foreign Policy', *Foreign Affairs,* vol. 74. no. 4. July-August 1996. Donally, Thomas. "Rebuilding America's Defenses: Strategy, Forces and Resources For a New Century'. A *The Project for the New American Century Report.* Washington DC, September 2000. The Project for the New American Century. *Statement of Principles.* Washington DC. The Project for the New American Century. June 3, 1997. Kagan, R., 'Power and Weakness', *Policy Review*, vol. 113, June–July 2002.

13 President Bush, *Remarks at 2002 Graduation Exercise of the United States Academy, West Point, New York*, The White House. Washington, DC: Office of the Press Secretary, 1 June 2002.

14 National Security Council. National Security Decision Directive NSDD 277. 'National Policy and Strategy for Low Intensity Conflict'. Washington DC: The White House. June 15, 1987. p. 1; see also National Security Council. NSDD 159. 'Covert Action Policy Approval and Coordination Procedures'. Washington DC: The White House.18 January 1985.

15 Netanyahu, B. (ed.), *Terrorism: How the West Can Win*, New York: Farrar, Straus and Giroux, 1986, pp. 16–17, 23.

16 See Secretary of State Condoleezza Rice. 'President's National Security Strategy'. Wriston Lectures, Manhatan Institute, New York: Office of Press Secretary, The White House. 1 October 2002

17 President George W. Bush, *The National Security Strategy of the United States of America*, Washington, DC: The White House, September 2002, pp. 6 and 12.

18 See Guertner, G., 'European Views of Preemption in US National Security Strategy' *Parameters*, Summer 2007, pp. 31–44.
19 President George W. Bush, *The National Security Strategy of the United States of America*, Washington, DC: The White House, September 2006, p. 23.
20 President William Clinton. *The National Security Strategy of Engagement and Enlargement*. Washington, DC: The White House, July 1994; 'The successor to a doctrine of containment must be a strategy of Enlargement, Enlargement of the world's free community of market democracies'. See Lake, Anthony. 'From Containment to Enlargement'. Washington DC: US Department of State, vol. 4, no. 39, 27 September 1993.
21 For a wider explanation of the concept of imperial Primacy and the 'peace through primacy' motto, see Garcia Cantalapiedra, David, *'Peace through Primacy': la Administración Bush, la política exterior de EEUU y las bases de una Primacía Imperial*, Madrid, UNISCI Papers, no. 30, December 2003.
22 Secretary of Defense Donald Rumsfeld. Guidance and Terms of Reference for the 2001 Quadrennial Defense Review. Washington DC: Department Of Defense, 22 June 2001, p. 1.
23 However, academics such as Kenneth Waltz announced the demise of NATO as the embodiment of transatlantic relations as early as 1993. See Waltz, Kenneth, 'The Emerging Structure of International Politics', *International Security*, vol. 18, no. 2, 1993, pp. 44–79.
24 'UN General Assembly, 'A more Secure World: Our Shared Responsibility', *Report of the High-level Panel on Threats, Challenges and Change*, A/59/565, 2005', New York: United Nations Department of Public Information.
25 For an American vision see Haass, Richard N., *Intervention: The Use of American Military Force in the Post-Cold War World*, Washington, DC: Brookings Institution, 1999, p. 71.
26 For a review of this process see García Cantalapiedra, David, *Una Estrategia de Primacía: la Administración Bush, las relaciones transatlánticas y la creación de un Nuevo Orden Mundial 1989–1992*, Madrid, UNISCI Papers 23–24, 2002, and García Cantalapiedra, David, *'Peace through Primacy': la Administración Bush, la política exterior de EEUU y las bases de una Primacía Imperial*, Madrid, UNISCI Papers 30, December 2003–February 2004.
27 Independent Task Force. 'European Defense: A Proposal for a White Paper'. Paris, EU Institute for Security Studies, 2005, p. 9.
28 Owen, J., 'How Liberalism Produces Democratic Peace', *International Security*, vol. 19, no. 2, Fall 1994.
29 Deutsch, K., *Political Community and the North Atlantic Area*, Princeton, NJ: Princeton University Press, 1957.
30 In this sense, this analysis is aware of the theoretical framework in which Peter Jervis and other 'defensive realists' work.
31 In this vein, see Waltz, Kenneth, 'Structural Realism after the Cold War', *International Security*, vol. 25, no. 1, 2000.
32 Welsh, Jennifer M., *Canada-United Kingdom Colloquium*, School of Policy Studies, Queen's University at Kingston, Quebec City, Canada, 18–21 November 2004, 2005, p. 20.
33 Krauthammer, Charles, 'The Unipolar Moment', *Foreign Affairs, America and the World 1990–91*, vol. 70, no. 1, Winter 1990/91, pp. 23–33.
34 The Economist: *A Nation Apart, A Survey on American Exceptionalism,* 8–14 November, 2003.
35 Jervis, Robert, 'Cooperation under the Security Dilemma', *World Politics*, vol. 30, no. 2, January 1978, pp. 168–214. Jervis concedes that differences among states, especially in the priority given to security in relation to other domestic concerns and the degree of threat perceived, will affect the severity of the security dilemma

by shaping the costs associated with the sucker's payoff. Geography, commitment to particular beliefs, and technology also affect the degree to which the security dilemma prevails. Specifically, the offence–defence balance and the ability to differentiate between offensive and defensive strategies alter the likelihood of spiralling security-related behaviour.

36 Snyder, Glenn, 'The Security Dilemma in Alliance Politics', *World Politics*, vol. 36, no. 4, July 1984, pp. 461–62.

37 For instance, Waltz, Kenneth, *Theory of International Politics*, Reading, MA: Addison-Westley, 1979, p. 172.

38 In this sense, see Walt, Stephen, *Taming American Power*, New York: Norton, 2005.

39 Rodman, Peter, *Uneasy Giant: The Challenges to American Predominance*, Washington, DC: Nixon Center, 1999, p. 2.

40 See Jervis, Robert, 'Cooperation Under the Security Dilemma', *World Politics*, vol. 30, no. 2, January 1978, pp. 167–214.

41 Snyder, Glenn, 'The Security Dilemma in Alliance Politics', *World Politics*, vol. 36, no. 4, July 1984, pp. 461–95.

42 Ibid., p. 461.

43 See Sarotte, M. E., 'Transatlantic Tension and Threat Perception', *Naval War College Review*, vol. 58, no. 4, Autumn 2005.

44 Jervis, R., *Perceptions and Misperceptions in International Politics*, Princeton, NJ: Princeton University Press, p. 113. He uses these terms to discuss the problems with the deterrence and spiral theories.

45 Snyder, Glenn, 'The Security Dilemma in Alliance Politics', *World Politics*, vol. 36, no. 4, July 1984. p. 468.

46 NATO/IMS. "NATO's Military Concept for Defense against Terrorism', released October 2003, updated 14 April 2005   www.nato.int/ims/docu/terrorism.htm consulted 20/08/2007

47 Scheuer, Michael F., former Chief, Bin Laden Unit, CIA 1995–99. *Extraordinary Rendition in U.S. Counterterrorism Policy: The Impact on Transatlantic Relations*. Statement before the House Committee on Foreign Affairs, Subcommittee on International Organizations, Human Rights, and Oversight. Subcommittee on Europe. 17 April 2007 (Washington, DC: Government Printing Office, 2007), p. 2.

48 Glaser argues that, beside perceived conflicts of interests generated by misunderstandings, conflicts of interests between states are also possible as a result of uncertainty about motives. Glaser, Charles L., The Security Dilemma Revisited', *World Politics*, vol. 50, no. 1, October 1997, pp. 171–201.

49 This argument is developed in Gordon, Philip H. and Shapiro, Jeremy, *Allies at War: America, Europe and the Crisis over Iraq*, New York: McGraw-Hill, 2004.

50 Snyder, Glenn, 'The Security Dilemma in Alliance Politics', *World Politics*, vol. 36, no. 4, July 1984. p. 471.

51 Christensen, T. and Snyder J., 'Chain Gangs and Passed Bucks: Predicting Alliance Patterns in Multipolarity' *International Organization*, vol. 44, no, 2, Spring 1990, pp. 139.

52 Julianne Smith, Director and Senior Fellow, Europe Program, CSIS, *Extraordinary Rendition in U.S. Counterterrorism Policy: The Impact on Transatlantic Relations*, Statement before the House Committee on Foreign Affairs, Subcommittee on International Organizations, Human Rights, and Oversight, Subcommittee on Europe, 17 April 2007, Washington, DC: Government Printing Office, 2007, p. 3.

53 Kennedy, Craig and Bouton, Marshall M., 'The Real Trans-Atlantic Gap: US and European Public Opinion Differences', *Foreign Policy*, November–December 2002.

54 Snyder, Glenn, op. cit., pp. 471–77.

55 Oudraat, Chantal de Jonge, 'US Attitudes evolve about EU Security Ambitions', *European Affairs*, vol 8, n. 2–3. Summer–Fall 2007

56 Welsh, Jennifer M., *Canada–United Kingdom Colloquium*, School of Policy Studies, Queen's University at Kingston, Quebec City, Canada, 18–21 November 2004, 2005, p. 29.

57 For a European view, see Bozo, Frederic, 'The Effects of Kosovo and the Danger of Decoupling' in Jolyon Howorth and John T. S. Keeler (eds), *Defending Europe: The EU, NATO and the Quest for European Autonomy*, New York: Palgrave McMillan, 2003.

58 'We are determined to take new steps in our common battle against the scourges of international crime, drug trafficking and terrorism. We commit ourselves to active, practical cooperation between the U.S. and the future European Police Office, EUROPOL'. See The New Transatlantic Agenda. Joint Action Plan. "II. Responding To Global Challenges". Brussels, European Commission. 3 December 1995.

59 NATO/IMS. 'NATO's Military Concept for Defense against Terrorism', released October 2003, updated 14 April 2005   www.nato.int/ims/docu/terrorism.htm consulted 20/08/2007

60 See also EU Council. Conclusions adopted by the Council (Justice and Home Affairs), Brussels, 20 September 2001. SN 3926/6/01; European Council. Conclusions and Plan of Action of the Extraordinary European Council meeting on 21 September 2001. SN Brussels, 23 September 2001; Agreement between the United States and the European Police Office. 6 December 2001, Brussels, Europol, December 2001; 2002 G-8 Summit. Global Partnership against the Spread of Weapons and Materials of Mass Destruction. Kananaskis, 27 June 2002; National Commission on Terrorist Attacks on the United States, *The 9/11 Commission Report*, New York: Norton, 2004.

61 For the origin of this concept, sometimes erroneously identified with the first wider (later broader) Middle East initiative, see Garcia Cantalapiedra, David, *'Peace through Primacy': la Administración Bush, la política exterior de EEUU y las bases de una Primacía Imperial*, Madrid, UNISCI Papers, no. 30, December 2003.

62 Shanker, Thom. 'Gates halts cut in Army Force in Europe', *The New York Times*, 21 November 2007.

63 Secretary of Defense Donald Rumsfeld. Remarks at the National Press Club. Washington DC, Office of the Assistant Secretary of Defense (Public Affairs). US Department of Defense 2 February 2006.

8 The End of the Euro-Atlantic Pluralistic Security Community? The New Agenda of Transatlantic Security Relations in the Global Political System

Carla Monteleone

The crisis in Iraq undoubtedly signalled one of the lowest points in transatlantic relations. This is particularly evident when looking at public opinion polls that, besides showing European disapproval towards the current American administration, highlight a dramatic decrease in European support towards American leadership in international affairs.[1] Although the negative trend cannot be said to be typical of only the European region,[2] the rhetoric embedded in the usage of terms such as 'old Europe' to refer to European countries not willing to align with American positions, or 'imperialist' and 'unilateralist' to refer to America was not a great help in transatlantic political communication[3] as it heightened the impact of negative expectations on perceptions[4] and it increased the risk of misperceptions.[5]

Even before the Iraq war, though, the high number of transatlantic disputes in all fields of the relationship that occurred since the end of the Cold War had led some scholars and analysts to issue warnings about a widening of the gap between Americans and Europeans. The transatlantic relationship has been often characterized in terms of a *drifting apart* of the two partners, and the estrangement process has been often attributed to the end of the common threat provided by the Soviet Union. It has been said that what is lacking is the *glue* that kept allies together during the Cold War, to use an expression that was fashionable in the 1990s and has become a hallmark of the political rhetoric on transatlantic relations after the crisis over Iraq during 2003–2004. The absence of a common threat has highlighted such a radical estrangement that the hypothesis has been advanced that Americans come from Mars while Europeans are from Venus.[6] In *Paradise and Power*, Kagan starts by saying that it is time to stop pretending that Europeans and Americans still see the world in the same way because they differ on the essential question of power: how effective, moral, and desirable it is. Kagan affirms that Europe is turning its back on power as it has entered into a post-historical world of peace and relative wealth: a Kantian world. However, the US still exerts power in an anarchic world in which laws and international rules are not dependable and security still depends on the use of force: a

Hobbesian world. According to this analysis, divergences are not the result of a temporary situation, but they have to be considered as a structural phenomenon. Other scholars have pointed to responsibilities of the current political leaders, but even in that case the main question has been whether the transatlantic relationship could survive.

Today, however, after the first visit of an American president to the European Union, but thanks to more conciliatory tones and to the greater visibility of cooperation, not only between American and Europeans in general, but specifically between the US and the EU, on diverse issues ranging from Iran to Darfur, from the Middle East to Afghanistan, from terrorism to Iraq even, some sort of 'friendship sparkle' seems to be in the air again. So much so that recently the US Deputy Assistant Secretary for European and Eurasian Affairs, Kurt Volker, declared:

> If you had asked a year and a half ago about our relationship with Europe, I would have said that we share common objectives on a number of issues ... Objectives, but not necessarily common strategies and joint actions. We wanted the same thing, but we had different strategies for how we were trying to get there. If I go through that same list of issues today, we not only have some broad common objectives, but much more clearly defined common strategies and common actions.[7]

Further, the US–EU summit that took place on 21 June 2006 was one of the most successful in the history of US–EU summits, and showed real convergence on some key issues and the global extent of the transatlantic partnership. In particular, in the political and security field a very high level of cooperation has been reached in a number of areas ranging from democracy promotion, which seems to be the issue currently on top of the American and European agenda, to 'regional issues', no longer limited to the European area but now ranging from the Balkans to the broader Middle East to all the areas now included in the European Neighbourhood Policy, to Africa, Latin America, and East Asia, to the still sensitive and most controversial issue of all: Iraq. The political and economic support provided by the EU to Iraq and its stabilization after the official end of the war – and in particular after the co-hosted US–EU conference on Iraq held in Brussels during June 2005 – led George W. Bush to express his gratitude at the 2006 EU–US summit. This positive trend was confirmed at the 30 April 2007 US–EU summit in Washington, and then again at the 10 June 2008 US–EU summit in Ljubljana.

The contrast between the perception of an irreversible transatlantic divergence and the maintenance – and even rebirth – of transatlantic cooperation reminds us that 'perceptions of the world and of other actors diverge from reality in patterns that we can detect and for reasons that we can understand'.[8] This leads to questions regarding the possible existence of two different security cultures and relational models, as well as the evolution of these models and their relationship, in order to understand how incompatible they really are. But it also leads us to start questioning the real character of transatlantic divergences and crises since the end of the Cold War, how much they are the result of evoked sets[9] that may have affected the Euro-Atlantic pluralistic security community, and how much the current mixed picture of conflict and cooperation can be explained by pressures at the systemic level.

It is important not to forget that the recent crises are not the first, nor a sporadic, episode in transatlantic relations. Disagreements started emerging not long after the end of World War II on issues such as the nuclear military strategy of NATO or the absence of consultations. The disagreements started to increase during the De Gaulle era, and became an almost regular feature from the 1970s and, even more, the 1980s. It would be fair to say that they were so acute that if the Marshall plan stimulated the European integration process, opposition to American policies stimulated the European integration process in the field of foreign and security policy. However, these divergences never led to a real break-up.

It would be of no analytical value to deny the frequency, seriousness, and meaningfulness of disagreements between the United States and the European Union since the end of the Cold War, and more acutely since the terrorist attacks against the US in 2001. However, it is also important to look at the transatlantic relationship from a global and longer-term perspective and in light of the changes that have taken place – both inside the two actors and at the international system level – and that are leading to a redefinition of the transatlantic relationship. It will be here claimed that, despite the increasing number of differences since the end of the Cold War, looking at the transatlantic relationship from a broader perspective, it is still possible to notice the creation of a new transatlantic agenda which builds on the agenda of the Atlantic Alliance but is not immediately identifiable with it, and the creation of a new communication channel, autonomous from the one already existing between the US and the Member States of the European Union.

This chapter aims to analyse security relations between the US and the European Union, as reflected in the new agenda of transatlantic security relations, which is still mostly framed by the framework of New Transatlantic Agenda (NTA) of 1995, and in its outcomes. Even if the European Union is still dependent on American military presence for its own security in strictly military terms, it has been allowed to play an important role especially in the soft security sector. This in turn reflects the emerging of a different sensitivity towards security challenges not strictly of a military type, most often of a transnational nature, and its new capabilities provided by its Member States. This creates an incentive for the two – potentially – most powerful actors to cooperate in order to confront the new security crises and conflicts. The new transatlantic agenda, bringing attention to the regulative principles and to a new distribution of capabilities, is therefore a useful indicator of the changes in – and the structure of – the contemporary international system.

The analysis of transatlantic cooperation developed in this chapter in the field of security will adopt an evolutionary perspective and a multi-dimensional definition of security. Within this framework, the new transatlantic agenda is seen as a response by the US and the EU to a new international order in which, despite occasional – nevertheless relevant – divergences, there is increasing consensus on the opportunity and need to work together to face global problems, and in which the United States is developing new alliances to build new alliances around a new set of issues.

This chapter will first analyse the similarities and differences in the contributions of the EU and the US as international actors, and show how these similarities and differences are reflected in their security strategies. Finally, the chapter will present an empirical analysis of the answers given by the two actors to the international security crises that occurred during the period 1990–2000, as well as a similar analysis of the cooperation in conflict management that occurred during the period 1990–2001 in order to assess the scope and depth of transatlantic cooperation. The analysis will show an established trend of global cooperation between the US and the EU, and an increase in cooperation also in areas that are not traditionally of interest for the EU.

Differences in international actorness

The divergences noted so far are the result of differences in the international actorness and in the security cultures of the two actors. These divergences reflect issues of interests, values and identity but also material disparities. The most relevant dissimilarity lies in the international actorness of the US and the EU. It is sometimes forgotten that while the US is a traditional state actor that has played a main role in the organization of the contemporary international system, the EU is not, and its international actorness has been questioned for a long time. This implies not only a different decision-making process, with the resulting higher probability of internal splits and incapacity to deliver in controversial cases, but also a difference in the tools available.

Divergence in the posture of the US and the EU also comes from a very relevant disparity in resources, especially of military resources, that allows the US to impose itself as a military hyper-power that can rely on its military capacities and, therefore, also on hard security. The US defence budget, after a period of decrease in the 1990s, has been privileged over other lines in the US budget. This is not to say that the US agenda is only military focused. In the National Security Strategies of the Bush administration security challenges of a non-military type are clearly identified. The role of deterrence – and therefore of an exclusively military reaction – is recognized as being less useful than it was during the Cold War. And idealist goals such as the promotion of democracy and human rights are clearly stated. Nevertheless, US military spending is not only unparalleled, but it is also on the rise.[10]

On the other hand, the EU, lacking autonomous military resources, has developed its foreign and security policy using instruments of soft security; it has acted mostly as a civilian power capable of using not only the instruments of the CFSP or the ESDP, but more often its economic and commercial relations, its development cooperation and humanitarian policies, enlargement, and even, especially today, instruments of cooperation in justice and home affairs. This is not to say that the EU has been left totally powerless, as the very high number of ongoing peacekeeping missions reminds us that foreign policy is maybe the most successful European integration field, even at a time of crisis for the EU due to the failure of ratification of the European constitution and the Lisbon Treaty. However, inevitably, its approach to crises and conflicts has often been associated with civilian instruments, therefore the EU has had to privilege political dialogue, conditionality, and sanctions, and has tended to adopt an approach of structural prevention of crises, aimed at eliminating factors of instability that are at the basis of conflicts, at the promotion of democratic systems, at the respect of human rights and of sustainable development, at the reduction of economic imbalances, and at the reconstruction of societies devastated by conflicts. The latest interventions, though, show the first signs of a possible different regional and organic approach that allows the EU to start projecting its own military and police capacity. Indeed, only recently the EU has added the use of military tools to its options for crisis management. Most of the EU's operations can be characterized as police operations, but the trend to use more and more military instruments points to a possible change of the EU from a civilian power to a 'normal' one.

The EU has also started to become more relevant within multilateral fora and to be seen increasingly as a unitary actor within them. EU Member States have progressively changed their behaviour in multilateral fora, so as to allow the EU to gain a more or less direct participation even in international organizations in which the EU only has observer status and not full membership. National foreign policies have not disappeared, but next to the logic of divergence it is possible to find a logic of convergence because of the advantages of the politics of scale, external demands and perceptions, common values, etc.: all of these factors push national governments to find a common political line.[11] The *practice* of cooperation in foreign policy has created a *habit* of cooperation, and EU Member States try to present themselves as a common front and make efforts to at least present a common stance.

The European habit of coordination and consensus-creation can be seen in the EU relationship with the US. The convergence of voting patterns between the EU and the US at the UN General Assembly in roll call votes has been slowly but definitely decreasing in the past few years (Figure 8.1), signalling differences that seem to point to an inevitable drifting apart. However, the voting convergence between the US and EU Member States is by far the highest among all political groups, and this indicates the persistence of common interests, values, strategies, and, most of all, of a similar

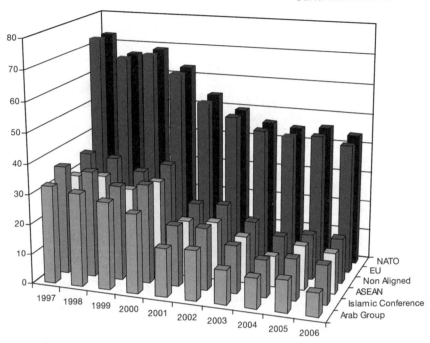

Figure 8.1 Percentage of voting coincidence with the US at the UN General Assembly (roll call votes) – by political groups

agenda. The voting convergence becomes higher on issues that the US con-siders to be 'important matters' (Figure 8.2). Significantly, in 2005 the voting convergence between the US and the EU in important matters returned to very high levels, around 80 per cent. What is truly remarkable is not the gap between the American and European positions, but the persistent and con-stantly widening gap between the US and EU Member States on the one hand, and all other groups of countries on the other. Considering the width of issues debated at the General Assembly, this clearly indicates that, no matter how acute their disputes become, Americans and Europeans still share other interests, values, and strategies much more than they do with any other groups of countries. But it is also a signal that their agenda may be less likely to be accepted by other countries.

Jørgensen and Laatikainen notice that in the UN Security Council there is even greater coincidence between the US and EU Member States, but this is a reflection of the practice of consensus at the UN Security Council. On the basis of an empirical analysis not only of European and American behaviour but also of their speeches, they argue that:

> There is not much difference in the values that are held by the US and the EU, though US national interests have led to some divergent positions,

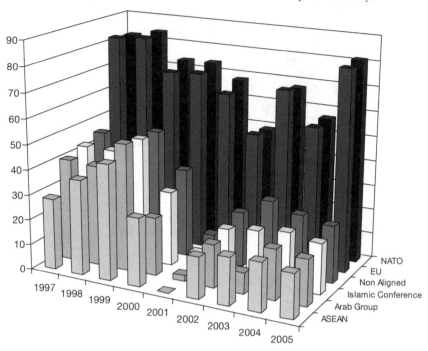

Figure 8.2 Percentage of voting coincidence (roll call votes) with the US at the
UNGA – important votes by political groups (adapted from: Department
of State 2000–2005)

notably on the Middle East and Cuba. There is a difference in tone, with
the US acting as a stern taskmaster with regard to UN operations and the
EU being much more nurturing of UN activities and more expansive in
articulating multilateral priorities. However, the 'difference machine' that
Manners and Whitman [2000] argue distinguishes the EU from the United
States and others is tenuous at best when it comes to values and principles.[12]

The same can be said of the persistence of common interests. Similar
dynamics can be found when we turn to other organizations today more
associated with regional and global governance such as the G8 or the OSCE.
Within them relations between the US and the EU are particularly close and
are considered to be very important by the US, not only for the meaningful
weight exercised by the EU within the organization, but also because both
the US and the EU have consistently showed their common interests in
keeping on top of the agenda issues such as democratization and respect for
human rights. This is the reason why 'the U.S. Mission works closely with
the EU Presidency and individual EU states, meeting regularly to exchange
views, share draft agreements, and coordinate priorities for the OSCE'
(Department of State 2004).

Differences in the Strategic Culture and Threat Perception: The National Security Strategy and the European Security Strategy

Another main reason for concern and the cause of disputes in transatlantic relations has been long-standing differences in the security cultures and threat perceptions. This difference is especially evident now when the American use of force is associated with a new sense of vulnerability that comes from the terrorist risk but that does not seem to be perceived in the same way by all Europeans. Apart from the Mars and Venus model of Kagan,[13] other analysts have highlighted identity and cultural differences that characterize the US as a warrior state reflecting the priorities of states belonging to the Westphalian model, whose policies tend to be coercive and to express a preference for intervention, and the emphasis of which is on threats, risks, and the development of hard power capacities in pursuit of control over the future world order in view of the design and control of the world order. On the other hand, the EU emphasis on institutions, on legitimacy, and on reciprocity reflects the priorities of a postmodern trading state committed to a negotiated global order.[14]

The idea that culture could influence national security policies has become more and more prominent since the 1970s, when strategic culture was defined as a set of ideas, emotional responses, and behavioural patterns that the members of a strategic community shared in relation to strategy.[15] More recent definitions refer to collective models of authority or identity of a nation state, represented in customs or law; to norms, values, and cognitive standards, such as rules and models that define which entities and actors exist in a system, how they act, and how they are interrelated[16] in the field of security. In order to better assess similarities and differences in strategic culture and threat perceptions, a comparison of the US National Security Strategy (NSS) and the European Security Strategy (ESS) can therefore be of some help.

The 2002 NSS and the 2003 ESS reveal profound differences.[17] The 2002 NSS is the response to the 9/11 attacks; it fully expresses the American sense of vulnerability and has a proactive character. On the other hand, the 2003 ESS is an attempt to bridge internal differences among EU Member States after deep divisions on the war against Iraq; it expresses the European sense of security in the world and has a reactive character. The American *war* on terrorism therefore becomes just a *fight* for Europeans; one that has to be conducted with instruments typical of law enforcement and intelligence-sharing and not of ideational and military warfare as indicated in the American strategy. Despite the little recognition achieved, the 2002 NSS not only has elements of unilateralism, but also has elements of multilateralism. Clearly stated in the 2002 NSS is the importance of cooperating with other international actors, especially those operating in areas of conflict. The kind of cooperation offered, though, was based not so much on existing multilateral institutions, but on coalitions of the willing and able, which might change depending on the issue. However, the ESS expresses the European commitment towards an 'international order based on effective multi-lateralism'. Although both the NSS and the ESS share the goal of promotion of freedom and democracy, the character of the NSS is more realist, repeating the importance of seeking a 'balance of power that favors freedom' and relying on preponderant power and military primacy, as opposed to the more liberal internationalist ESS that relies mostly on socio-economic instruments.[18]

The two documents also have similarities. There is a similar identification of threats. The NSS acknowledges the risk of the possibility that weapons of mass destruction might come into the hands of terrorists through rogue states, while the ESS is more conscious of the link between 'terrorism committed to maximum violence, the availability of weapons of mass destruction, organized crime, the weakening of the state system and the privatization of force'. Nevertheless, not only terrorism and the proliferation of weapons of mass destruction are on both actors' list, but the dynamic of the threats is acknowledged in a similar way. As far as the instruments to react to the identified threats are concerned, although the NSS stresses the military instrument more than the ESS, and the ESS seeks to address the root causes more than does the NSS, both documents identify the need to use the full spectrum of instruments. This means that both the US and the EU acknowledge the importance of acting globally and of preventing the rise of threats by using all instruments available, including the use of force. This is why the EU, challenging its traditional nature of civilian power, commits itself to use the military instrument if needed, although always in a multilateral framework and with a UN mandate. Neither the US nor the EU any longer bases its strategy on deterrence, preferring to *pre-empt* (US) or *prevent* (EU).[19] Both the US and the EU recognize the importance of the promotion of democracy as a stabilization tool and set normative goals. More importantly, both the NSS and the ESS express the nature and ambition of *transformational* and *revolutionary* powers of the US and the EU. They both see the world as in desperate need of transformation and they both present themselves as '*models* of stability, freedom and prosperity and as *agents* of transformation with a vocation to change the world in their own images'.[20]

Interestingly, the NSS of 2006 is somehow showing clear signs of convergence with the ESS. The new National Security Strategy highlights even further the American commitment towards promotion of democracy and the construction of a community of democracies, and explicitly states the importance of transformational diplomacy. However, compared to the previous strategic document, it also puts less emphasis on the military factor and stresses the importance of fighting terrorism *with* allies. Like the ESS it points out the causes of terrorism and gives more attention to regional conflicts. That is why, in an effort of reconciliation and in order to stress that attention should not be focused on the military campaign only, in July 2005 the 'global war on terror' was officially renamed 'global struggle against violent extremism'. The use of pre-emption is confirmed, but with limits. Also, the three priorities identified are convergent with the ESS: reform of the UN; strengthening and promoting democracy through international and multilateral institutions; establishing results-oriented partnerships to face the new challenges and opportunities. An example of the last priority was the November 2006 NATO Riga Summit, during which the US tried to revitalize NATO as the main aggregation centre for wider coalitions not restricted to the European area.

The Euro-Atlantic Pluralistic Security Community

So far the Euro-Atlantic area has been defined in the terms of a pluralistic security community:[21] there are dependable expectations of peaceful change, and we can find the elements that Deutsch (1957) considered essential for the construction of a security community, i.e. compatibility of major values and mutual responsiveness. We can also find at least some of the indicators that Adler and Barnett (1998) used to define a tightly coupled pluralistic security community, i.e. a mutual aid society in which members have constructed collective security arrangements, and in which a sort of post-sovereign system, with common supranational, transnational, and national institutions and some form of a collective security system has been realized.[22] The sharing of fundamental constitutive norms and the increase of the institutionalization process are therefore at the basis of the maintenance of the Euro-Atlantic security community and its institutions.

Socialization within the Euro-Atlantic community is particularly important. After World War II, Americans and Europeans built such a strong sense of belonging to the Western community and such a strong relationship that this influenced the construction of the collective identity of its member states, Americans included. During the Cold War, despite the differences in power and status, Europeans managed to influence American policies during moments of American unilateralism through: (1) norms that tied allies to consultation; (2) unacceptability of the use of military supremacy to solve internal disputes; and (3) presence of transnational and trans-governmental coalitions.[23] An extremely important role in the construction of the identity of the community is played by international organizations and institutions, i.e. those social institutions and material practices that, by establishing behavioural norms, monitoring mechanisms and sanctions in case of non-application of the established norms, can push the members of the security community to develop mutual expectations and therefore to identify with each other.

The existence of a security community framework does not cancel the asymmetry of power nor the exercise of power within the community: it just rules out the use of its most coercive form.[24] Likewise, a security community does not rule out divergences or even clashes between the community members: not only rules are subject to interpretation, but they are meant to solve conflicts peacefully, not to avoid them. Nevertheless, the pluralistic security community framework allows the peaceful redefinition of relationships amongst its members, no matter how harsh the tone becomes during a dispute. That is why disputes internal to the Euro-Atlantic community cannot be seen as a military threat from the other members of the community, nor will they lead to new internal alliances to balance the system.[25]

Unrecognized differences in evoked sets of issues normally lead to misperception even among actors who have a history of communication and cooperation.[26] As a result, a decrease in European public opinion support of American foreign policy has followed. However, a closer look at public opinion polls in recent years also shows that in all the EU Member States polled feelings towards the US are still the warmest towards any non-EU country (the average is 53), while in the US, feelings towards the EU are the warmest (60) after those towards Israel (61).[27] Disapproval is more directed towards the current American administration (76 per cent) than towards the US as a country[28] and, in line with world public opinion, the war on Iraq is the most disapproved foreign policy action.[29] Interestingly, although disaffection towards the US and reluctance to follow the US have grown in Europe, European elites still have a positive view of the American leadership and of the transatlantic alliance. Even if only 16 per cent of European public opinion believes that transatlantic relations have improved,[30] European elites are more keen on believing that they have improved (40 per cent of members of the European Parliament and 38 per cent of officials of the European Commission) and, although more critical towards the Bush Administration than citizens, 71 per cent of members of the European Parliament and 75 per cent of officials of the European Commission still think that US leadership is at least 'desirable' (CIRCaP 2006).

Americans and Europeans still tend to identify the same global threats, amongst which prevention of nuclear proliferation and international terrorism play an important role. Even on issues that have been highly divisive, such as global warming, public opinions in both Europe and America are in agreement that the issue represents a threat.[31] Americans and Europeans also tend to identify the same goals, and among them democracy promotion is certainly prominent.[32] The existing collective security arrangements are still valued as important as NATO is considered essential by 54 per cent of Europeans and 61 per cent of Americans. Public opinion polls also show that a great majority of Europeans (80 per cent in 2005) wants to build a stronger Europe, not to compete but to cooperate with the US.[33] As pointed out by Isernia (2005), overall the structure of public opinion looks more stable than it may be thought to be. Choices made at the end of World War II still form the basis of divisions, but they reflect slow and progressive adaptation to different historical experiences and geopolitical positions, not just recent events.[34]

However, serious disputes have taken place between Americans and Europeans, especially since the end of the Cold War and they might have long-term effects on the identity of the Euro-Atlantic pluralistic security community, on its 'we-ness', as well as on the existing forms of collective security and on the level of military integration. An analysis of current systemic pressures on the transatlantic relationship can therefore help to better understand its prospects.

An Evolutionary Interpretation

If the security community framework emphasizes values and institutions, an explanation of the current phase of transatlantic relations that underlines the presence of systemic pressures on the actors and on cooperation is based on Modelski's theory on the cycles of world leadership and the political learning process inscribed into it.[35]

Analysing the past 500 years of global politics, evolutionary theory identifies the existence of a role of global leadership – 'a position that is sanctioned by a systemic, collective process, and is not merely a matter of individual effort and national power or superior productive potential … whose elements need to be acquired via an extended learning process'[36] – exercised within the framework of succession of four-phase cycles. Each long cycle represents a political selection process of the global leader and can also be described as a four-phase learning process.

During the *agenda-setting* phase there is the weakening – more in terms of legitimacy and consent than in material terms – of the global leader, the fading away of old agendas and the emergence of new problems, which create increasing dissatisfaction for old alignments and alliances. New actors, who have acquired political or economic capabilities, arise. In the *coalition-building* phase the global leader is weakened even more and there is an increasing awareness of the existence of new global problems. This sets in motion 'a reshuffling of established coalitions and the construction of new alliances around a new set of issues'.[37] The loss of global concentration gives rise to multipolarity and lower concentrations that favour flexibility of alignments and new alliance systems based on common concerns and proposals for the restructuring of the global system. In the *macro-decision* phase at least two coalitions confront each other to choose amongst the rival agendas as to which one of these will be adopted by the global leader. While in the past this phase has been characterized by a generation-long period of global warfare, there is no reason to believe that in the future it could not assume a different form. 'There are reasons to believe that such substitutes can in fact emerge from within the democratic community' as this has become, according to Modelski,[38] the focus of coalition-building. Once the macro-decision process has ceased, the *execution* phase starts, during which the global leadership has unrivalled and unquestioned weight and influence; it is powerful and it has legitimacy.

As for the phases of the current American cycle, although there is no neat division between phases; the execution phase lasted approximately from 1945 to the beginning of the 1970s, and it reflected the peak of American hegemony and legitimacy. The agenda-setting phase took place in the period from around 1973 to around 2000, and saw the Europeans openly disassociating themselves from the Americans on a wide range of issues and policies and launching their own initiatives.[39] Although elements of the agenda-setting phase are still present, we should currently be in the coalition-building phase, which should last for approximately two more decades and which seems to be focused on the building of a democratic community. Given the effect of the spread of democracy, Modelski[40] considers it possible that a global democratic community will evolve, possibly around a US–EU nucleus.

According to evolutionary theory, it should therefore be possible to interpret the current phase of transatlantic relations as a reflex of a relative weakening (not in terms of material capabilities but, in terms of international legitimacy, as witnessed by the decline of the global leader in voting coincidence at the UN (Figure 8.1) and the construction of new alliances (or the rebuilding on new foundations of old ones) around a new agenda and a new set of issues. This does not mean that the US and the EU necessarily have to always share exactly the same values and an identical vision of their goals or of the best instruments to achieve them. What it implies is that they share a similar vision of the global order and an analogous commitment to solve what they have identified as global problems.

The outcomes of transatlantic cooperation

According to both the pluralistic security community and evolutionary theoretical frameworks, behind transatlantic divergences we should expect that, despite the end of the Cold War and the lack of *glue* that was given by the common Soviet threat, transatlantic relations will adapt to the new circumstances. Differences will emerge, but the existence of common institutions, common values and a common agenda will prevent a permanent divergence.

Consistent with this framework is the increase in the number and level of institutional contacts between the US and the EU since the end of the Cold War, i.e. the creation of a cooperation structure that has been progressively institutionalized and that helps both to solve internal disputes (or to avoid their degeneration) and to promote coordinated actions in sectors recognized as of common responsibility and interest. Although the enormous number of formal and informal contacts makes it difficult to map it, the US–EU dialogue has established some regular meetings, especially since the signing of the New Transatlantic Agenda in 1995. New levels and contacts are continually added to the structure and as a result it has proved capable of adapting itself. At the same time, the presence of the Commission in almost all institutionalized meetings inserts an element of continuity and reflects the capacity of the Commission to exert its power not only in the economic sector but also in all grey areas of foreign policy.

According to an analysis of the institutionalized meetings since 1995, which was conducted in an independent study for the European Commission (2005), the driving force by issue was the US in 39 cases, the EU in 32 cases, but both could be considered the driving force in 99 cases. The nature of discussions was considered to be promising in 106 cases, conflictual in 62 cases, and discontinued only in 9 cases. The objectives were achieved in 76 cases, partially achieved in 61 cases, and not achieved in 33 cases. According to this analysis, the relationship between the US and the EU proves to be 'broadly healthy and, in some areas, thriving', and the continuous transatlantic dialogue proved to be extremely useful in helping to limit the political fall-out of important crises such as the one over Iraq.

However, the above-mentioned results of cooperation concern all areas of the transatlantic relationship. In order to measure the extent of cooperation in the security field, an empirical analysis has been conducted of the answers given by the US and the EU to international security crises that occurred in the period 1990–2000, i.e. after the signing of the Transatlantic Declaration.[41] Security crises (according to a wider definition of security) have been identified in order to verify the impact on them of the answers provided by the US and the EU in relation to their solution. In order to operationalize the wider definition of security, the crises considered fall into the sectors originally provided by the so-called Copenhagen school: political, military, societal, economic, and environmental. Although the military sector will still be considered as the most important one, in the last three sectors, in an effort to find objective and quantifiable factors, crises will be considered when they can be linked directly or indirectly to causes of tension capable of provoking violence or the breaking up of the system, and where there is on the one hand a material external threat and on the other direct and intentional human responsibility. Therefore security crises in this context will mostly refer to phenomena such as massive migratory and refugee flows, for the societal sector, economic crises capable of threatening the existence of the economic system or of provoking serious internal or international tensions, for the economic sector, and environmental crises provoked by human intervention, such as nuclear accidents, but also famines caused by desertification, all of which are phenomena where the important responsibility of human intervention has been proven.

As for the concept of international crisis, considering that there is no definition of international crisis universally accepted, and 'each researcher has defined the concept in a manner suitable to his preferred methodological orientation or the chosen focus of study',[42] crisis will be here defined as an event capable of threatening existentially a referent object, characterized by an initial turning point and by a descendent phase, which can take the form of a cessation of the threat, a natural decline and disappearing of the crisis, or a stalemate. In order to keep the character of crisis, i.e. of structural anomaly and emergence, the discriminating factor to distinguish between two crises that occur in the same period with similar characteristics will be the existence of a period of at least one year of inactivity in between the end of a crisis and the beginning of the following one. The international character of the crisis will be given by the contemporary presence of or threat against several international actors or communities that perceive themselves as distinct.

These criteria have been applied to a screening of the *Keesing's Record of World Events* for the period November 1990 (when the first transatlantic document, the Transatlantic Declaration, was adopted) to December 2000 in order to verify the impact of transatlantic cooperation in the field of security of the NTA. In order to find elements of the relationship between events and reactions of the US and the EU, the Department of State's *Dispatch* and the *Foreign Policy Bulletin*, and the *EC Bulletin* and the European University Institute (EUI) online database on EPC (European Political Cooperation)/ CFSP have also been used for US and EU actions respectively.

In order to operationalize the reactions of the US and the EU, the study used a widely accepted definition of cooperation understood as a variation in the preferences of the actors through a negotiating process.[43] Following the negotiating processes, actions or declarations classified as *joint and/or coordinated* are those that were discussed and negotiated by the two actors, even if this did not automatically guarantee the adoption of identical actions. Actions defined as *non-coordinated* are those that were not discussed by the US and the EU, neither during summits and high level meetings established within the framework of the Transatlantic Declaration (TD) or the NTA, nor during multilateral international meetings, but in which they both intervened. *No recorded answer* indicates that no reaction could be found in any of the above-mentioned collections of documents and materials used. *US + others* indicates that the US was involved either alone or together with actors different from the EU. *EU + others* indicates that the EU was involved either alone or together with actors different from the US in the second case.

Disaggregating these results by sector (Figure 8.3), i.e. by the nature of crisis, it is possible to note that in the period 1990–2000 the US and the EU worked together in 44 per cent of politico-military crises, in 83 per cent of economic crises, in 65 per cent of societal crises, and in 33 per cent of environmental crises. This confirms the tradition of cooperation in the economic sector, due to the greater capacities that the EU has in this sector, but also due to the great importance that the maintenance of the tradition of cooperation in the economic sector has for both actors. The virtually total cooperation in facing international security crises in the economic sector in the second sub-period, in cases such as the Asian, Russian, or Latin American crises which in the second half of the 1990s put at risk the existence of the international economic system in its present form, shows that both the US and the EU share the same view of and interest in the importance of preserving the international economic system as it is today. Comparing the

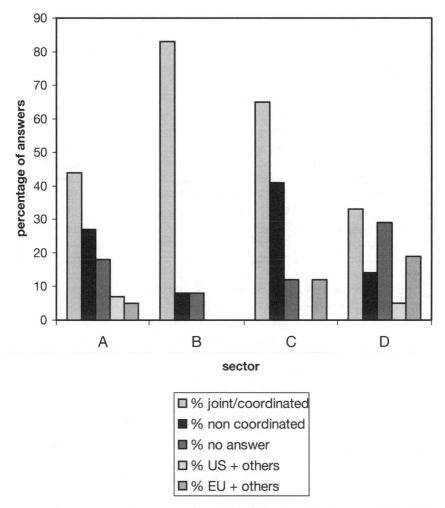

Figure 8.3 Percentage of answers to international security crises by sector 1990–2000

sub-periods 1990–95 and 1996–2000, i.e. after the adoption of the NTA, an increase also emerges in the politico-military cooperation from 37 per cent to 47 per cent, due to the acquisition of greater capabilities in this sector by the EU. Also, in the societal sector there has been an increase in cooperation between the first and the second the second sub-period, which shows the greater capacity of the EU to act in humanitarian crises and to display capabilities that are more adequate to dealing with *soft* security. But a decrease emerges in the environmental sector (from 56 per cent to 21 per cent), even though in this sector inaction seems to be the prevalent mode.

Disaggregating data by geographical area (see Figure 8.4) and comparing the two sub-periods, it is possible to note a more significant increase in cooperation and effectiveness in some geographical areas than in others. However, data show that the sphere of action of the EU is not exclusively regional, and the EU has been called upon to cooperate with the us in crises both within Europe and beyond. In absolute numbers most of the cooperation took place in Europe and Africa, but if we look at percentages of cooperation within the region, it is clear that the US and the EU cooperated the most in the Middle East. This can be explained by the fact that in Africa the European colonial tradition still carries some weight and, therefore, the EU tends to be more active and it can better display its instruments of humanitarian and development aid. As for the Middle East, although Americans and Europeans often have serious and relevant divergent views on how to reach a goal, the US and the EU have always shared the same objective and, indeed, burden, as the long-term cooperation on the Israeli–Palestinian question shows. Even in the case of the clash on Iraq, everybody always agreed that the dispute concerned the means question more than the goals question. As Figure 8.4 shows, though, cooperation was the prevailing answer in all regions.

In the European region, the level of consultation/cooperation between the EU and the US reaches a very high level, 55 per cent, with an increase in the level of cooperation after the introduction of the NTA from 50 per cent to 58 per cent. This, however, could be explained by considering the very long tradition of cooperation between Americans and Europeans in the European region. That is why transatlantic cooperation in security crises is more

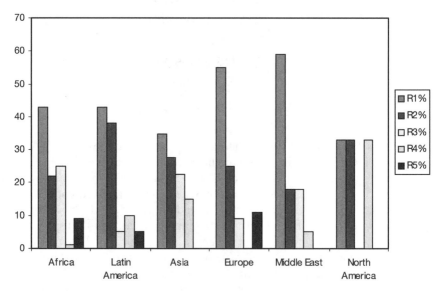

Figure 8.4 Percentage of all answers to international security crises by region 1990–2000

remarkable in the political and economic sector, the two traditional sectors of cooperation of the Atlantic relationship.

In the African region the US and the EU consulted and cooperated in 42 per cent of the crises during the period 1990–2000, but in the period 1996–2000, cooperation increased from 38 per cent to 42 per cent, showing a greater impact of the transatlantic cooperation within the framework of the NTA. In this region there has been a more marked cooperation in case of societal and environmental security crises. The increase of transatlantic cooperation in this area reflects the strengths and weaknesses of the EU, which is capable of showing unity, autonomy, resources, weight, and management capabilities in the field of soft security, and therefore of attracting the attention of the United States. According to the Americans, however, the EU is still incapable of going beyond this point.[44]

In Asia, the level of cooperation in international security crises has been relatively low – 35 per cent – but this is also one of the regions that benefited the most from the stimulus given by the NTA: cooperation jumped from 24 per cent in the first sub-period to 43 per cent in the second. This is particularly evident in the political sector where joint/coordinated actions moved from 24 per cent to 57 per cent. Again, these data are probably the result of greater capabilities of the EU, which in Asia is engaged not only in the Association of South-Eastern Asia Nations (ASEAN) Regional Forum together with the US, but also in a bilateral dialogue (Asia–Europe Meeting (ASEM)). Still, in Asia the EU plays a secondary role compared to that of the US, but it is strongly engaged in projects that have a direct impact on hard security, such as the Korean Peninsula Energy Development Organization (KEDO). Interestingly enough, the European involvement in KEDO saw a particularly active role on the part of the European Commission. Both hypotheses are proved at the regional level.

The Latin American region is the other region where it was possible to register the biggest impact of cooperation induced by the NTA: from 29 per cent to 42 per cent. This underlines a growing interest and greater involvement of the EU in the area, especially in the political sector where cooperation increased from 17 per cent to 33 per cent. Although this is still the backyard of the US, the EU has increased its role through agreements with regional organizations and with Central American countries.

However, that analysis adopted a multidimensional definition of security, which left open the question whether similar results could be repeated in the more traditional field of security, i.e. armed conflicts and, in particular, conflict management. In order to verify the existence of a *habit of cooperation* between the US and the EU in the field of conflict management, Monteleone and Rossi conducted a quantitative analysis of the *answers* given by the two actors in relation to the management of armed conflicts. In particular, the research carried out an empirical assessment of the *reactions* of the EU and the US to all armed conflicts that took place between 1990 and 2001.[45]

Out of the 83 armed conflicts that took place in the considered period, and most of which were internal, in 7 cases there was no recorded reaction by either of the two actors, while the number of conflicts in which a non-cooperative intervention was recorded (2 for the US (+ others) and 3 for the EU (+ others)). On the other hand, the American and European presence was highly prominant, sometimes separate (26 cases), but most often in coordination. The US and the EU intervened in a joint or coordinated manner in 45 out of 83 armed conflicts. The two actors intervened with a cooperative approach in 54 per cent of the cases, indicating that, as soon as the EU acquires new competences in the field of conflict management, the habit of cooperation that already exists in other issues is transposed to the area of conflict management (Figure 8.5).

Disaggregating data by region, in absolute numbers Africa is the region where cooperation occurs the most, followed by the Middle East (Figure 8.6). However, looking at the percentages of cooperation, the Middle East is the region in which there is the highest level of cooperation (9 conflicts out of 11 or 82 per cent) (Figure 8.7). In all the regions the attitude towards working together is equal (Africa) or higher than 50 per cent, with the only exception of Asia (37 per cent). This could be because the limited coopera-tion of Americans and Europeans in Asia does not create the best environment in which a multilateral operation can be 'constructed'.

Multilateral intervention was recorded only in 35 cases out of the total of 83 armed conflicts, or 42 per cent of the cases. This limited intervention

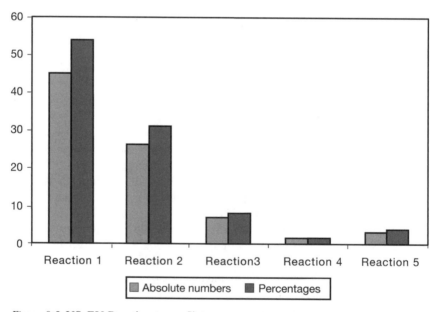

Figure 8.5 US–EU Reaction to conflicts

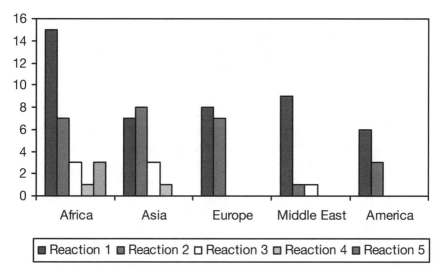

Figure 8.6 Reactions by region (absolute numbers)

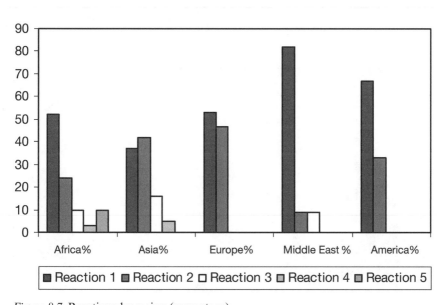

Figure 8.7 Reactions by region (percentage)

should be considered within a framework where the majority of conflicts were internal conflicts and where a significant number of conflicts were minor-intensity conflicts. Multilateral intervention is also significantly more frequent than it was before the end of the Cold War. The disaggregation of data by type of intervention (Figure 8.8) shows a remarkable figure: out of 35 multilateral interventions only one was realized without the active role of either the US or the EU (Papua New Guinea), while not one was realized unilaterally by the US or the EU. In 34 cases out of the 35 in which multilateral intervention was recorded, *both* the US and the EU had an active role, either acting separately (7 cases or 20 per cent) or, more often, acting jointly or in a coordinated way (27 cases or 77 per cent).

In all types of intervention, apart from traditional peacekeeping, the intervention was decided on the basis of an environment in which the EU and the US had some sort of cooperative arrangement (Figure 8.9). This does not necessarily mean that the agreement between the two actors is in a direct causal relationship with the decision to intervene, but it is a signal that cooperation between the EU and the US may create a favourable environment for launching multidimensional initiatives in the field of conflict management. This is particularly evident when we look at peace enforcement, which occurred in 11 cases out of 35, but we can also notice that, out of those 11 cases, in 10 cases (or 91 per cent) a cooperative *answer* was recorded. The exception is traditional peacekeeping where both actors have to be present, but direct cooperation was limited to 50 per cent of the cases.

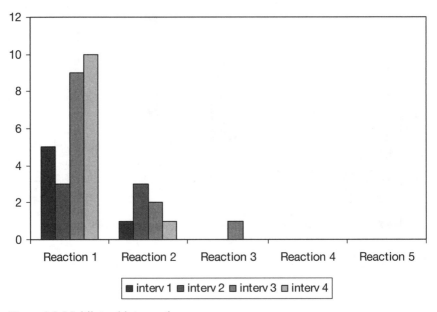

Figure 8.8 Multilateral intervention

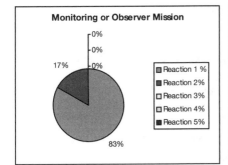

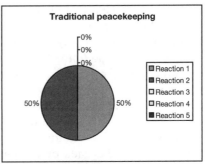

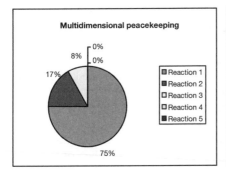

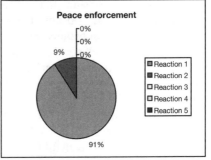

Figure 8.9 Intervention

Conclusions

Despite crises and numerous calls for the end of the transatlantic relation-ship that started after the end of the Cold War, despite differences in actor-ness, roles and material capabilities, despite partial differences in security culture and threat perceptions, the transatlantic relationship has benefited from the complementarities of the EU and the US as international political actors, of the persistence of common interests and values, of the willingness of the EU to play a global role and of the search by the US of global part-ners. A US–EU cooperation nucleus built on the long practice of the Atlan-tic cooperation is often also present in the security field, especially in multilateral fora, and in particular in the case of international security crises and of conflict management. Especially in the latter case, transatlantic cooperation has often proved to be the basis of a wider socialization process that is capable of creating an environment in which multilateral intervention is more likely to occur. This is consistent with the persistence of common values and institutions typical of pluralistic security communities. The crea-tion of a cooperation nucleus is also consistent with Modelski's theory of evolutionary politics in that it shows some of the features typical of the shift from the agenda-setting phase to the coalition-building one, signalling some weaknesses in the legitimacy and international consensus of the global leadership and the need to build a new consensus on a new agenda of global politics. Along this path, differences and even crises between Americans and Europeans are and will be inevitable. However, no matter what differences exist, Americans and Europeans are still closer to each other than they are with any other actor, both have a *transformational* agenda, based on common interests and values, and so far mostly directed at the promotion of a democratic community. At the same time – and as confirmed by voting patterns at the UN – the gap between them and the other actors is increasing.

Further research needs to be done to assess the creation and evolution of a new transatlantic agenda over a longer period, and to understand whether the terrorist attacks of 11 September 2001 brought about a change in the transatlantic relationship that will lead towards a permanent drifting apart of Americans and Europeans. The recent crises and clashes were particularly harsh in tone and substance and seemed to be symptomatic of two totally different views of the world and approaches to the solution of problems. The difference in international actorness, roles, and resources seemed to combine with differences on the sense of vulnerability and on the position to adopt. Nevertheless, the widespread perception of radical divergence is not fully confirmed by the analysis of the European Security Strategy and of the National Security Strategies of 2002 and – even more – 2006, that, despite relevant and meaningful differences, still expressed a number of common interests and values and a similar transformational view of the world. Moreover, as shown by the totally different tone of official speeches in 2006 and by empirical analysis of the results of cooperation[46] and of reaction to international security crises and conflict management, the pattern of transatlantic cooperation – despite the absence of the *glue* given by a common threat – remains important and solid.

A redefinition of transatlantic relations is taking place to adapt it to the new circumstances of the international system. Although recurring clashes should still be foreseen in this phase, if the highlighted pattern of transatlantic cooperation proves in the long run to be stronger than the disassociation tendencies, and the collaborative nucleus of the US and the EU manages to be attractive to other democracies, the possibility of the establishment of a new organization of the political system in which the transatlantic partnership is still active cannot be ruled out.

Notes

1 From 64 per cent in 2002 to 37 per cent in 2006; *Transatlantic Trends Survey*, 2006, at www.transatlantictrends.org.
2 World Public Opinion (2007) shows that in the 25 countries polled in 2007, 49 per cent of the population thinks that the US is playing a mainly negative role in the world. Moreover, the trend in the 18 countries polled regularly since 2005 shows an increase in the negative view of the US from 46 per cent in 2005 to 52 per cent in 2007, and a decrease in the positive view of the US from 40 per cent in 2005 to 29 per cent in 2007 'World View of US Role Goes From Bad to Worse', 22

January 2007, at http://www.worldpublicopinion.org/pipa/articles/international_security_bt/306.php?nid = &id = &pnt = 306&lb = btis.

3 Jervis points out that: 'Not being aware of the inevitable influence of beliefs upon perceptions often has unfortunate consequences. If a decision maker thinks that an event yields self-evident and unambiguous inferences when in fact these inferences are drawn because of pre-existing views, he will grow too confident of his views and will prematurely exclude alternatives because he will conclude that the event provides independent support for his beliefs.' Jervis, R., *Perceptions and Misperceptions in International Politics*, Princeton, NJ: Princeton University Press, 1976, p. 181.

4 On the impact of expectations on perceptions see Jervis (ibid., p. 145): 'expectations or perceptual sets represent standing estimates of what the world is like and, therefore, of what the person is likely to be confronted with.' Jervis adds: 'expectations create predispositions that lead actors to notice certain things and to neglect others, to immediately and often unconsciously draw certain inferences from what is noticed, and to find it difficult to consider alternatives.'

5 '[I]f an actor does not understand others' beliefs about international relations and about the actor, he is not apt to be able to see what inferences others are drawing from his behavior. And if he is incorrect in his estimates of the other's beliefs or if he thinks that perceptions are influenced only by the immediate stimulus, he will be confident that he knows how the other is seeing him, and he will be wrong.' Jervis, op. cit., p. 187.

6 Kagan, R., *Of Paradise and Power*, New York: Random House, 2003.

7 'Transatlantic Security: Addressing Global Challenges Together', speech delivered on 28 March 2006 at the University of San Francisco, Center for Public Service and the Common Good, San Francisco.

8 Jervis, 1973, p. 3.

9 As Jervis (1976, pp. 153, 206) highlighted: 'Context is supplied not only by the situation, but also by the concerns and information that dominate the person's thought at any particular time. ... Whatever creates the predisposition, the result is that, if an actor expects a phenomenon to appear, he is likely to perceive ambiguous stimuli as being that phenomenon.' Differences in evoked sets may create misperceptions not only under conditions of hostility, but 'even when there is complete common interest between the actors, when deception is neither intended nor suspected, and when both actors wish to communicate accurately'.

10 Damro, C., 'Security Strategy and the Arms Industry', in R. Dannreuther and J. Peterson (eds), *Security Strategy and Transatlantic Relations*, London and New York: Routledge, 2006

11 Hill, C., 'Convergence, Divergence and Dialectics: National Foreign Policies and the CFSP', in J. Zielonka (ed.), *Paradoxes of European Foreign Policy*, Dordrecht: Kluwer Law International, 1998, pp. 35–53.

12 Jorgensen, K. E. and Laatikainen, K. V., 'The EU @ the UN: Multilateralism in a New Key?', paper presented at the Second Pan-European Conference on EU Politics, Bologna, 24–26 June 2004.

13 Kagan, R., *Of Paradise and Power*, New York: Random House, 2003.

14 Smith, M., (2004), 'Between Two Worlds? The European Union, the United States and World Order', *International Politics*, 2004, 41(1), pp. 95–117.

15 Snyder, J. L., *The Soviet Strategic Culture: Implications for Limited Nuclear Operations*, Santa Monica: RAND, 1977.

16 Jepperson, R. L., Wendt, A. and Katzenstein, P. J., 'Norms, Identity and Culture in National Security', in P. J. Katzenstein (ed.), *The Culture of National Security: Norms and Identity in World Politics*, New York: Columbia University Press, 1996, p. 56.

17 Among others Berenskoetter, F. S., 'Mapping the Gap: A Comparison of US and European Security Strategies', *Security Dialogue*, 2005, 36(1), pp. 71–92; Molloy, S., 'Security Strategy and the "war on terror"', in R. Dannreuther and J. Peterson (eds), *Security Strategy and Transatlantic Relations*, Milton Park and New York, Routledge, 2006; Wyllie, J. H., 'Measuring Up: The Strategies as Strategy', in R. Dannreuther and J. Peterson (eds), *Security Strategy and Transatlantic Relations*, Milton Park and New York: Routledge, 2006.
18 Wyllie, ibid.
19 Interestingly, the first draft of the ESS also mentioned the importance of *pre-emption.*
20 Dannreuther, R. and Peterson, J. (eds), *Security Strategy and Transatlantic Relations*, Milton Park and New York: Routledge, 2006, p. 180.
21 Adler, E., 'Imagined (Security) Communities: Cognitive Regions in International Relations', *Millennium*, 1997, 26(2), p. 256; Pouliot, V., 'The Alive and Well Transatlantic Security Community: A Theoretical Reply to Michael Cox', *European Journal of International Relations*, 2006, 12(1), pp. 119–27. For opposite views see Cox, M., 'Beyond the West: Terrors in Transatlantia', *European Journal of International Relations*, 2005, 11(2), pp. 203–33, and 'Let's Argue about the West', *European Journal of International Relations*, 2006, 12(1), pp. 129–34.
22 Other indicators of tightly coupled pluralistic security communities that we can apply to the Euro-Atlantic area are: (1) decision-making procedures tend to be consensual and to incorporate the interests of all members; (2) borders are not protected against the risk of an attack from a member of the community; (3) military plans are not conceived on the basis that other members of the community are considerd possible military threats; (4) threats still tend to be commonly defined (divergence is more on how to face those threats than on their definition, and sometimes Europeans tend to disagree among themselves as much as with Americans on this point); (5) discourses and language are still about the 'Atlantic community', though sometimes identified with the 'Western civilization'; (6) cooperative and collective security is still present; (7) although the Revolution in Military Affairs and the divergence between their defence budgets are remarkable and will probably bring about significant change, the level of military integration is still high. More lacking are other elements of tightly coupled security communities and, in particular: (a) policy coordination against 'internal' threats; (b) free movements of populations; (c) internationalization of authority; and (d) a 'multiperspectival' polity.
23 Risse, 1995.
24 Adler and Barnett, 1998, p. 428.
25 On this point, see also Risse, T., 'A Liberal World Order: The Democratic Security Community and U.S. Power', paper presented at the conference *American Unipolarity and the Future of the Balance of Power*, Woodrow Wilson Center, Washington, DC, 19 May 2000.
26 Jervis, 1976, p. 214.
27 Interestingly, though, Spain has warmer feelings towards Russia and China than it has towards the US. Also in Portugal, Slovakia, and Bulgaria, Russia is loved as much as or even more than the US (Transatlantic Trends 2006).
28 It includes Turkish public opinion (Transatlantic Trends 2006).
29 Disapproval rates range from 52 per cent in Poland to 92 per cent in France, but the average of EU countries polled is 78 per cent (World Public Opinion 2007).
30 According to European public opinion polls, 41 per cent believes that they have remained the same and 35 per cent that they have gotten worse (Transatlantic Trends 2006).
31 According to European public opinion polls, 90 per cent of Europeans and 82 per cent of Americans believe that global warming is an extremely important or an important threat (Transatlantic Trends 2006).

32 In the 2006 public opinion polls, however, there has been a decrease in US public opinion support of democracy promotion.
33 On this point see, especially, Transatlantic Trends (2005 and 2006).
34 Isernia, P, 'Le fratture transatlantiche e l'opinione pubblica: continuità e mutamento negli orientamenti del pubblico americano ed europeo', *Rivista Italiana di Scienza Politica*, 2005, 35(1), p. 73. See also Asmus, R., Everts, P. P., and Isernia, P., 'Power, War and Public Opinion: Looking Behind the Transatlantic Divide', *Policy Review*, 2004, (123), pp. 73–88.
35 Modelski, 1987; 1999.
36 Modelski, 1999: 13
37 Ibid., p. 17.
38 Ibid., p. 18.
39 Among others, the Euro-Arab dialogue, the disapproving of the Latin-American policy of Reagan, and the initial American policy towards the Soviet Union
40 Modelski and Thompson 1999.
41 Monteleone, 2003.
42 For a review of the literature on crisis see Brecher1993; Lebow 1981: 7.
43 Keohane 1984: 51.
44 Interview with an official of the Department of State, December 1998.
45 What follows is built on Monteleone and Rossi (2004). The chosen source for armed conflicts is the PRIO/Uppsala Armed Conflict Dataset as it covers the most recent period. Data on international interventions to manage armed conflicts were drawn-up mainly by the Doyle and Sambanis Dataset, updated to 2001. Interventions by the international community for the management of *international* conflicts in the period under consideration were added (Rossi 2003). The type of international intervention in the conflicts was classified according to Doyle and Sambanis' and Fortna's datasets and, following the latter, international commitment was distinguished in: *monitoring or observer mission, traditional peacekeeping, multidimensional peacekeeping* and *peace enforcement*. See more extensively in Monteleone and Rossi (2004).
46 European Commission 2005.

9   Terrorism and Homeland Security

Carlos Echeverría Jesús

Introduction

This chapter addresses the problems stemming from the different visions and perceptions that Americans and Europeans have on how to define the threat posed by terrorism, and particularly on the instruments needed to deal with this threat. What is especially important is that although there is a growing consensus over how to define the threat addressed here, namely Jihadist-Salafist terrorism, transatlantic disputes over how to deal with it are increasing due to a number of issues such as the Guantanamo prison, the Central Intelligence Agency (CIA) flights using European airports, and the war in Iraq, among others.[1] Traditionally international politics have been characterized by differing perspectives and perceptual distortions among nations but, as Professor Robert Jervis states, these misperceptions are perhaps more dangerous among allies than among adversaries because allies have high expectations of mutual understanding and cooperation.[2]

The argument in this chapter supports the idea that not only do Europe and the United States need to win this war – the global war on terror or terrorism, in US lingo – but so too do the Arab/Muslim governments and their peoples who are being attacked by this extremely bloody violence on a daily basis.[3] Moreover, this war or effort against terrorism needs to be won because the price of defeat would be very high and because the evolution of scenarios in places such as Afghanistan or Iraq demands a rapid reaction. Along this line, we also support the idea that any appeasement policy coming from either Western or Arab/Muslim governments will reinforce the determination of Jihadist-Salafist terrorists to win their war – there is no doubt that for them it is a war – against us all.

Reactions against terrorism since the 9/11 attacks

Like the Cold War, which was a struggle that lasted for 45 years, the global war on terror is, according to the official US perspective, of indefinite duration. As a national crisis, 9/11 imposed rhetorical and leadership demands on the White House, and President George W. Bush talked about retaliation as a clear indication that the United States would mount military operations in order to seek restitution for the assault against it But retaliation against whom? Against terrorists, Bush said, making no distinction between terrorists and the governments that supported them.

President Bush, in a speech on 20 September 2001, spoke about the opportunities of a changed world. On the same day, the UN Security Council passed two resolutions: one condemning terrorism, and the other establishing a Committee on Counterterrorism (CTC). But it was unable to define terrorism. This raises questions about how effective international institutions can be in dealing with this global threat. We could define terrorism as the use or the threatened use of force against non-combatants or property for political reasons, which is the basic definition provided by the US Department of State, but a number of Arab/Muslim violent groups and even a number of Arab/Muslim states refuse to accept that definition. They define some violence as freedom-fighting when applied to actors such as Hamas in Palestine, Hizbollah in Lebanon, or various groups of 'insurgents' in Iraq.[4]

Some Arab/Muslim sectors do not believe 9/11 was terrorism or even that it was carried out by Arab/Muslims. Even in the West, 12 years after the radical Islamist attacks perpetrated by the Algerian Islamic Armed Group (GIA, using its French acronym) in Paris,[5] we are still having problems defining the enemy. In America, for example, it took President Bush several months to finally give a face to the main enemy that the US is fighting, which is not terrorism in general, but mainly Jihadist-Salafist terrorism.

In Europe, during the middle of the 1990s, GIA plots – like the attack against the St Michel Metro Station in Paris in July 1995 – were largely devised by outside groups operating within Europe, as was the case with 9/11. Until the emergence of radical Islamist terrorism on European soil in the 1990s, Western terrorism was basically nationalist or anarchist and Marxist-Leninist in origin and ideology. Groups such as ETA (Basque Land and Freedom) in Spain, the Irish Republican Army (IRA) in Northern Ireland and the rest of the United Kingdom, the Baeder-Meinhoff gang in Germany, the Red Brigades in Italy, the 17 November Group in Greece, Action Direct in France, and others, saw themselves as the vanguard of the working class or the armed supporters of marginalized national minorities. These groups targeted (or continue to target in the case of ETA) authorities of the states that they targeted, and also civilians, and all of the groups had or have limited reach.

Now, the most radicalized Islamist terrorism, which involves myriad Jihadist-Salafist cells and groups, including Al Qaeda as the network of all the networks, have global reach and different goals and methods. For instance, the 11 March 2004 attacks in Madrid were carried out by a number of cells dominated by Moroccans, some of whom had been established in Spain for years. Their goal was not to destroy a symbol of a state, but rather it had religious, political, strategic and cultural elements aims. In the United Kingdom, three-quarters of the terrorists who acted in London on 7 July

2005 were of Pakistani background, some of whom had been established in the country for years or had even been born in the UK. The bombings in London and the alleged London-based plot uncovered in August 2006 to blow up airliners flying between the UK and the US also involved disaffected British youths of Pakistani descent, some of whom had travelled to Pakistan for family visits, study, and perhaps training.[6]

The problem we are facing now in Europe, as well as in the United States, is that while most Muslims are not terrorists, most terrorists acting today are Muslims. Many in the West deny that there is something called a clash of civilizations, but it is hard to deny such a conflict when on the other side the terrorists declare it exists. Only small minorities within the Arab/Muslim world support or participate in terrorism but, in fact, these small minorities have large numbers according to the perspective of the various security forces. In addition, the Jihadist-Salafist version of radical Islamism is an ideology with religious and geopolitical goals.

So, how can we, Europeans at large and Americans, contribute to deal with this threat? First, we must assume that a structural problem exists, which is the inability or unwillingness of the mainstream Arab/Muslim communities to deal with the issue. For some religious leaders in the Sunni faction of Islam, solidarity with fellow Muslims is more important to them than taking decisive steps to isolate the extremists. For political reasons, even in countries such as Algeria or Egypt, where radical Islamist terrorism was strongly confronted in the past, recent political decisions such as wide-ranging amnesties, mainly in Algeria in 2006, are reinforcing terrorism. Secondly, some European governments and even the US government, which was tolerant with radical Islamist ideologists and militants in the past – to the extent of providing political asylum to some of them – are changing their attitudes; intergovernmental cooperation is growing, but they must improve and reinforce this attitude. The dissemination of videos showing the slaughter of people in Algeria, Chechnya, or Iraq and the free activism for years of radical preachers such as Abu Hamza Al Masri at the Finsbury Park Mosque in London persuaded many young Muslims to join the combatant Jihad.[7]

Governments must start to assume that the Jihadist-Salafist version of Islamism is a totalitarian ideology with a religious background, and not a religion or a culture. They must also reinforce their knowledge about the threat and coordinate their efforts better among them in order to combat it. Unfortunately, extraditions take years, even between close countries like the UK and France, and some radical Islamist groups remain tolerated in the West, in the EU, and also in the US, for example those operating in Chechnya, in Central Asia (such as the Hizb ut Tahrir), or against the Pakistani government. For the time being, the experience of more than six years of global effort against Jihadist-Salafist terrorism shows that Europeans and Americans continue to mislabel many Islamist groups that constitute a real security threat to their security and to democratic regimes in general.[8]

What is the threat?

The threat is an ideology and a web of cells formed by groups and individuals who believe in building a better world based on what they consider the only pure community in world history, that of the Islamic Prophet and his companions. The problem is that nobody knows what original Islam was like and they recreate the period, mainly that of Medina after the Prophet escaped Mecca and became a warrior as they wish.

Having tried this peacefully or violently through the twentieth century, these Jihadist groups tried to overthrow the so-called 'near enemy', the local regimes, killing, for instance, President Anouar El Sadat in October 1981, and tried to overthrow the Algerian regime during the 1980s and the 1990s. They also contributed to fight the 'far enemy' abroad, either the Soviets in Afghanistan in the 1980s or the French or the Americans in the 1990s in Algeria or in Iraq until now. In Afghanistan, during the Jihad of the 1980s, they developed a global view of the problem defining the 'far enemy' as communists in Afghanistan in the 1980s and Westerners in Iraq or even in Afghanistan now.

Al Qaeda captured the leadership of this movement, becoming the most militant of the militants. But the picture was completed with a number of local or national terrorist groups such as the GIA in Algeria, the local Combatant Islamist Groups in Morocco, Tunisia, and Libya, the Abu Sayyaf Group in Philippines, and others. The Salafist Group for Preaching and Combat (GSPC, its French acronym) was founded in Algeria early in 1998 by a splinter group of GIA members and it is becoming now the most important Al Qaeda arm in the Maghreb, in the Sahel strip, and even in Europe.[9] The Moroccan Islamic Combatant Group (GICM, its French acronym) has been designated as an Al Qaeda affiliate by the US Department of State since November 2002. Since January 2007, the GSPC has been renamed 'Al Qaeda in the Land of the Islamic Maghreb' which entails the pursuit of much more ambitious aims.[10]

During the 1990s, the demobilized *Moudjahidin* (holy warriors of the Jihad) remained along the Afghanistan–Pakistan border and in Central Asia, participating in national events or returning to their communities for action as they did in the Maghreb countries. Some of them accepted invitations to Khartoum where Hassan El Turabi and Osama Bin Laden tried together to reinforce the global network until 1996 when Bin Laden left Sudan.[11] From 1996 until 2001, Al Qaeda controlled training camps in Afghanistan and started to indefine the components of the global threat: the Al Qaeda first circle or central staff was largely composed by Saudis and Egyptians;[12] the Maghrebians or second-generation individuals from Europe started to coordinate amongst themselves; and the Asians, from Indonesia to the rest of Southern Asia, started to coordinate their plans and actions through Jemaah Islamiya and encompassing groups like Abu Sayyaf in the Philippines.[13] In operational terms, mobilization was and is spontaneous and self-organizing, and individuals become more and more radicalized collectively under the umbrella of different propaganda spaces including the Internet.

Unfortunately, the existence of a Jihadist-Salafist offensive during the 1990s, with one of its epicentres in Algeria, was not recognized by the West. In fact, Algeria had to fight on its own against this terrorism because it did not find allies that understood the true dimension of the threat. The European countries considered themselves as mere terrorist rearguards and not targets of the terrorists. These countries were unable to decipher the Jihadist-Salafist messages, such as the GIA attacks against France, or how the terrorists nurtured the Jihad in places such as Bosnia, Chechnya or Kosovo from within the West in general.

After 9/11, the West woke up and the US-led coalition attempted to eliminate the militants' sanctuary in Afghanistan, attempted to cut of funding for terrorist groups, monitored communications, and killed or captured many of the leaders of the network. Six years after 9/11, we are seeing the emergence of home-grown Jihadist-Salafist groups who are not under the supervision of the Al Qaeda elite. Anyone who wants to be a Jihadist can be, often with funds raised by drug-trafficking and other illegal activities, and with the Internet for communications. The Internet is obviating the need for leaders or training camps. We are moving quickly towards a global Jihad – a leaderless Jihad where attacks like those in Madrid in 2004 and London in 2005 could become frequent.

The actual global threat is Jihadist-Salafist, a minority within Islam. They believe that Islam must have political power and that a revived Muslim rule – the recreation of the Caliphate – can only be achieved violently. They believe they are the only true believers and they declare other Muslims unbelievers, as they did in Algeria in the 1990s. If they declare someone 'Apostate' that person must be killed, even if they are a baby or a woman. The central idea of Jihadist-Salafist Islamists is that there is only one god – the *Tawhid*, the original name of Abu Mussab al Zarqawi's group in Iraq – and they must obey only that god's law. According to their way of thinking, if you obey the laws of another person, you are committing idolatry. In this way of thinking, democracy becomes the centre of all that is evil in the world because it lets people establish their own laws, and that is not desirable for the Iraqis or the Palestinians in the Middle East or for Maghrebians in the western part of the Holy Land of Islam.[14]

Al Qaeda wants to bring back to the Caliphate and this is its central strategic long-term goal.[15] Osama Bin Laden considers the war that they are now fighting began in 1924 with the dissolution of the Caliphate and the signing of the League of Nations covenant that imposed foreign governors on former Ottoman lands through the Mandates and through the occupation and administration of Palestine by the British. In Al Qaeda's cause, Bin Laden tries to disrupt the US so that it will withdraw from the Islamic world. The US is perceived by Al Qaeda and others as the remaining superpower supporting Israel and Arab/Muslim regimes that are considered as apostates. In addition, Bin Laden and his 'number two', Ayman Al Zawahiri, consider that the Shiites betrayed Islam to its 'infidel' foes and they have declared the war against all the Shiites, thus provoking bloody killings, such as those in Iraq and Pakistan. The recovery of what was once Islamic territory – applied as in Spain, the Balkans, southern Russia, India, and western China – should be achieved in parallel to the development of a struggle against apostates and infidels across the world.

In their struggle the Jihadist-Salafists are universalists; they are unable to constrain the fight to within national borders because they reject that notion. Let us keep in mind that Al Qaeda has contempt for the Palestinian Hamas and Islamic Jihad because, according to the terrorist network's leaders and ideologists, those groups have the pitiable objective of creating an Islamic state confined only to historic Palestine. The terrorist activity observed during the last two years in Egypt, particularly that in the Sinai Peninsula and the so-called 'Al Qaeda-Palestine Jihad Brigades in the Border Land', shows the desire of the Al Qaeda leadership to seize the Palestinian battlefront that is traditionally in the hands of Al Fatah, Hamas and Islamic Jihad.

As a single country and the only remaining superpower, the United States has been limited by many fewer external restraints than the European countries in terms of response to the threat. Given that most of the European countries cannot mount significant military power and that the European Security and Defence Policy (ESDP) is not defined as a combat instrument, it is to be expected that these countries will continue to denigrate the military instrument in their fight against the Jihadist-Salafist terrorism. Professor Jervis states that maybe if the Europeans had been attacked on 9/11, they might not have maintained their aversion to the use of force against the Jihadist-Salafist terrorism.[16] In fact, European countries such as France and Spain have also been attacked by Jihadist-Salafist terrorists before and after the 9/11: France avoided a 9/11 style attack against Paris when a GIA commando hijacked an Air France Airbus in Algiers in December 1994, and Spain suffered the 11 March 2004 attacks, the bloodiest terrorist action produced in an European country in history.[17] Neither France nor Spain have adopted offensive actions against Jihadist-Salafist terrorism apart from strong police and judicial efforts, and other European countries that never suffered a direct terrorist attack on their soil, such as Denmark, are much more engaged in military actions against terrorism in battlegrounds such as Afghanistan. The EU member countries are making a huge effort to try to act in a coordinated manner, forgetting anachronistic ideas such as that those who supported the terrorists in Algeria or Chechnya, or more recently in Iraq, as that those permitted terrorists act protected by freedom of speech. In any case, much has been achieved in Europe since 9/11; more than 700 arrests in connection with Al Qaeda were made between the attacks in the US and the end of 2004, with an evident disruptive effect on the terrorist organization. But much more needs to be done by the Europeans.[18] In addition, what is needed now is better harmonization of the European efforts with those of the United States in order that the anti-terrorist efforts can be made more efficient.

American perceptions that the 9/11 attacks were organized by the Hamburg cell, centred on the Al Quds Mosque seemed to be borne out by events in the Summer of 2006. Then, another group of Jihadist-Salfist terrorists tried to attack American interests from European soil. In August 2006, the British security services disrupted an apparent multiple transatlantic airline bombing plot, which, had it been successful, could have caused casualties on the scale of the 9/11 attacks in New York, crashing some nine commercial airplanes flying between the US and the UK in the middle of the Atlantic.[19]

In terms of European perceptions, the April 2007 issue of the Europol's *EU Terrorism Situation and Trend Report* showed that the members of the EU who are providing information to Europol for coordination among the EU members' police forces consider the Islamist threat the most dangerous and pressing one. The high number of arrests of Jihadist-Salafist suspects rightly reflects the level of the threat faced, and the fact that Jihadist attacks are very much worth disrupting and halting. The numerous police operations undertaken against Jihadist-Salafist cells illustrate their obsession with Europe as a place to attract and indoctrinate members, to get financing through diverse illicit activities, to find havens to rest and hide away, through which to funnel some members to other destinations, such as Iraq or Afghanistan, in order to carry out terrorist activities, to undertake attacks on European soil as well as anywhere else, as and when required. In addition, some of the failed attacks in Europe were planned against American interests, such as the attacks in Germany and Austria in September 2007.[20]

Since late 2007, Al Qaeda seems to have been revitalizing its infrastructure in the Pakistani-Afghan tribal areas, promoting violence in both Afghanistan and Pakistan. While facing insurmountable challenges in some Arab countries where it has deployed, it is also trying to attack European soil directly as well as reinforcing its presence in areas such as the Maghreb and the Sahel in Africa.[21] To face this terrorist redeployment, new efforts from the US, Europe, and the Arab/Muslim world are needed.

Areas where Americans and Europeans should work together

First, the fight against Jihadist-Salafist terrorism should include a common effort by Americans and Europeans in ideological and counter-propaganda terms. The April 2007 Europol Report did note that there was a marked increase in propaganda activities by Islamist groups, notably in the form of video statements by the senior Al Qaeda leadership including Osama Bin Laden, Ayman Al Zawahiri, and Adam Gadahn, the latter a former US citizen from California who converted to Islam and became a relevant media adviser for Al Qaeda.[22] Such videos are becoming more professional, and could point to ' ...a coordinated global media offensive from Islamist terrorists'.[23] The spread of this ideology through the Internet and channelled by the very professional Global Islamic Media Front – producer of programmes such as *The Voice of Caliphate* and *As Sahab* – is a threat in itself because it is promoting extreme violence across the world. Where the Jihadist-Salafist terrorists have succeeded in Europe – in Madrid in 2004 and in London in 2005 – they have put their ideological comrades in the shade in terms of indiscriminate killing and destruction.[24] For the time being, counterterrorism efforts in Europe have not been able to deeply penetrate the process of radicalization and recruitment within Jihadist-Salafist networks and cells. In November 2006, Dame Eliza Manningham-Buller, the Director General of the MI5, disclosed that intelligence officers were watching 1,600 people 'who are actively engaged in plotting, or facilitating, terrorist acts here and overseas' and had identified nearly 30 plots that 'often have links back to Al Qaeda in Pakistan and through those links Al Qaeda gives guidance and training to its largely British foot soldiers here'. During summer 2007 two failed attacks in the UK, one of them a suicide attempt made by two doctors of Pakistani origin against the Glasgow Airport, confirmed the previous MI5 chief's evaluation.[25]

In geographical terms, one of the areas of potential common effort against a common threat should be Northern Africa and the Sahelian region, where a rapid response to the progressive fusion of the various local Jihadist-Salafist groups in Al Qaeda in the Land of Islamic Maghreb (AQMI in its French acronym) is needed.[26] A number of European countries have established relations with the regimes in the area and the US is developing a cooperation effort on security and counterterrorism with most of the countries there: the Pan-Sahel Initiative between 2002 and 2004, and the much more ambitious Trans Saharan Counterterrorism Initiative (TSCTI) for the period 2005–9.

The Pan-Sahel Initiative was launched in late 2002 and until the end of 2004 trained military and law enforcement units within the four participant nations, Chad, Mali, Mauritania, and Niger. In 2005, the United States developed the TSCTI which was designed to provide organic and logistics support under the US European Command. The TSCTI headquarters are in Stuttgart, Germany. With a US$500 million budget for a five-year programme, $100 million per year, it already includes – in addition to the four participating Sahelian nations – Algeria, Morocco, Nigeria, Senegal, and Tunisia. The first military exercise on the ground under the TSCTI command took place from 6–26 June 2005. It was called 'Flintlock-2005' and included the participation of up to 1,000 US Special Forces troops.

The TSCTI carries out daily training activities by US Special Forces troops for the participating countries' armed forces and much-needed intelligence work in light of the existence of mobile training camps belonging to AQMI in the middle of the desert. Other activities will doubtless be boosted after the creation of the US Africa Command (USAFRICOM), sixth among the US regional military commands in the world, after an executive order signed by President Bush on 8 February 2007.

These efforts developed by a number of EU countries and the US are meant to be complementary to each other but also, in a wider area, should involve the Maghreb and Sahelian countries.[27] The suicide attacks in Casablanca and Algiers in April 2007, the Maghreb and Sahelian areas where there are Al Qaeda-supported training and projection, the direct threat by AQMI against 'the European and American crusaders', and, last but not least, the relevant figures of Maghrebians fighting in Iraq against the Iraqi government and the Coalition Forces[28] all presuppose good reasons for a much more coordinated effort among Europeans, Americans, and Arab/Muslims in their necessarily unique struggle against this specific terrorism. In addition, the Maghreb countries do not cooperate among themselves, a fact that has facilitated the cooperation among terrorist groups belonging to the five member states of the Arab Maghreb Union (AMU) created in 1989. The death of four suicide bombers in Casablanca on 10 April 2007, and the bomb attacks in Algiers on the following day, perpetrated by three suicide bombers, must be considered as one more step in the unstoppable surge that the Jihadist-Salafist threat means for all of us – Arab/Muslims, Americans, and Europeans – regardless of who are the victims each time.[29] The former GSPC – today's AQMI – has settled not only in Algeria but it is also extending its tentacles to neighbouring countries in the Maghreb and the Sahel, following the model provided by Bin Laden, and it requires a global response. In terms of direct US interest, in December 2006 in Algiers a terrorist attack against a Halliburton bus used by the American company's workers injured a number of foreigners and domestic nationals and was a sign of this global war that the Jihadist-Salafist terrorists have declared. The mobile training camps in the Maghreb, the Sahel, and Nigeria that the AQMI/GSPC terrorists organize to welcome terrorists from other countries also requires urgent common approaches and reactions.[30]

Last but not least, it is important to say that any appeasement policy is always perceived by the Jihadist-Salafist terrorists as a sign of their enemy's weakness and it emboldens their will to fight. Amnesties in the Maghreb countries, mainly in Algeria in 2006 when almost 2,600 Jihadists were released in six months, but also some releases of Jihadist prisoners in Morocco and other Maghreb countries, together with the weakness of penal codes in some EU member countries, are eroding the fight against terrorism in terms of coordination and mutual reinforcement.[31]

Conclusions

For the time being, the global war led by the US against Jihadist-Salafist terrorism – involving not only direct military and police actions against terrorist cells but also military intervention in Iraq, the Guantanamo prison, and the clandestine arrests of foreign citizens abroad – has provoked disputes within the West and negative reactions in the Arab/Muslim world.

The Bush administration's major departure was to state that the United States makes no distinction between those who commit acts of terror and those who harbour terrorists. This came after years of US indecision over what to do about terrorism, not only in Afghanistan but also in Iraq. Since 9/11, the US government considers that the first priority is no longer apprehending terrorists in order to prosecute them, but preventing attacks. Some supporters say that the US, in order to preserve the integrity of terrorism prosecutions, must build a high wall separating counterterrorism work from law enforcement and prosecutorial work.[32]

The other players included in this study, Europeans and Arab/Muslims, mainly EU Member States and Maghreb countries, also have combat experience against Jihadist-Salafist terrorism. This variety of terrorism has been very important in the Maghreb in terms of recruitment, improving its training techniques whilst executing its criminal activities on the ground as exporting its methods to places like Europe, the Sahel, Iraq or Afghanistan.

All these players have experienced direct attacks on their soil – 9/11 in New York and Washington, DC, in Casablanca, in Madrid, in London, and in Algiers – but they are not able to arrive at a common definition of the threat and consequently common strategies and responses are lacking.

It is about time that Americans, Europeans, Maghrebians, and those in other Arab/Muslim countries work together as one against the threat affecting us all. At this level it is important that Europeans and Maghrebians cooperate with the US, taking advantage of the positive aspects that Washington's interest could have in the Maghreb region at a moment so critical in the fight against a threat that sees itself more daring and emboldened than ever.

Finally, notwithstanding defeatist trends that point to problems in Western culture, the Arab authors of the four UN Development Programme (UNDP) reports published between 2002 and 2007 concluded that most of the problems in the Arab world are of their own making. No dialogue or conciliation must be searched vis-à-vis a worldwide terrorist actor – Jihadist-Salafist terrorism – that preaches the ideology of genocide through the elimination of apostates and infidels. This is an existential struggle against fanatics and has nothing to do with debates and even disputes between the Arab/Muslim world and the West. Those debates and disputes are important and not very well recognized either in Europe or even in some circles in the Arab/Muslim world. But it must be placed in the context of present discussions about diplomatic proposals such as the European and American initiatives towards the Arab/Muslim countries and regions,[33] the Spanish and Turkish initiative to create an alliance of civilizations, and at the same time as defining areas of common activity in the fight against Jihadist-Salafist terrorism, which is a self-declared enemy of all these and other efforts focused on dialogue and cooperation between Islam and the rest of the world.

Notes

1 See on the definition of the threat Walid Phares: 'Projecting Future Jihadi Terrorism Five Years After 9/11', 8 September 2006, in http://counterterrorismblog. org/2006/09/projecting_jihadi_terro.php.

2 See the Robert Jervis' chapter in this book. See also his classic *Perception and Misperception in International Politics* Princeton, NJ: Princeton University Press, 1976.

3 A good reference about the bloody terrorist experience in Algeria during the 1990s is the book by Mohamed Mokeddem, *Les Afghans algériens. De la Djamaâ à la Qa'îda*, Algiers: Éditions ANEP, 2002.

4 The political and military wings of Hamas and at least one leader of Hizbollah – but not Hizbollah as a group – have been included in the EU list of terrorist organizations and persons for number of years. This list is currently updated by the EU Council. See a 2003 version of the list in 'Council Common Position 2003/906/CFSP of 22 December 2003' in *Official Journal of the European Union* L 340, 24 December 2003, pp. 77–80, and the updated version dating from June 2007 in *Official Journal of the European Union* L 169, 29 June 2007 in http://eur-le x.europa.eu/LexUriServ/site/es/oj/l169/16920070629es00690074.pdf.

5 The GIA carried out terrorist attacks on French soil between 1995 and 1996. The bloodiest of them claimed ten lives and injured dozens in June 1995 in the Saint Michel Metro station in Paris.

6 Elaine Sciolino and Stephen Grey, 'British Terror Trial Traces a Path to Militant Islam', *The New York Times*, 26 November 2006, in www.nytimes.com/2006/11/ 26/world/europe/26crevice.html?_r = 1&ref = worldcile Hennion, 'Omar Bakri, un cheikh qui vous veut du bien', *Jeune Afrique/l'Intelligent*, no 2125, 2–8 October 2001, pp. 26–28, and Matthew Crosston, 'The Hizb Al-Tahrir in Central Asia: How America Misreads Islamist Threats', *MERIA Journal*, 11(3), Article , September 2007.

7 The role played by radical prayers such as Abu Qutada and Omar Bakri, both in London, or Mohamed El Fizazi, in Morocco, must be pointed out in terms of transborder indoctrination.

8 See two distant analyses in chronological terms for confirming this reality. Cécile Hennion, 'Omar Bakri, un cheikh qui vous veut du bien', *Jeune Afrique/l'Intelligent*, no. 2125, 2–8 October 2001, pp. 26–28, and Matthew Crosston, 'The Hizb Al-Tahrir in Central Asia: How America Misreads Islamist Threats', *MERIA Journal*, 11(3), Article 3/8, September 2007.

9 Craig Whitlock, 'Salafist Group Finds Limited Appeal in Its Native Algeria', *Washington Post Foreign Service*, 5 October 2006.

10 Carlos Echeverría Jesús, *Casablanca and Algiers: Terrorism that Strikes Against all of us*, Madrid: Grupo de Estudios Estratégicos (GEES)-Colaboraciones Number 1639, 17 April 2007, in www.eng.gees.org/imprimir.php?id = 205 .

11 Carlos Echeverría Jesús, 'Radical Islam in the Maghreb', *Orbis. A Journal of World Affairs*, 48(2), Spring 2004, p. 357.

12 The Egyptian Islamic Jihad merged with Al Qaeda in the second half of the 1990s, at the very moment when Al Zawahiri, together with Bin Laden, launched the International Islamic Front Against Crusaders and Jews in 1998.

13 See an updated report on the Jihadist-Salafist activism in South Asia in Bruce Vaughn (Coordinator), *Terrorism in Southeast Asia*, Washington, DC, Congressional Research Service (CRS) Report for Congress, Order Code RL34194, 11 September 2007.

14 See two recent examples of Jihadist-Salafist activism against democratic processes in two distant Arab countries, Yemen and Morocco, in Mohamed Sudam, 'Yemen says oil site attacks linked to al Qaeda', *Reuters*, 16 September 2006, in http://news. yahoo.com/s/nm/20060916/wl_nm/security_yemen_attack_dc&printer = 1   and Olivier Guitta, 'The Islamization of Morocco. Extremism is displacing moderation in the North African kingdom', *The Weekly Standard*, 12(3), 10 February 2006.

15 See Jean-Pierre Filiu, 'Ghosts of the caliphate', *Prospect Magazine*, Issue 140, November 2007.

16 See Professor Robert Jervis' chapter in this book.

17 The crash of the Air France Airbus on Paris was avoided due to the intervention of the French National Gendarmerie special forces when the aircraft landed for technical reasons in Marseille. See Jean-Claude Bourret, *Groupe d'Intervention de la Géndarmerie Nationale (GIGN). Vingt ans d'actions. Les nouveaux défis*, Paris: Éditions Michel Lafon, 1995, pp. 273–300.

18 Julian Richards, *Terrorism in Europe: The Local Aspects of a Global Threat*, Jihad Monitor Occasional Paper No. 7, 10 April 2007, p. 7, in www.jihadmonitor. org. In terms of the lack of a common approach among Europeans it is important to remember that France spent more than ten years obtaining the extradition of Rachid Ramda from the UK; Ramda is an Algerian citizen accused of helping in the GIA terrorist attack against the Saint Michel Metro station in Paris.

19 Julian Richards, *Europe and the Nature of the Terrorist Threat in 2007*, 30 June 2007, pp. 4–5, in www.gees.org.

20 On 5 September 2007 a Jihadist-Salafist group was arrested in Germany when they were planning terrorist attacks against various targets including Ramstein US Air Base. In addition, a terrorist attack against the US Embassy in Vienna was aborted on 1 October 2007. See a detailed analysis about a large number of failed Jihadist-Salafist attacks in Europe in C. Echeverría Jesús, *Ataques yihadistas frustrados en Europa*, Análisis GEES Number 228, 17 October 2007, in www. gees.org/autor/251.

21 In 2007, Al Qaeda in Iraq faced an internal revolt by Sunni tribes who supported the Iraqi government and even the Coalition efforts against Al Qaeda's extreme violence. In Lebanon, the Jihadist Palestinian group Fatah al Islam, a pillar of Al Qaeda and based in the Nahr El Bared camp in Tripoli, was defeated by the Lebanese Army in September 2007 after two months of clashes.

22 Craig Whitlock, 'Converts To Islam Move Up In Cells', *Washington Post Foreign Service*, 15 September 2007.

23 Europol, *EU Terrorism Situation and Trend Report 2007*, The Hague (The Netherlands): Europol, April 2007, p. 4.

24 A good example of how a sustained fight against Jihadist-Salafist terrorist propaganda must be maintained and coordinated is the item posted on Islamist websites hosted in Minnesota on 26 August 2007, and entitled 'How to Join Al-Qaeda'. The item called on every Muslim to regard Jihad as a personal duty and to take initiative to establish a terrorist cell without waiting for recognition from Al-Qaeda. See *Islamist Websites Hosted in Minnesota on How to Join Al-Qaeda, Form a Jihad Cell, and Select a Western Target*, in MEMRI Special Dispatch Series Number 1702, 31 August 2007, in www.memri.org/bin/opener_latest.cgi?ID = SD170207.

25 See Sciolino and Grey, op. cit.

26 See Jonathan Dahoah-Halevi, 'Al-Qaeda. The Next Goal Is to Liberate Spain from the Infidels', *Jerusalem Issue Brief*, 7(16), 11 October 2007, in www.jcpa.org

27 Echeverría Jesús, *Casablanca and Algiers*, op. cit., p. 3.

28 Nawaf Obaid and Anthony Cordesman, *Saudi Militants in Iraq: Assessment and Kingdom's Response*, Washington DC: Center for Strategic and International Studies (CSIS), 19 December 2005, p. 5.

29 Echeverría Jesús, *Casablanca and Algiers*, op. cit., p. 1.

30 C. Echeverría Jesús, 'El terrorismo yihadista a las puertas de España: los campos de entrenamiento en el Sahel', *Análisis del GEES*, Number 202, 5 July 2007, in www.gees.org/autor/251.

31 In Morocco, a number of suicide terrorists who acted in spring 2007 in Casablanca, and even Hassan Al Khattab, the leader of the Jihadist-Salafist cell Ansar Al Mahdi' which was dismantled by the Moroccan police at the end of July 2006, had spent some years in prison in the aftermath of the suicide bombings in

Casablanca on 16 May 2003. They were released by the application of annual royal amnesties. See Matthew Chebatoris, 'Islamist infiltration of the Moroccan Armed Forces', *Global Terrorism Analysis*, 5(3), 15 February 2007, in www.jamestown.org/terrorism/news/article.php?articleid = 2370252.

32 For a good description of this strategy, see John Lehman, 'We're Not Winning This War', *The Washington Post*, 31 August 2006.

33 We include here: the Euro-Mediterranean cooperation within the Barcelona Process; the European Neighbourhood Policy (ENP), involving a number of Arab countries among the states bordering the enlarged EU: the Broader Middle East Initiative launched by the US; the NATO Mediterranean Dialogue; the OSCE Mediterranean Dialogue; the initiatives involving the EU and the Arab League or the Islamic Conference Organization; the various sectorial and subregional frameworks of dialogue in the Mediterranean basin; and others.

10 Putin's Energy Policy in European and Transatlantic Perspective

Alex Marshall*

The end of the Cold War at Soviet initiative would, it was widely antici-pated, help herald in a new era of greater Russian–American cooperation and trust. Following mutual disappointment in the 1990s, the new 'global war on terror' to which Russia rapidly signed up appeared to be a new opportunity to forge a closer partnership and alliance, but this opportunity was again squandered. In this chapter, using the statements of American 'public intellectuals' and policy think-tanks themselves as evidence, I argue that the dominant American discourse towards Russia has in fact for a long time been excessively negative, and that the gap between the dominant mode of discourse and the reality of facts and perceptions on the ground is now glaring. This has become particularly noticeable of late in three main areas – namely in the 'managed democracy' debate regarding Russia, in the discussion of Russia's so-called 'energy weapon' vis-à-vis the EU, and in the rhetoric of the 'New Great Game' in the Trans-Caucasus and Central Asia. The conclusion calls for Europeans to help initiate a new form of public discourse regarding Russia that would be more appropriate for a multipolar world and more likely to foster mutual trust and confidence on all sides.

The Russian–Ukrainian gas dispute of 2005–06 has placed the energy policies of the Russian government at the heart of both Russian–European and transatlantic relations. In turn, this has provoked a public discourse that relies upon the dramatic manipulation of perception – a discourse in which the United States flatters new allies, playing down their various sins, whilst amplifying its criticism of any and every perceived Russian transgression. The most famous recent outburst along these lines was that of US Vice-President Dick Cheney in Vilnius on 4 May 2006, in a speech in which he criticized alleged Russian backsliding from democratic reform and 'energy blackmail', whilst at the same time never even mentioning that the neigh-bouring Estonian government continues to erect monuments to local fascists from World War II.[1] This speech is perhaps the clearest example of a new discourse being developed in American policy-making circles about Russia. The formulation of such a dominant discourse is of course a central part of politics of all shades; 'facts' in such a discourse are never objective, but are utilized within an organized system of meanings, as Foucault famously demonstrated:

> ... relations of power cannot themselves be established, consolidated nor implemented without the production, accumulation, circulation and functioning of a discourse.[2]

Critical to discourse formation is not an absolute factual reality, but a series of vital and absolute antagonistic dichotomies – state/society, totalitarianism/democracy, control/freedom, order/disorder, tradition/modernity. Such discourses invariably entail the conscious attempt to create a *perception* that attempts to influence public opinion whilst also satisfying various political stakeholders, business interests, and lobby groups. They are, in short, inevitably shaped by national perspective. Such dichotomies are only *ever* functional and sustainable given strong emphasis on certain facts and 'necessary silences' on other issues. Rhetorical discourse plays a strong role in current American policy-making in the same manner that it did for Imperial France in Napoleon's time or for the Soviet Union before 1985, and for broadly similar reasons – a desire to shape power relations and assume a leadership role in international relations. The new American discourse regarding Russia is largely hostile, and reliant both upon exaggerations of nuance, and a whole series of inconsistencies and 'necessary silences'. Thus, current American discourse will condemn alleged democratic back-sliding in Russia, but *not* growing signs of authoritarianism in Georgia or Poland; it will condemn alleged Russian interference in Ukrainian elections, but defend passionately what is arguably similar types of behaviour by America in Venezuela or other Latin American countries, such seen most recently where Washington bluntly warned Nicaraguan voters that they might lose US aid if they dared elect Daniel Ortega into office. Finally, American discourse will condemn Russia for 'outdated' geopolitical thinking whilst also, in its own quadrennial defence review, regularly and openly engaging in grand strategic geopolitical perspectives itself. Accusations of peculiar American hypocrisy over such matters misses the point; when it comes to the formulation of political discourse for policy formation, all countries throughout history in a similar position of seeking hegemony have made similar rhetorical choices and efforts to shape mainstream perception. The key issue for Europeans is that it lies with them independently as sovereign nations to make their own judgement as to how far America's current discourse regarding Russia reflects real political realities in that country today. How far are do the perceptions being shaped by this discourse correspond to reality?

In this chapter I wish to propose that current heightened rhetoric over Russia and its future orientation has become particularly agitated by three main issues: (1) questions over the state of 'managed democracy' in Russia itself, most recently condemned in a US Council of Foreign Relations report chaired by John Edwards and Jack Kemp, which itself as a consequence advocated 'selective cooperation' with Russia in future rather than any kind of 'broad partnership, which is not now possible';[3] (2) speculation over the future of Russian energy policy and its implications for Europe; (3) speculation over EU/NATO expansion, the global war on terror, and the alleged 'Great Game' unfolding in Central Asia and the Transcaucasus over military basing rights and pipeline access. These three areas of course overlap in many instances, again creating within the current discourse a series of perceptions that ultimately affects strategic decision-making. At the moment this very circle of perception and decision-making has led some commentators to worriedly speculate that, without careful handling, we are facing a new Cold War.[4] Yet, for the purposes of this chapter, I wish to treat these three areas individually and sequentially before in my conclusion then setting forth my *own* perception of the present state of play.

With regard to the first issue here, the doubts expressed over 'managed democracy' in Russia, most Western commentary on this can be traced back to the year 2000 and concern over President Putin's own rise to power. This in itself however is a serious misperception on the part of most media commentators. The first clearly 'managed' election in Russian politics was the 1996 election that returned President Boris Yeltsin to office. Without heavy unofficial Western backing and the support of his own narrow circle of corrupt oligarchs, there exists very little doubt that the discredited and increasingly dissolute Yeltsin, who in 1993 had bombarded his own parliament and then inaugurated a disastrous first war in Chechnya just a year later, would have lost that election; the vast majority of the Russian electorate at that time would have voted for either communist or nationalist candidates, the so-called 'red-brown coalition'. Nonetheless this was a turn of affairs with which many in the West merely turned a blind eye. Yeltsin, with his market reform programme (which, in its earliest Western-backed 'shock therapy' phase, inflicted a massive demographic and healthcare disaster on Russia from which it has not yet fully recovered), was seen as an indispensable asset, although in practice mutual misunderstanding and distrust on both sides also led to deep disappointment within Russia itself in the wake of the 1998 rouble devaluation and the international Kosovo crisis. The American academic Stephen F. Cohen has eloquently criticized this particular chain of events that formed part of the so-called 'who lost Russia?' debate of the late 1990s, so therefore I will not cover it extensively here.[5]

Accepting therefore that 'managed democracy' began in 1996 rather than in 2000, President Putin in Russia today, by contrast with President Yeltsin, is a genuinely popular figure. After a short but difficult period in late 2004, he continues today to bask in 70 per cent personal approval ratings compared to Yeltsin's pitiful 35 per cent in the first round of the 1996 elections. For many people abroad however, President Putin's own openly acknowledged background as a former member of the KGB simply made him an unacceptable candidate for election in a democratic country, and a great deal of subsequent interpretation of President Putin's own behaviour has been guided by knowledge of his former background and *perceptions* about how that background will make him behave. The perception that Mr Putin was an instinctive authoritarian was increased by the language and vocabulary he used, particularly in regard to the Second Chechen war, where his famous declaration that he would kill Chechen terrorists in the outhouse if necessary both increased his popularity in Russia domestically and, in a pre-September 11 world, caused revulsion amongst certain liberal circles in the West. Here at least it must be admitted that assessment of Putin and his statements was coloured in the West by liberal interpretations of the Chechen wars themselves (which are in and of themselves a powerful self-contained 'discourse'). These were conflicts in which, in Western circles at least, the Russian armed forces were for a time almost always portrayed as the sinners and the Chechen insurgents as near-saints. Whilst in this chapter it would be inappropriate to go down a byway into discussing either the rights and wrongs of the Chechen wars, where, as in all wars, crimes have been committed by both sides; some insight countering the dominant Western discourse can be gained from Paul Murphy's deeply flawed but still important book *The Wolves of Islam*, which depicts many of the less attractive aspects of the Chechen insurgency both in 1994–96 and today. Amongst the other factors that Murphy details is very clear evidence of Chechen contacts with Al Qaeda during the 1990s, multiple atrocities in the interwar period including barbaric and well-publicized public beheadings (which briefly shocked even the Western media at the time), rampant slave- and drug-trafficking, explicit plans by Shamil Basaev to turn the whole of the North Caucasus into a Muslim caliphate, and even stated plans in 1996 to fly planes into the Kremlin itself.[6] Though Murphy's work remains deeply unsatisfactory due to its tendency, in places, towards exaggeration and statements lacking corroboration, few who have studied the Chechen conflict in detail would be able to deny that the threat from Islamic extremism in Chechnya is also a very real one and which has claimed many victims.

Although the subsequent global war on terror has diminished Western and particularly American criticism of Russian actions in Chechnya, criticism of Russian democracy under Putin has continued on a number of fronts, recently and most notably over the Khodarkovskii trial, the treatment of foreign NGOs in Russia, and Putin's moves after the Beslan tragedy to appoint, rather than have elected, regional governors in Russia. Thus, although the subject of criticism changed, the dominant mode of discourse did not, suggesting as I have already stated that, as in any discourse, facts are only to be used to fit and facilitate judgements and actions that have to a significant degree already been made and resolved upon. The latest round of American criticism of Russia was made ceremonially evident in the 2005 tour of President Bush to Latvia, Moscow, and Georgia, during which the President criticized Russian democracy but lavished praise on the current near-dictator of Georgia, Mikhail Saakashvili. Following President Bush's display of double standards in relation to Saakashvili, Cheney followed his recent speech in Vilnius by then flying on to Kazakhstan to glad-hand President Nazarbaev, a leader who has increasingly turned 'managed democracy' in his own country into a modern art form. Yet of course Nazarbaev was important to America, both because of the Baku-Tiblisi-Ceyhan (BTC) pipeline recently completed in the Transcaucasus, which I will consider shortly, and because of Kazakhstan's pivotal role in the Shanghai Cooperation Organisation, a group whose influence in Central Asia the American government has found increasingly irritating.

Looking back then at international criticism, suspicion, and media perception of the democratic process in Russia, as part one of this survey, what are we Europeans left with in practice when estimating the gap between current American discourse and Russian reality? We have a government in Russia today which is at least as democratic as, if not in some regards even more democratic (in terms of genuinely reflecting the national mood) than, the often-praised Yeltsin regime was. We certainly see some state control of the Russian media and a degree of self-censorship by the media themselves, but we also see mass participation in the political process and an extremely healthy and vibrant public press (including some 5,000 political newspapers, and vibrant regional television and radio broadcasters), a phenomenon unimaginable in the Soviet period. Kremlin manipulation of the media and political 'spin' certainly often occurs, but not on a scale any greater than in the UK under 'New Labour' or in America today through the Fox News Channel. In short, though there are undoubtedly negative elements in the state-media relationship in Russia today, these are often in many instances rather 'normalized' elements when compared to other, much older Western democracies. More troubling is the murder rate amongst Russian journalists – 13 since Putin came to office – a terrible phenomenon, but even here figures need to be looked at in proportion in relation to the overall population.[7] We certainly also have in the Kremlin a government that still occasionally feels the need to employ prophylactic measures against rich oligarchs who would otherwise use their considerable power and influence to corrupt the democratic process, something we saw all too much of during the 1990s in Russia, and which we continue to see in the Ukraine even today, as well as in the frequent pronouncements and actions abroad of Boris Berezovskii. Putin inherited this problem from Yeltsin; he did not create it. But I would argue that we are not, facing a government that is significantly backsliding on its democratic commitments; rather, it is trying to create a structured democracy that conforms to Russian historic and cultural traditions, contested though that approach may be.[8] The appointment of local governors is an example where Western media misperception has arguably obscured what are actually attempts to create more responsive regional administrations. Whilst governors are now appointed by the Kremlin, they must also meet the approval of locally elected legislatures, and they are in reality arguably more rather than less accountable than their predecessors were. Contrary to some accounts that the governors are there to 'serve Putin's whim', appointed governors serve an important function in areas like the North Caucasus where the appointment system effectively leapfrogs into office capable men who otherwise would be forever blocked by local corruption and petty regional political rivalries.

Russia today is certainly far from perfect (what state is?), but for reasons that often actually fall outside the dominant official mode of American discourse. There certainly remain significant areas where it would be desirable for both Russians and Europeans to see considerable improvement – most notably in reducing bureaucracy, investing greater amounts in state healthcare, and in making Russia a more secure legal environment for international investment, an area in which China, with a much less democratic record, is ironically today actually much further ahead. Better ways also have to be found to increase legitimate employment opportunities and local incomes in critical regions, of which the North Caucasus is again the best example– official unemployment figures in Dagestan in 2003–2004 ran at 24.9 per cent, in Kabardino-Balkaria at 28.7 per cent and in Ingushetia at 49 per cent. All republics remain heavily subsidized, with Ingushetia in 2005 covering 88.3 per cent of its budget from Federal subsidies.[9] The North Caucasus is a region where pure 'hard' security measures – to the neglect of 'soft' power – will clearly only perpetuate local unrest, and in this regard the rebuilding of Groznyi itself with federal funds marks an important first step down a long road. But even given all this, it is nonetheless, in my view, extremely hard to make the intellectual leap, as Freedom House, the independent American NGO now does, that Russia today merits being downgraded from the status of 'partly free' to 'not free', or that Russia should be ejected from the G8 for its alleged sins.[10] We are, in other words, now in a very dangerous area of public debate, where the mainstream dominant perception represents an extremely simplified and deliberately cropped version of a complex picture, and where critical rhetoric of Russia is now considerably removed not just by one but by several degrees from the actual.

Moving on to the second part of my study – speculation over Russian energy policy and its implications for Europe – we again come to consider an area where, I would argue, the gap between the perceptions fostered in mainstream discourse and actual reality have reached something of an extreme. President Putin undoubtedly possesses a consistency of purpose that many Western commentators and politicians find slightly unnerving. Even before becoming president he used one of his first speeches in 1999 on Russian strategy in the 21st century to emphasize what he saw as the central importance of energy to Russia's future as a great power.[11] High world oil prices since the onset of the Iraq war in 2003 have domestically facilitated the creation in Russia of the so-called 'stability fund' that is designed for two purposes – the greater provision of social welfare and better housing for the Russian people, and the slow rebuilding of more modern military capabilities in the Russian army. Recently announced moves to float the rouble on the international exchange market reflect a degree of renewed domestic confidence. The position of Gazprom today on the world stage meanwhile is the direct product of a series of consistent actions taken by Putin since coming to office in 2000. Gazprom today controls 16 per cent of the world's known natural gas reserves, and is the top global supplier of gas, as well as a top-20 oil company. Meanwhile, against this background, energy security has also become a primary EU concern.

Imports account for approximately 50 per cent of the EU's energy consumption and this figure is expected to rise to some 70 per cent in 2030, and in the case of oil products to 90 per cent. Russian disputes over energy payments from Belarus and Ukraine, with accompanying periodic cut-offs, have sparked concern in EU circles over Russia's so-called 'energy weapon', creating much comment about a perceived Putin policy some describe as the 'single minded pursuit of *realpolitik* by energy blackmail'.[12] Yet, until now, this debate has been the subject of a number of common misperceptions. First, the contracts that Gazprom and other Russian companies have signed with the EU are long-term deals without corrupt middlemen – deals that are mutually satisfactory to both sides. The EU possesses substantial legal leverage against breach of contract, whilst Russian companies receive the world market price for their products from the EU. Honouring these contracts and obtaining the income they bring is extremely important to Russian financial stability. The situation with regard to the Ukraine, Georgia, Belarus, and other states on Russia's immediate periphery is altogether different due to the Soviet legacy of subsidized pricing, local nationalist agendas, corrupt middlemen, and powerful criminal elements. To a greater or lesser degree these countries are all still receiving subsidized oil and natural gas much as they did in the days of the Soviet Union. Ukraine today, which continuously shrieks about Russian energy blackmail, is in reality even now paying only 40 per cent of the world market price for natural gas. This lies at the heart of the dispute with the Ukraine, where the extreme nationalist leadership has recently appeared time and again incapable of understanding even basic market economics – if they do not desire to have a 'special relationship' with Russia then, to most Russians at least, it seems eminently natural that they pay world market prices. Moreover, greater 'normalization' of the pricing structure has been on Gazprom's agenda for some considerable time, leading to an earlier dispute with Belarus (a country politically much closer to the Kremlin than Kiev at present). Where EU oil and gas supplies have suffered is incontrovertibly in instances related to Russian pricing disputes with the Ukraine, which is a country highly dependent on gas but also incredibly wasteful, like Russia itself, in using it within its Soviet-era heavy industries and heating infrastructures. In December–January 2005–06, Kiev chose not to pay a long-planned and warned about price increase, chose to refuse Russia's corresponding offered loans, and chose instead to steal transited gas from other European countries. Thus it seems to me the problem is not Russia, but the Ukraine and the unstable government of that still deeply divided country. Nonetheless, more alarmist prognostications about Russian energy policy continue in some circles and have a clearly identifiable geographical source – on 30 April 2006, the Polish Defence Minister Radek Sikorski compared a recently concluded Russian–German gas pipeline deal to the 1939 Molotov-Ribbentrop pact.[13] Hopefully, the EU will not have its Russian policy shaped by the likes of Poland, Ukraine, and the Baltic states. The wider issue is that Russia and the EU are in fact mutually dependent. Although successfully diversifying its supplies and pursuing effective energy-efficiency strategies, the EU still needs Russian oil and natural gas, and Russia in turn needs EU investment and access to high technology in order to exploit deeper fields near the Arctic circle. Without wider geological exploration and the tapping of new deposits, many experts argue that the Russian energy sector faces a stark crisis within the first 50 years of the 21st century. This crisis will emerge as the days of 'easy oil', or in other words the easily exploited but previously untapped Siberian fields that existed as a legacy of Russia's market crisis in the 1990s, come to an end. The International Energy Agency (IEA) estimates that to maintain and develop Russia's energy infrastructure, investment of just under US$1 trillion is necessary until 2030.[14] Within this context, and given the very real interest in investment in Russian energy from alternative sources such as China, India and America it would seem to me natural that on the one hand the EU should cease to mollycoddle states like the Ukraine, Estonia, Latvia, Lithuania, and Poland, and on the other should continue and, if possible, accelerate the positive form of partnership pioneered by Germany with Russia. Greater maturity and less hysteria in the relationship will be to the immense benefit to all sides concerned.

Turning now to the third and final part of this chapter – the emergence of a so-called 'new Great game' discourse in the Transcaucasus and Central Asia – we again come across a striking amount of perceptual manipulation by all sides. The American administration has repeatedly stated that it does not see its involvement in Central Asia as part of a new 'Great Game', but rather that democratization and greater access to the region is to the benefit of the whole world community. Yet many American projects in the region have also enlisted the support of some of America's most noted geopolitical thinkers. Best known of these perhaps is Zbigniew Brzezinski, President Carter's former National Security Adviser, and a man who was critical of initiating American financial support to the Afghan *moudjahidin* in July 1979 (five months *before* the Soviet invasion). It is at the very least unfortunate that, in this case, Brzezinski, as they say, has form. When asked during the 1990s by a French journal whether he regretted such lavish support during the 1980s of the *moudjahidin*, he was unrepentant, revelling instead in the fact that he had, as he himself admitted, created a situation deliberately designed to draw in and entrap the Soviet Union, thus creating a 'Soviet Vietnam'. He then added 'what is more important, a few agitated Muslims or the liberation of Eastern Europe and the end of the Cold War?', a remark that perhaps could only have been made in a world that had not yet experienced 11 September or the London and Madrid bombings.[15] Brzezinski is unfortunately best known in Russia today for his 1997 book *The Grand Chessboard* which has been translated into Russian and gone through multiple editions. It lays out a geopolitical design for, as he puts it, 'extending American pre-eminence into the 21st century' via gaining control of the Eurasian landmass and fulfilling the proclamation of British geopolitician Sir Halford Mackinder that 'Who rules the World-Island rules the World.' As Brzezinski put it in 1997 in a famous *Foreign Affairs* article, 'in a volatile Eurasia, the immediate task is to ensure that no state or combination of states gains the ability to expel the United States or even diminish its decisive role'.[16] Amongst a Russian public and a military elite who are currently intensely, I would say perhaps even unhealthily, obsessed by geopolitics, it is very easy to see how Brzezinski and anything he is associated with today is interpreted as strategic aggression of the worst kind.

The project with which Brzezinski is currently most closely associated is the so-called 'New Silk Road Project', which is the development of an extensive network of pipelines, railroads, highways, ports, airports, and telecommunications intended to serve as a 'Silk Road' to link the East and West into the third millennium. Within America this project has assumed considerable institutionalized form and structure in the shape of the Central Asia-Caucasus Institute Silk Road Studies Program, which as an American–European institute has affiliated offices in Johns Hopkins University in Washington and Uppsala University in Sweden.[17] Brzezinski has, however two close associates who have in recent years overshadowed even his own contribution to the current debate: these are the American–Israeli scholar Dr Ariel Cohen and Professor Stephen Blank, Professor at the US Army War College. It fell to Ariel Cohen in 1997 to set out the founding theses of the Silk Road Project, namely: that the Caucasus and Central Asia ceased to be in the Russian sphere of influence with the collapse of the Soviet Union; that, consequently, America must grant most-favoured-nation status to Azerbaijan and encourage internationalization of such as those in Nagorno-Karabagh and the recently (2008) revived conflict in South Ossetia; and that in addition it should focus in the Transcaucasus; that it should focus on providing assistance for implementing market reforms, encourage industrial and agricultural privatization, help develop the rule of law by creating functioning legal systems, boost educational exchanges, and strengthen civil society. According to Cohen's programme, this Silk Road strategy should include diplomatic cooperation as well as military, security, and political support for the newly independent states in the southern tier, especially countries like Azerbaijan and Georgia. This would allow American companies to help develop the region's natural resources. It would also help secure the sovereignty of the new independent states (NIS) and, Cohen openly admitted, seek to foster pro-American, pro-Western orientations in Georgia, Azerbaijan, Armenia, and other countries in the region.[18] Over time such views have become more developed and entrenched. Professor Blank in April 2005, reflecting on new American bases in Afghanistan and Central Asia, argued that Central Asia was America's strategic future, proclaiming that:

> It does not suffice to be able to deploy and sustain long-range strike forces in the theatre, the theatre itself must be cooperatively reordered by the US, its other partners, and host governments, working together to stabilise it and legitimise US presence and a political order that has a genuine chance to evolve in a liberal, democratic direction enjoying popular support. America must also develop an appropriate long-term and multi-dimensional strategy for retaining permanent access to the area.[19]

For many local rulers in the region, not just the Russians and Chinese, the physical evidence of America's new strategy came in the form of the 'colour revolutions' that rocked Georgia, the Ukraine, and Kyrgyzstan. President Karimov of Uzbekistan's suspicion that nebulous American forces were manoeuvring to topple him arguably played as much a role in the subsequent break in Uzbek–American relations as the actual events in the so-called Andijan massacre of May 2005. The loss by the Americans of Khanabad air base in Uzbekistan, alongside Uzbekistan's embrace of Russia and China in the Shanghai Cooperation Organization (SCO) and the opening of a new Russian airbase in Kyrgyzstan are all now interpreted and accepted by all sides as the shifting of local pawns in what is, in all but name, a new Great Game. The opening of the Russian 'Blue Stream' gas pipeline with Turkey is likewise now seen as a natural competitor to the American and UK-backed BTC pipeline project, and American suspicion of Turkey's Islamist government and resentment of Turkey's refusal to provide bases for the 2003 attack on Iraq has arguably done nothing but foster a warming of Russian–Turkish relations.[20] The irony of the situation is in the two-faced treatment by American scholars and policy planners of the situation; whilst publicly frequently announcing that they are not interested in pursuing a Great Game, many of their most vocal proponents, such as Stephen Blank, frequently use and even relish employing the rhetorical discourse of gamesmanship. S. Frederick Starr, a prominent member of Central Asia-Caucasus Institute Silk Road Studies Program, has recently courted ridicule by going through public contortions to argue that President Karimov's actions in Andijan were in fact a legitimate response to a planned Islamic rebellion in the Fergana valley, which are statements inevitably bound to be viewed as attempts to lever American influence back into favour in Uzbekistan.[21] However the changes in Stephen Blank's approach to the situation have been, if anything, even more revealing. In 2002, Blank had presented the project he called 'Reconstructing Inner Asia' as an exercise in gaining Russian trust and forging a new era of peaceful international cooperation.[22] By 2005, however, the language for establishing and maintaining American hegemony had become more strident in Blank's writings, and his efforts to undermine trust in Russia and to belittle the SCO had become more and more blatant. In the online Eurasianet website, Blank in 2006 castigated the SCO as a paper tiger, opining that:

> Since China and Russia show signs of wanting to use the SCO to pursue their own interests at the expense of smaller members and external powers, it is quite possible that differences will grow behind the facade of unity. Washington must be alert to exploit any openings to gain geopolitical advantage. While the political, ideological, and military dimensions of the *New Great Game* [emphasis added] in Central Asia continue to heat up, it should be clear to all players that plenty of time remains in the contest. The SCO now appears to have momentum on its side, but such an advantage can dissipate quickly.[23]

Here I wish to emphasize that Blank now was by then quite open in identifying the local contest as a 'New Great Game', despite earlier American rhetoric that that was precisely what they wished to avoid. Ariel Cohen meanwhile attempted to portray the SCO as a doomed alliance, and in June 2006 formulated a new American strategy for breaking it apart:

> The U.S. can demonstrate to Beijing that Russia is dragging it into an anti-American bloc, which is counter to China's long-term interests. Russia is a high cost oil producer, and Middle Eastern instability keeps its oil prices high and its budget revenues higher. China, on the other hand, is an energy-starved economic powerhouse dependent on cheap Middle East oil. China has an interest in seeking peace in the Gulf to ensure the security of its growing energy investments.[24]

In short, American anxiety has grown, and their own rhetorical identification that they are indeed fighting a 'New Great Game' has correspondingly grown louder and more strident.

Summing up very briefly: we face a situation in all three areas surveyed where exaggerated and alarmist perception is now playing every bit as great a role as political reality itself. American discourse towards Russia, even in the absence of ideological conflict, has become ever more hostile in a manner that appears irrational and disproportionate unless one also takes into account America's own geopolitical discourse and perceived national interests. Nonetheless, for Europeans there exists a serious and glaring contradiction in American political rhetoric and policy statements towards Russia and the other states of Eurasia. The Quadrennial Review produced by the United States Department of Defence has for some considerable time now stated as an article of faith that American global hegemony is good for the world, and that the main aim of all American policy should be to prevent the potential emergence of any and all peer competitors, which is a goal that

I would describe as distinctly utopian. American policy tries to sweeten this pill by arguing that America promotes forms of democratic expression, free market reform and resource diversification that are to the visible benefit of all states. Yet when rhetoric meets reality, America appears time and again to be interested mainly in advancing its own national interests, which is a sensation that inevitably creates resentment amongst regional players and fosters the creation of anti-American alliances. The cause is not helped when American policy commentators themselves use the very language of the Great Game that they claim to be trying to transit away from. America is also facing a serious crisis in the world today where, through Guantanamo Bay and the events at Abu Ghraib, it has lost the aura of unquestionable moral superiority it undoubtedly once enjoyed amongst many in the international community. The programme of supporting democratization itself has become associated with and discredited by the rather sleazy parade of 'colour revolutions' in which one corrupt elite leapfrogs over another by the use of well-organized and well-televised pressure and public blackmail, exchanging one external sponsor for another in the process. For Europeans, it remains important to maintain a discourse regarding Russia that can separate itself from this increasingly overheated transatlantic campaign of perception; one that can continue to recognize that Russia remains on track for integrating with the global economic community (seen most recently in its campaign to join the World Trade Organization (WTO)), that the Russian Federation remains a democracy, albeit of a culturally specific type, and that the Kremlin has repeatedly stated its lack of interest in actual territorial aggrandizement or reviving the Soviet Union. If Russians continue to long for greater respect to be shown towards their perceived geopolitical sphere of influence, one is left to ponder if that is not their natural legacy anyway given the immense disparity between the Russian Federation's economic resources and those of some of its nearest neighbours – Georgia today for example has a per capita GDP of just US$1,000. It will remain vital for Europeans to maintain a healthy distance from the manipulative transatlantic perspective will remain vital since, if America and Europe genuinely wish to avoid a new Cold War, the boundaries of both legitimate political influence and acceptable political rhetoric will therefore clearly ultimately have to be rethought at some point in the near future in order to produce strategies more appropriate for a multipolar 21st century.[25]

Notes

* The views expressed in this paper in no way shape or form reflect the views either of the Ministry of Defence or indeed any other branch of the UK government.
1 For the text of the speech, see: http://www.whitehouse.gov/news/releases/2006/05/20060504–1.html; accessed 01 August 2006.
2 Michel Foucault, *Power/Knowledge: Selected Interviews and Other Writings, 1972–77*, Sussex: Harvester, 1980, p. 93.

3 http://www.cfr.org/content/publications/attachments/Russia_TaskForce.pdf; accesses 28 August 2006.
4 See for example the views of the editor of the George Soros-backed Eurasianet website: Justin Burke, 'The United States is Ill-Prepared to Wage a New Cold War' at http://www.eurasianet.org/departments/insight/articles/eav050806.shtml , accessed 28 August 2006, and Stephen F. Cohen, 'The New American Cold War', *The Nation*, 17 July 2006, at http://www.thenation.com/doc/20060717/cohen_charlierose_video, accessed 28 August 2006.
5 Stephen F. Cohen, *Failed Crusade: America and the Tragedy of Post-communist Russia*, New York: W. W. Norton & Company, 2001. Strobe Talbott in his memoirs has mounted a sustained defence of his Russian policy at this time: *The Russia Hand, A Memoir of Presidential Diplomacy*, New York: Random House, 2003.
6 Paul Murphy, *The Wolves of Islam. Russia and the Faces of Chechen Terrorism*, Washington, DC: Brassey's Inc, 2004.
7 http://www.newssafety.com/hotspots/countries/russia/miscagencies/russia280307.htm, accessed 1 April 2007.
8 See for example the recent Financial Times interview with Russian Deputy Prime Minister Sergei Ivanov, who stated that 'Russia will never take its model of management completely, 100 per cent, from the Anglo-Saxon political elite. Whether you like it or not is a different question but I am telling you how it is.' http://search.ft.com/ftArticle?queryText=ivanov+cold+war+rake&aje=true&id= 070418 010488, accessed 20th April 2007.
9 Jeronim Perovic, *The North Caucasus on the Brink,* Zurich: ISN, 2006, p.7.
10 http://www.freedomhouse.org/template.cfm?page=16&country=6818&year= 2005, accessed 28 August 2006.
11 Vladimir Putin, *First Person*, London: Hutchinson, 2000, p. 216.
12 Dr Andrew Monaghan, 'Russian Oil and EU Energy Security', *Conflict Studies Research Centre*, November 2005, Russia Series p. 1 quoting a 2005 article from *International Affairs*.
13 http://service.spiegel.de/cache/international/0,1518,413969,00.html, accessed 28 August 2006.
14 Monaghan, 'Russian Oil and EU Energy Security', p. 11.
15 http://www.commondreams.org/views–30.htm, accessed 28 October 2006.
16 Z. Brzezinski, 'A Geostrategy for Eurasia', *Foreign Affairs*, September/October 1997, Volume 75 Issue 5, p. 52.
17 Their website is http://www.silkroadstudies.org/new/ .
18 http://www.btinternet.com/~nlpwessex/Documents/silkroad.htm, accessed 29 October 2006.
19 Professor Stephen Blank, 'After Two Wars: Reflections on the American Strategic Revolution in Central Asia', *Conflict Studies Research Centre*, April 2005, Central Asian Series , frontispiece.
20 Fiona Hill and Omer Taspiner, 'Turkey and Russia: Axis of the Excluded?' *Survival*, 2006, 48(1), pp. 81–92.
21 http://www.eurasianet.org/departments/civilsociety/articles/eav051806.shtml, accessed 28 August 2006.
22 Professor Stephen Blank, 'Reconstructing Inner Asia', *Conflict Studies Research Centre*, August 2002, K34, pp. 1–2.
23 http://www.eurasianet.org/departments/insight/articles/eav062106.shtml, accessed 22 June 2006.
24 http://www.heritage.org/Research/RussiaandEurasia/wm1124.cfm, accessed 28 August 2006.
25 http://www.eurasianet.org/departments/insight/articles/eav062207b.shtml

Bibliography

Abramsky, S., 'Supporting the troops, doubting the war', *The Nation*, 4 October 2004

Adler, E., 'Imagined (Security) Communities: Cognitive Regions in International Relations', *Millennium*, 26, 1997: 249–78.

Adler, E. and Barnett, M. (eds), *Security Communities*, Cambridge: Cambridge University Press, 1998.

Aggestam, L., 'A Common Foreign and Security Policy: Role Conceptions and the Politics of Identity in the EU', in Aggestam, Lisbeth and Hyde-Price, Adrian, eds, *Security and Identity in Europe: Exploring the New Agenda*, London: Macmillan, 2000, pp. 86–115.

Ajami, F., *The Foreigner's Gift: The Americans, the Arabs, and the Iraqis in Iraq*, New York: Free Press, 2006

Alexander, M., (ed.), *Knowing Your Friends: Intelligence Inside Alliances Coalitions From 1914 to the Cold War*, London: Frank Cass, 1998.

Allen, D., Smith, M., 'Western Europe's Presence in the Contemporary International Arena', *Review of International Studies*, vol. 16, 1990: 19–37

Andrews, D. M. (ed.) *The Atlantic Alliance under Stress: US-European Relations after Iraq*, Cambridge: Cambridge University Press, 2005.

Arbel, D., Edelist, R., *Western Intelligence and the Collapse of the Soviet Union, 1980–1990*, London: Frank Cass, 2003

Art, R., *A Grand Strategy for America*, Ithaca, NY: Cornell University Press, 2003.

Ashton, N., *Kennedy, Macmillan, and the Cold War: The Irony of Interdependence*, New York: Palgrave, 2002.

Asmus, R., Everts, P. P., and Isernia, P., 'Power, War and Public Opinion: Looking Behind the Transatlantic Divide', *Policy Review*, n. 123, 2004: 73–88.

Attina, F., 'Transatlantic Relations in Post-Iraq War Global Politics', in Jean Monnet WP in Comparative and International Politics, (JMWP no. 50), University of Catania, 2003, http://www.fscpo.unict.it/EuroMed/jmwp50.htm.

Baker, J., Young, R., 'False Statements and False Claims,' *American Criminal Law Review*, vol. 42, 2005: 427–62

Barbé, E. (ed.), *Existe una brecha transatlántica? Estados Unidos y la Unión Europea tras la crisis de Irak*, Madrid: Catarata, 2005.

Barner-Barry, C., Rosenwein, R., *Psychological perspectives on politics*, Englewood Cliffs, NJ: Prentice Hall, 1985.

Barnhart, M., *Japan Prepares for Total War*, Ithaca, NY: Cornell University Press 1987.

Beach, L. R. *Image theory: Decision making personal and organizational contexts*, New York: Wiley, 1990.

Bem, D. J., 'Self-Perception Theory,' in Leonard Berkowitz, ed., *Advances in Experimental Social Psychology,* vol. 6, New York: Academic Press 1972: 1–62.

Berenskoetter, F. S., 'Mapping the Mind Gap: A Comparison of US and EU Security Strategies', FORNET Working Paper, 2004, no. 3, http://www.fornet.info.

——'Mapping the Gap: A Comparison of US and European Security Strategies', *Security Dialogue,* 36, 2005: 71–92.

Bertram, Ch., in Lindstrom, Gustav and Schmitt, Burkard (ed.), *One year on: lessons from Iraq,* Chaillot Paper No. 68, 2004, Institute for Security Studies, Paris: 21–27

Betts, R., *Surprise Attack,* Washington, DC: The Brookings Institution, 1982.

——'Striking First: A History of Thankfully Lost Opportunities,' *Ethics and International Affairs,* vol. 17, no. 1, 2003: 17–24.

Bildt, Carl (2004), in Lindstrom, Gustav and Schmitt, Burkard (ed.), *One year on: lessons from Iraq,* Chaillot Paper No. 68, Institute for Security Studies, Paris, March, pp. 21–27.

Blandy, Ch. W., 'North Caucasus: On the Brink of Far-Reaching Destabilization.' *Conflict Studies Research Centre,* August 2005 Caucasus Series 05/36.

Blank, S., 'Reconstructing Inner Asia', *Conflict Studies Research Centre,* August 2002 K34:1–2.

——'After Two Wars: Reflections on the American Strategic Revolution in Central Asia', *Conflict Studies Research Centre,* April 2005, Central Asian Series 05/14.

Boer, M. Den, Monar, J., 'Keynote Article: 11 September and the Challenge of Global Terrorism to the EU as a Security Actor', in Geoffrey Edwards and Georg Wiessala (eds), *The European Union: Annual Review of the EU 2001/2002,* Oxford: Blackwell, 2002: 11–28

Bono, Giovanna, 'The Parliamentary Accountability Gap in EU-Led External Security Engagements: Issues, Visions and Proposals', paper presented at the UACES Annual and Research Conference, Zagreb, Croatia, September 2005.

Bourret, J. C., *Groupe d'Intervention de la Géndarmerie Nationale (GIGN). Vingt ans d'actions. Les nouveaux défis,* Paris: Éditions Michel Lafon, 1995.

Bozo, Frederic, 'The Effects of Kosovo and the Danger of Decoupling' in Jolyon Howorth and John T. S. Keeler (eds), *Defending Europe: The EU, NATO and the Quest for European Autonomy,* New York: Palgrave McMillan, 2003.

Brecher, M., *Crises in World Politics,* Oxford: Permanent Press, 1993.

Brewster Smith, M., Bruner, Jerome S. and White, Robert W., *Opinions and personality,* New York: Wiley, 1956.

Brimmer, E. (ed.), *Transforming Homeland Security. U.S. and European Approaches,* Center for Transatlantic Relations, Washington, DC: J. Hopkins University, 2006

——*Seeing Blue: American Visions of the European Union.* Challiot Paper, 2007, n. 105. Intitute for Security Studies. European Union.

——(ed.) *Changing identities and Evolving Values: Is There Still a Transatlantic Community?,* Washington, DC: Center for Transatlantic Relations, J. Hopkins University, 2006.

Brooks, David, 'The Age of Skepticism', *The New York Times,* 1 December 2005.

Brzezinski, Z., 'A Geostrategy for Eurasia.' *Foreign Affairs* September/October 1997.

——*El gran tablero mundial,* Barcelona: Paidós, 1998.

——*The Grand Chessboard: American Primacy and its Geostrategic Imperatives.* New York: Basic Books, 1997.

Bull, H., 'Civilian Power Europe: A Contradiction in Terms', in Tsoukalis, Loukas, ed., *The European Community – Past, Present and Future*, Oxford: Blackwell, 1983, pp. 150–70.

Burke, J., 'The United States is Ill-Prepared to Wage a New Cold War' at http://www.eurasianet.org/departments/insight/articles/eav050806.shtml, accessed 28 August 2006

Burchill, Scott, Linklater, Andrew, Devetak, Richard, Donnelly, Jack, Paterson, Matthew, Reus-Smit, Christian and True, Jacqui *Theories of International Relations*, 3rd edition revised and updated, Palgrave, 2005

Bush, George W., Public Papers, Remarks at the Aspen Institute Symposium in Aspen Colorado. August 2, 1990, pp. 1190–94

——*Toward a New World Order*. Address by President Bush before a Joint Session of the Congress. September 11, 1990. US Department of State Current policy no. 1298

Bushm George H. W., Remarks at 2002 Graduation Exercise of the United States Academy. West Point, New York. June 1, 2002. Office of the Press Secretary. Washington, DC: The White House.

——*National Security Strategy of the United States*, Washington, DC: The White House, August 1991, pp. 4, 7.

——*The National Security Strategy of the United States of America*, Washington, DC: The White House, September 2002, pp. 6, 12.

——*The National Security Strategy of the United States of America*, Washington, DC: The White House, September 2006, p. 23.

Carr, E. H., *The Twenty Years' Crisis: 1919–1939*, New York: Harper Torchbooks, 1946.

Carter, J. R., *Airpower and the Cult of the Offensive*, Maxwell Air Force Base, AL: Air University Press, 1998.

Cederman, L. E., 'Political Boundaries and Identity Trade-Offs', in Cederman, L. E., ed., *Constructing Europe's Identity: The External Dimension*, Boulder, CO: Lynne Reiner, 2001, pp. 1–32.

Chaiken, S., "Heuristic Versus Systematic Information Processing," *Journal of Personality and Social Psychology*, 1980, vol. 39: 752–66

Chebatoris, M., 'Islamist Infiltration of the Moroccan Armed Forces' *Global Terrorism Analysis* vol. 5, Issue 3, February 15, 2007, in http://www.jamestown.org/terrorism/news/article.php?articleid = 2370252.

Christensen, T. and Snyder, J., 'Chain Gangs and Passed Bucks: Predicting Alliance Patterns in Multipolarity', *International Organization*, vol. 44, no. 2, Spring 1990

CIRCaP, *European Elites Survey 2006*, available http://www.gips.unisi.it/circap/ees_overview (accessed 30 June 2007).

Clinton, W., 'Clinton's State of Nation Message', *New York Times*, 26 January 1994. p. A17.

——National Security Strategy of Engagement and Enlargement, Washington, DC: The White House, July 1994, GPO.

——National Security of Engagement and Enlargement, Washington, DC: The White House, February 1996, p. 2.

——National Security for a New Century, Washington, DC: The White House, 1998, p. 5.

Clymer, A., 'European poll faults US for its policy in Mid-East', *New York Times*, 19 April 2002.

Cohen, S. F., *Failed Crusade: America and the tragedy of post-communist Russia*, USA: W. W. Norton Company, 2001.

——'The New American Cold War', *The Nation*, 17 July 2006, at http://www.thenat ion.com/doc/20060717/cohen_charlierose_video, accessed 28 August 2006.

Communication de la Commission au Conseil et au Parlement Européen, *Union Européenne et Nations Unies: le choix du multilatéralisme, com*, (2003) 526 final de 10.9.2003.

Cooper, R., *The Breaking of Nations: Order and Chaos in the Twenty-First Century*, New York: Atlantic Monthly Press, 2003.

Cooper, R. N., *The Economics of Interdependence: Economic Policy In the Atlantic Community*, New York: Columbia University Press for the Council on Foreign Relations, 1968.

Copeland, D., *The Origins of Major War*, Ithaca, NY: Cornell University Press, 2000

Cornish, P., Edwards, G., 'Beyond the EU/NATO Dichotomy: The beginnings of a European Strategic Culture', *International Affairs*, 2001, vol. 77, no. 3.

——'The Strategic Culture of the European Union: A Progress Report', *International Affairs*, vol. 81, no. 4, 2005: 801–20.

Cox, M., 'Beyond the West: Terrors in Transatlantia', *European Journal of International Relations*, 2005, 11: 203–33.

——'Let's Argue about the West', *European Journal of International Relations*, 2006, 12: 129–34.

Cowe, B., "The Significance of the New European Foreign Minister", *Fornet, CFSP Forum*, 2004, vol. 2, issue 4: 1–4

Crosston, M., "The Hizb Al-Tahrir in Central Asia: How America Misreads Islamist Threats", *MERIA Journal*, vol. 11, no. 3, Article 3/8, September 2007.

Crowe, B., 'A common European foreign policy after Iraq?', *International Affairs*, 2003, vol. 79, no. 3: 533–46.

Damro, C., 'Security Strategy and the Arms Industry', in R. Dannreuther and J. Peterson. (eds), *Security Strategy and Transatlantic Relations*, London and New York: Routledge, 2006.

Dannreuther, R. (ed.) *European Union Foreign and Securtiy Policy: Towards a Neighbourhood Strategy*, London: Routledge, 2003

Dannreuther, R. and Peterson, J. (eds), *Security Strategy and Transatlantic Relations*, London and New York: Routledge, 2006.

Daadler, I. H., "The End of Atlantism", *Survival*, vol. 45, no. 2, 2004: 147–66.

Daalder, I. and Lindsay, J. M., *America Unbound: The Bush Revolution in Foreign Policy*, Washington, DC: Brookings Institution, 2003.

Dahoah-Halevi, J., "Al-Qaeda. The Next Goal Is to Liberate Spain from the Infidels", *Jerusalem Issue Brief*, vol. 7, Number 16, October 11, 2007, in http://www.jcpa.org.

Dassu, M., in Lindstrom, Gustav and Schmitt, Burkard (ed.), *One year on: lessons from Iraq*, Chaillot Paper No. 68, 2004, Institute for Security Studies, Paris.

Deighton, A., 'The European Security and Defence Policy', *Journal of Common Market Studies*, vol. 40, no. 4, 2002: 731.

Department of State, Report to Congress *U.S. Policy and the Organizations for Security and Cooperation in Europe*, March 2004.

Department of State, *Voting Practices in the United Nations*, Washington DC, 2005.

——*Voting Practices in the United Nations*, Washington DC, 2006.

——*Voting Practices in the United Nations for 2000*, Report to Congress, 2000, at http://www.state.gov/p/io/rls/rpt/2000/vtg/

——*Voting Practices in the United Nations for 2001*, Report to Congress, 2001, at http://www.state.gov/p/io/rls/rpt/2001/vtg/

——*Voting Practices in the United Nations for 2002*, Report to Congress, 2002, at http://www.state.gov/p/io/rls/rpt/2002/vtg/

——*Voting Practices in the United Nations 2003*, Report to Congress, 2003, at http://www.state.gov/p/io/rls/rpt/2003/c12061.htm

——*Voting Practices in the United Nations, 2004*, Report to Congress, 2004, at http://www.state.gov/p/io/rls/rpt/c14622.htm

——*Voting Practices in the United Nations 2005*, Report to Congress, 2005, at http://www.state.gov/p/io/rls/rpt/c17894.htm

Deutsch, K.W. *et al.*, *Political Community in the North Atlantic Area*, Princeton, NJ: Princeton University Press, 1957.

de Schoutheete, P., *La coopération politique européenne*, 2nd edition, Brussels: Labor, 1986.

de Wijk, R., in Lindstrom, Gustav and Schmitt, Burkard, eds, *One Year On: Lessons from Iraq*, Chaillot Paper No. 68, Paris: Institute for Security Studies, 2004, p. 107;

Díez, T., 'Constructing the self and Managing Others: Reconsidering "Normative Power Europe"', *Millennium: Journal of International Studies*, vol. 33, no. 3, 2005: 613–36

Doyle M. and Sambanis N., 'International Peacebuilding: A Theoretical and Quantitative Analysis', *American Political Science Review*, 94, 4, pp. 779–801. Also available at http://econ.worldbank.org/WBSITE/EXTERNAL/EXTDEC/EXTRES EARCH/0,contentMDK:20701031~pagePK:64214825~piPK:64214943~theSiteP K:469382,00.html

Duchêne, F., 'Europe in World Peace', in Mayne, Richard (ed.), *Europe Tomorrow*, London: Fontana and Collins, 1972.

Duke, S., *The Convention, the Draft Constitution and External Relations: Effects and Implications for the EU and its International Role*, European Institute of Public Administration Working Paper No. 2003/W/2, Maastricht: European Institute of Public Administration, November 2003; www.eipa.nl, p. 7.

Echeverría Jesús, C., "Radical Islam in the Maghreb", *Orbis. A Journal of World Affairs*, vol. 48, no. 2, Spring 2004.

——'El terrorismo yihadista a las puertas de España: los campos de entrenamiento en el Sahel', *Análisis del GEES*, Number 202, July 5, 2007, in http://www.gees.org/autor/251.

——*Ataques yihadistas frustrados en Europa*, Análisis GEES Number 228, October 17, 2007, in www.gees.org/autor/251

——*Casablanca and Algiers: Terrorism that strikes against all of us*, Madrid: Grupo de Estudios Estratégicos (GEES)-Colaboraciones, Number 1639, April 17, 2007, in www.eng.gees.org/imprimir.php?id = 205.

Elgström, O. and Smith, M. (eds), *The European Union's Roles in International Politics: Concepts and Analysis*, London: Routledge, 2006.

Elster, J., *Political psychology*, Cambridge: Cambridge University Press, 1993.

Etheredge, L. S., *Can Governments Learn?*, New York: Pergamon Press, 1985.

Europol, *EU Terrorism Situation and Trend Report 2007*, The Hague, The Netherlands: Europol, April 2007, p. 4

Erickson, J., *The Soviet High Command*, London: Macmillan, 1962.

Escribano, G., 'Geopolítica de la seguridad energética: concepto, escenarios e implicaciones para España y la UE', *Jornadas Energía e Infraestructura: la nueve agenda internacional de las regiones*, F. Manuel Giménez Abad, Fiedrich Ebert Stiftung, Zaragoza, 24–25 October 2007.

European Commission, *Review of the Framework for Relations between the European Union and the United States: an independent study*, 2005, available http://europa.eu.int/comm/external_relations/us/revamping/final_report_260405.pdf (accessed 30 June 2007).

European Council, *A Secure Europe in a Better World. European Security Strategy* Brussels: European Council, 12 December 2003.

Evera, S. Van, *Causes of War: Power and the Roots of Conflict*, Ithaca, NY: Cornell University Press, 1999.

Everts, Steven, Missiroli, Antonio, 'Beyond the Big Three', *International Herald Tribune*, 10 March 2004; at www.cer.org.uk/articles/everts_iht_10march04.html.

Everts, S., Keohane, D., 'The European Convention and EU Foreign Policy: Learning from Failure', *Survival*, vol. 45, no. 3, 2003: 167–86.

Farnham, B., *Roosevelt and the Munich Crisis: A Study of Political Decision-Making*, Princeton, NJ: Princeton University Press, 1997.

Fernández Sola, N., 'La subjetividad internacional de la Unión Europea', *Revista de Derecho Comunitario Europeo*, vol. 11, 2002: 85–112.

——'La política de seguridad y defensa como elemento constitucional de la Unión Europea', *Revista General de Derecho Europeo*, 2003, no. 2, online. Available http://www.iustel.com (accessed 4 August 2007).

Fernández Sola, N., Stavridis, S., 'Is a Constitutional framework really needeed for the development of a ESDP?', *Fornet Network*, Available http://www.fornet.info/CFSPforumworkingpapers.html

Ferguson, N., 'A World Without Power,' *Foreign Policy*, July/Aug. 2004.

Filiu, J.-P., 'Ghosts of the caliphate', *Prospect Magazine*, Issue 140, November 2007.

Finel, B., and Lord, K. (eds), *Power and Conflict in the Age of Transparency*, New York: Palgrave, 2000.

Fiske, A. P., Tetlock, P. E., 'Taboo Trade-Offs: Reactions to Transactions that Transgress the Spheres of Justice,' *Political Psychology*, 1977, vol. 18, 1997: 255–97.

Fiske, S. T. and Taylor, S. E., *Social Cognition*, New York: McGraw-Hill, 1991.

Forster, Anthony and Wallace, William, 'Common Foreign and Security Policy', in Wallace, Helen and Wallace, William (eds), *Policy-Making in the European Union*, Oxford: Oxford University Press, 1996, pp. 411–435.

Fortna, V. P., 'Does Peacekeeping Keep Peace? International Intervention and the Duration of Peace After Civil War', *International Studies Quarterly*, 48, 2, pp. 269–292

Foucault, M. *Power/Knowledge: Selected Interviews and Other Writings, 1972–77* Sussex: Harvester, 1980.

Freedman, L., 'Can the EU Develop an Effective Military Doctrine?', in Steven Everts, Lawrence Freedman, Charles Grant, François Heisbourg, Daniel Keohane and Michael O'Hanlon, (eds), *A European Way of War*, London: Centre for European Reform, 2004, p. 15.

Gaddis, J. L., 'Grand Strategy in the Second Term', *Foreign Affairs*, vol. 84, no. 1, 2005.

——*Reluctant Empire: British Policy on the South African Frontier, 1834–1854*, Berkeley, CA: University of California Press, 1963.

Galtung, J., *The European Community: A Superpower in the Making*, London: George Allen & Unwin, 1973.

Gammer, M., 'The road not taken: Daghestan and Chechen independence', *Central Asian Survey*, 24, 2, June 2005.

Gann, L. H. and Duignan, P., *Contemporary Europe and the Atlantic Alliance*, Oxford: Blackwell, 1998.

García Cantalapiedra, D., *EEUU y la construcción de un Nuevo Orden Mundial: la Administración Bush, las relaciones transatlánticas y la seguridad europea 1989–92*, PhD dissertation, Department of International Studies, Faculty of Political Sciences, Universidad Complutense de Madrid, Madrid, 2001, pp. 148–69.

——'Irak, la política exterior de EEUU y las elecciones de noviembre', *UNISCI Discussion Papers*, no. 6, October 2004, in http://www.ucm.es/info/unisci

——*Una Estrategia de Primacía: la Administración Bush, las relaciones transatlánticas y la creación de un Nuevo Orden Mundial 1989–1992*, UNISCI Paper no. 23–24. Madrid: Unisci, 2002

——'"Peace through primacy": la Administración Bush, la política exterior de EEUU y las bases de una Primacía Imperial.' UNISCI Paper no. 30, Madrid: Unisci, 2003.

——"La política Europea de seguridad y defensa y la seguridad nacional de los Estados de la Unión: un Jano problemático". *Cuadernos Constitucionales Catedra Fadrique Furió Ceriol*, no. 49 (0toño 2004), Valencia: Universidad de Valencia, pp. 81–96.

García Picazo, P., *¿Qué cosa es esa llamada Relaciones Internacionales? Tres lecciones deterministas y algunas consideraciones indeterministas*, Madrid: Marcial Pons, 2000.

García, S., ed., *European Identity and the Search for Legitimacy*, London: Pinter, 1993.

Gerber, A., Green, D., 'Bias,' *Annual Review of Political Science*, vol. 2, Palo Alto, CA: Annual Reviews Press, 1999: 189–210.

Giegerich, B., Wallace, W., 'Not Such a Soft Power: the External Deployment of European Forces', *Survival*, vol. 46, no. 2, 2004: pp 163–82.

Ginsberg, R. H., *Foreign Policy Actions of the European Community: The Politics of Scale*, Boulder CO: Lynne Rienner, 1989.

——*The European Union in International Politics: Baptism by FIRE*, Lanham MD: Rowman and Littlefield, 2001.

Glabraith, John S., 'The "Turbulent Frontier" as a factor in British expansion', *Comparative Studies in Society and History*, vol. 2, January 1960.

Gladwell, M., *Blink: The Power of Thinking Without Thinking*, New York: Little, Brown, 2004.

Glaser, Ch., 'The Security Dilemma Revisited', *World Politics*, no. 1, 1997.

Gnesotto, N., 'La PESC en antidote', European Union Institute for Security Studies *Bulletin*, no. 16, October 2005.

Gompert, D. (1997): "America as partner", in D.Gompert and F. S. Larrabee (eds), *America and Europe. A Partnership for a New Era*, Cambridge: Cambridge University Press, 1997: 143–65.

Goodby, J., Buwalda, P., Trenin, D., *A Strategy for Stable Peace: Towards a Euroatlantic Security Community*, Washington, DC: USIP, 2002.

Gordon, P., Shapiro, J., *Allies at War. America, Europe and the crisis over Iraq*. New York: McGraw-Hill, 2004.

Greenstein, F., 'The study of personality and politics: overall considerations', in Greenstein, F., Lerner, M., *A source book for the study of personality and politics*, Markham Political Science Series, 1971.

Guertner, G., 'European Views of Preemption in US National Security Strategy' *Parameters*, Summer 2007: 31–44.

Guitta, O., 'The Islamization of Morocco. Extremism is displacing moderation in the North African kingdom', *The Weekly Standard*, 12(3), 10 February 2006.

Guthman, E., Shulman, J., eds, *Robert Kennedy: In His Own Words*, New York: Bantam, 1971.

Haass, R. N., *Intervention: The Use of American Military Force in the Post-Cold War World*. Washington, DC: Brookings Institution, 1999.

Habermas, J., *Problemas de legitimación en el capitalismo tardío*, Madrid: Cátedra, 1973, p. 94.

—— *Verdad y justificación*, Madrid: Trotta, 1999, pp. 117–22.

Halper, S. and Clarke, J.*America Alone: The Neo-Conservatives and the Global Order*, Cambridge: Cambridge University Press, 2004.

Hamilton, D., 'Introduction: Transforming Homeland Security: A Road Map for the Transatlantic Alliance', in Brimmer, E., ed., *Transforming Homeland Security. U.S. and European Approaches*, Washington, DC: Center for Transatlantic Relations, The Johns Hopkins University, 2006, p. x.

Hamilton, D., Sundelius, B., Grönvall, J. (eds), *Protecting the Homeland: European Approaches to Societal Security. Implications for the United States*, Washington DC: Center for Transatlantic Relations, J. Hopkins University, 2005.

Hamilton, D. S. and Quinlan, J. P., *Partners in Prosperity: The Changing Geography of the Transatlantic Economy*, Washington, DC: Centre for Transatlantic Relations, Johns Hopkins University, 2004.

Hartmann, F., *The Conservation of Enemies: A Study in Enmity*, Westport, CT: Greenwood Press, 1982.

Hassner, P., in Lindstrom, Gustav and Schmitt, Burkard, eds, *One Year On: Lessons from Iraq*, Chaillot Papers, p. 81.

——*The United States. The Empire of Force or the Force of Empire?* Chaillot Paper, no. 54, European Union Institute for Security Studies, http://www.iss.europa.eu 2002, pp. 20–25.

Hastings, Max, *Bomber Command*, New York: Dial Press, 1979.

Hastorf, A. H.and Cantril, H., "They Saw a Game*," Journal of Abnormal and Social Psychology*, vol. 49, 1954: 129–34

Heisbourg, F.,'US-European Relations: from Lapsed Alliance to New Partnership?', 41 *International Politics*, 2004: 119–26.

Hennion, C., 'Omar Bakri, un cheikh qui vous veut du bien', *Jeune Afrique/l'Intelligent*, no. 2125, 2–8 October 2001: 26–28

Held, D. and Koenig-Archibugi, M. (2004) (eds) *American Power in the 21st Century*, Cambridge: Polity.

Hellman, G., Wolf, R., 'Neorealism, Neoliberal Institutionalism, and the Future of NATO,' *Security Studies* 3, no. 1, Autumn 1993: 17

Herf, J., *Reactionary Modernism: Technology, Culture, and Politics in Weimar and the Third Reich*, New York: Cambridge University Press, 1994

——'Historic Transgressions: The Uses and Abuses of German History,' *International Politik* vol. 7, Spring, Berlin: Transatlantic Edition, 2006.

Herrero de Castro, R., *La realidad inventada: Percepciones y proceso de toma de decisiones en Política Exterior*, Madrid: Plaza y Valdés, 2006.

——'La influencia de variables políticas y psicológicas en los procesos de información y decisión', *Inteligencia y seguridad: Revista de análisis y prospectiva*, vol. I, no. 2, 2007: 79–95.

Herwig, Holger H., 'Germany', in Richard F. Hamilton and Holger H. Herwig, eds, *The Origins of World War I*, Cambridge: Cambridge University Press, 2005

Hill, C., 'European Foreign Policy: Power Bloc, Civilian Model – or Flop?', in Rummel, R., ed., *The Evolution of an International Actor – Western Europe's New Assertiveness*, Boulder, CO: Westview Press, 1990, pp. 31–55.

—— 'The Capability-Expectations Gap, or Conceptualizing Europe's International Role', *Journal of Common Market Studies*, vol. 31, no. 3, 1993: 305–28.

——'Closing the Capabilities-Expectations Gap?', in Peterson, John and Sjursen, Helene (eds), *A Common Foreign Policy for Europe? Competing Visions of the CFSP*, London: Routledge: 18–39.

——'Convergence, Divergence and Dialectics: National Foreign Policies and the CFSP', in J. Zielonka (ed.), *Paradoxes of European Foreign Policy*, Dordrecht: Kluwer Law International, 1998: 35–53.

—— 'The Future of the European Union in World Politics', in Tsoukalis, Loukas, ed., *Globalisation and Regionalism – A Double Challenge for Greece*, Athens: ELIAMEP, 2001, pp. 97–107.

——'Renationalising or Regrouping? European Foreign Policy Since 11 September 2001', *Journal of Common Market Studies*, vol. 42, no. 1, 2004: 143–63.

Hill, C. and Smith, M. (eds), *International Relations and the European Union*, Oxford, Oxford University Press, 2005.

Hill, F., Taspiner, O., 'Turkey and Russia: Axis of the Excluded?' *Survival* 48, 1, 2006: 81–92.

Hoffmann, S., 'The crisis in transatlantic relations', Lindstrom, G. (ed.), Shift or Rift-Assessing US-EU relations after Iraq, European Union Institute for Security Studies Transatlantic book, Paris, 2003: 13–20.

Holsti, O., 'Cognitive dynamics and images of the enemy', in Farrell, John and Smith, Asa P., *Image and reality in world politics*, New York: Columbia University Press, 1968.

Howorth, J., *European Integration and Defence: The Ultimate Challenge?* Chaillot Paper 43, Paris: WEU Institute for Security Studies, 2000.

——'European defence and the Changing Politics of the European Union: Hanging Together or Hanging Separately?', *Journal of Common Market Studies*, vol. 39, no. 4, 2003: 765–90

Howorth, Jolyon, 'From Security to Defence: The Evolution of the CFSP', in Hill, Christopher and Smith, Michael, eds, *International Relations and the European Union* Oxford: Oxford University Press, 2005.

Hull, Isabel V., *Absolute Destruction: Military Culture and the Practices of War in Imperial Germany*, Ithaca, NY: Cornell University Press, 2005.

Ikenberry, G. J. (ed.), *America Unrivalled: The Future of the Balance of Power*, Ithaca, NY: Cornell University Press, 2002.

Isernia, P., 'Le fratture transatlantiche e l'opinione pubblica: continuità e mutamento negli orientamenti del pubblico americano ed europeo', *Rivista Italiana di Scienza Politica*, 35, 2005: 57–76.

Janis, I., Mann, L., *Decision Making: A Psychological Analysis of Conflict, Choice, and Commitment*, New York: Free Press, 1977.

Jepperson, R. L., Wendt, A. and Katzenstein, P. J., 'Norms, Identity and Culture in National Security', in P.J. Katzenstein (ed.), *The Culture of National Security: Norms and Identity in World Politics*, New York: Columbia University Press, 1996.

Jervis, R., *The logic of images in International Relations*, Princeton, NJ: Princeton University Press, 1970.

——*Perceptions and Misperceptions in International Politics*, Princeton, NJ: Princeton University Press, 1976.

——'Cooperation under the Security Dilemma', *World Politics* 30, no .2, 1978: 167–214.

——'Realism in the Study of World Politics', *International Organization*, 52 (4), Autumn 1998: 971–91.

——'Deterrence and Perception,' *International Security*, vol. 7, 1982/83: 3–30.

——'Was the Cold War a Security Dilemma?' *Journal of Cold War History*, vol. 3, Winter 2001: 36–60.

——'The Compulsive Empire'. *Foreign Policy*, July/August 2003.

——*American Foreign Policy in a New Era*, London: Routledge, 2005.

——'The Remaking of a Unipolar World', *The Washington Quarterly*, 29(3), Summer 2006: 7–19.

——'Reports, Politics, and Intelligence Failures: The case of Iraq,' *Journal of Strategic Studies*, vol. 29, 2006: 3–52.

——'Understanding Beliefs', *Political Psychology*, forthcoming.

Jervis, R., Lebow, R. N., Gross Stein, J., *Psychology and Deterrence*, Baltimore, MD: Johns Hopkins University Press, 1985

Joffe, J., 'A World Without Israel,' *Foreign Policy*, Jan/Feb 2005.

Johansson-Nogués, E., *The Voting Practice of the Fifteen in the UN General Assembly: Convergence and Divergence*, IUEE Observatory of European Foreign Policy, UAB Barcelona, Working Paper no. 54, January, http://www.uab.es

Johnson, Chalmers, *The Sorrows of Empire: Militarism, Secrecy, and the End of the Republic*, New York: Metropolitan Books, 2004.

Jørgensen, K. E., 'A Multilateralist Role for the EU?' in Ole Elgström and Michael Smith (eds), *The European Union's Roles in International Politics: Concepts and Analysis*, London: Routledge, 2006.

Jorgensen, K. E. and Laatikainen, K.V., 'The EU @ the UN: Multilateralism in a New Key?', paper presented at the Second Pan-European Conference on EU Politics, Bologna, 24–26 June 2004.

Kagan, R., 'Power and Weakness' *Policy Review*, no.113, June-July 2002

——(2003) *Of Paradise and Power: America and Europe in the New World Order*, New York: Knopf.

Kagan, R., and Kristol, W., *Present Dangers: Crisis and Opportunity in American Foreign and Defense Policy*, San Francisco, CA: Encounter Books, 2000

Kaldor, M., 2003 *Barcelona Report on European Security Capabilities*.

——*A European Way of Security: The Madrid Report of the Human Security Study Group Seminar* Madrid: CIDOB, The Centre for the Study of Global Governance, 8 November 2007.

Kant, I., *Perpetual Peace*, London: FQ Classics, 2007.

Kaufmann, C. D., 'Out of the Lab and Into the Archives: A Method for Testing Psychological Explanations of Political Decision Making,' *International Studies Quarterly*, vol. 38, 1994: 557–86.

Kegley, Ch. W., Raymond, G. A., "Global Terrorism and Military Preemption: Policy Problems and Normative Perils", *International Politics*, 41, 2004: 37–49.

Keeler, J., 'Transatlantic relations and European security and defense', *EUSA Review*, vol. 17, no. 2, 2004: 4–5.

Kennedy, Craig and Bouton, Marshall M., 'The Real Trans-Atlantic Gap: US and European Public Opinion Differences', *Foreign Policy*, November–December 2002

Keohane, D., *The EU and Counter-Terrorism*, CER Working Paper, Centre for European Reform, London, May 2005.

Keohane, R. O., *After Hegemony*, Princeton, NJ: Princeton University Press, 1984.

Keohane, R. O., 'Ironies of Sovereignty: The EU and the US', in Weiler, J. H. H., Begg, I. and Peterson, J. (eds) *Integration in an Expanding European Union: Reassessing the Fundamentals*, Oxford: Blackwell, 2003, pp. 307–30.

Keohane, R.O. and Nye, J.S. *Power and Interdependence: World Politics in Transition*, 3rd edition, Boston, MA: Little, Brown, 2001.

Keukeleire, S., 'The European Union as a Diplomatic Actor: Internal, Traditional and Structural Diplomacy', *Diplomacy and Statecraft*, 2003, vol. 14, no. 3: 31–56.

Krauthammer, Charles, "The Unipolar Moment," *Foreign Affairs, America and the World, 1990–91*, vol. 70, no. 1, Winter 1990/91, pp. 23–33.

—— 'The unipolar moment revisited', *National Interest*, 70, 2003: 5–20.

Kristol, W. and Kagan, Robert, 'Toward a Neo-Reaganite Foreign Policy', *Foreign Affairs*, vol. 74, no.4, July/August 1996.

Kupchan, Ch.,"The Waning Days of the Atlantic Alliance," in Bertel Heurlin and Mikkel Vedby Rasmussen (eds), *Challenges and Capabilities: NATO in the 21st Century*, Copenhagen: Danish Institute for International Studies, 2003.

Kugler, J., Lemke, D., *Parity and War: Evaluations and Extensions of the War Ledger*, Ann Arbor, MI: University of Michigan Press, 1996.

Laatikanen, K., Smith, K. (eds), *Intersecting Multilateralisms: The European Union at the United Nations*, Basingstoke: Palgrave, 2006.

Lake, A., "From Containment to Enlargement", Washington, DC: US Department of State, vol. 4, no. 39, 27 September 1993.

Larsen, H., 'The EU: A Global Military Actor?', Cooperation and Conflict, vol. 37, no. 3, 2002: 283–302.

Larson, D., *Origins of Containment*, Princeton, NJ: Princeton University Press, 1985.

——"Truman and the Berlin Blockade: The Role of Intuition and Experience in Good Foreign Policy Judgment," in *Good Judgment in Foreign Policy: Theory and Application,* ed. Deborah Larson and Stanley Renshon, Lanham, MD: Rowman & Littlefield, 2003: 127–52.

Lebow, R. N., *Between Peace and War: The Nature of International Crisis*, Baltimore, MD, and London: The Johns Hopkins University Press, 1981.

LeDonne, J., *The Grand Strategy of the Russian Empire, 1650–1831*, New York: Oxford University Press, 2004.

Leffler, M., *A Preponderance of Power: National Security, the Truman Administration, and the Cold War*, Stanford, CA: Stanford University Press, 1992.

Lehman, John, 'We're Not Winning This War, *The Washington Post*, 31 August 2006

Lejins, A., in Lindstrom, Gustav and Schmitt, Burkard, eds, *One Year On: Lessons from Iraq*, Chaillot Paper no. 68, 2004, Paris: Institute for Security Studies, p. 90.

Leonard, M., *Can EU Diplomacy Stop Iran's Nuclear Programme?* CER Working Paper, Centre for European Reform, London, November 2005.

Levy, J., "Declining Power and the Preventive Motivation for War," *World Politics*, 1987, vol. 40: 82–107.

Levy, J., Gochal, J., "Democracy and Preventive War: Israel and the 1956 Sinai Campaign," *Security Studies*, 2001/2, vol. 11: 1–49.

Lewis, B. *What Went Wrong? Western Impact and Middle Eastern Response*, New York: Oxford University Press, 2002.

Lieber, R., 'Die USA und der Nahe Osten,' *Internationale Politik* (Berlin), vol. 61, no. 9, 2006: 91–97.

——*The American Era: Power and Strategy for the 21st Century* New York: Cambridge University Press, revised edition, 2007.

Lieven, A. *America Right or Wrong: An Anatomy of American Nationalism*, Oxford: Oxford University Press, 2004.

Lindberg, T. (ed.), *Beyond Paradise and Power: Europe, America, and the Future of a Troubled Partnership*, London: Routledge, 2005.

Lindley-French, Julian, 'In the Shade of Locarno? Why European Defence is Failing', *International Affairs*, vol. 78, no. 4, 2002: 789–811.

—— 'Two Roads to the Same Place? The Diverging Pursuit of Values and Interests in the Transatlantic Relationship', in Hochleitner, E., ed., *Europa und Amerika-eine Beziehung in Wandel,*Vienna: OIES, 2003, pp. 69–70.

Lindstrom, G. (ed.), *Shift or Rift? Assessing EU-US Relations After Iraq*, Paris: European Union Institute for Security Studies, 2003.

Lindstrom, G., Schmitt, B. (ed.), *One year on: lessons from Iraq*, Chaillot Paper no. 68, 2004, Paris: Institute for Security Studies.

Link, A. *et al.* (eds), *The Papers of Woodrow Wilson*, vol. 48, *May 13–July 17, 1918* Princeton, NJ: Princeton University Press, 1985.

Lippmann, W., *Public Opinión*, New York: Macmillan, 1922.

Liska, G., *Nations in Alliance*, Baltimore, MD: Johns Hopkins University Press, 1962.

Lord, Christopher, 'Accountable and Legitimate? The EU's International Role', Hill, Christopher and Smith, Michael (eds) *International Relations and the European Union* Oxford: Oxford University Press, 2005.

Lott, Anthony D., *Creating Insecurity. Realism, Constructivism, and US Security Policy* Burlington: Ashgate, 2004, pp. 128–36.

Luck, E. C., 'American Exceptionalism and International Organization: Lessons from the 1990s', en Foot, R., Macfarlane, S. N., Mastaduono, M. (eds), US *Hegemony and International Organizations*, Oxford, 2003.

Lugar Survey on Nuclear Proliferation, June 2005; http://lugar.senate.gov/reports/NPSurvey.pdf.

Luhmann, N., *Teoría política en el Estado de bienestar*, Madrid: Alianza editorial, 1993.

Mahncke, D., "Transatlantic Relations", in D. Mahncke, A. Ambos, C. Reynolds (eds) *European Foreign Policy. From Rhetoric to Reality?*, College of Europe Studies, no.1, Brussels: P.I.E. Peter Lang, 2004, second printing 2006.

Mahncke, D., Ambos, A., Reynolds, C. (eds), *European Foreign Policy. From Rhetoric to Reality?* College of Europe Studies no. 1, Brussels, P.I.E. Peter Lang, 2006.

Manners, I., 'Normative Power Europe: A Contradiction in Terms?' *Journal of Common Market Studies*, vol. 40, no. 2, 2002: 234–58.

——'Normative Power Europe Reconsidered' *Journal of European Public Policy*, vol. 12, no. 6, 2005.

—— 'Normative Power Europe Reconsidered: Beyond the Crossroads', *Journal of European Public Policy*, 13 (2), 2006: 182–99.

Mandelbaum, M., *The Case for Goliath: How America Acts as the World's Government in the 21st Century*, New York: Public Affairs, 2005.

Maull, H., 'Germany and the Use of Force: Still a "Civilian Power"?', *Survival*, vol. 42, no. 2, 2000: 56–80.

Mearsheimer, J., *The Tragedy of Great Power Politics*, New York: Norton, 2001.

Medina, M., *The Coherence of European Foreign Policy: a Real Barrier of an Academic Term?*, IUEE Obs Working Paper no.27, September 2002; http://www.uab.es/iuee.

MEMRI, *Islamist Websites Hosted in Minnesota on How to Join Al-Qaeda, Form a Jihad Cell, and Select a Western Target*, in MEMRI Special Dispatch Series, Number 1702, 31 August 2007, in www.memri.org/bin/opener_latest.cgi?ID = SD170207.

Merton, R., *Sociological Ambivalence and other Essays*, New York: The Free Press, a division of Macmillan Publishing Co., Inc. 1976.

Modelski, G., 'Long Cycles in World Leadership', in Thompson, W. R., ed., *Contending Approaches to World System Analysis* London: Sage, 1983.

—— *Long Cycles in World Politics*, London: Macmillan, 1987.

—— 'From Leadership to Organization: The Evolution of Global Politics', in Bornschier, V. and Chase-Dunn, C. (eds), *The Future of Global Conflict*, London: Sage, 1999.

Modelski, G. and Thompson, W. R., 'The Long and the Short of Global Politics in the Twenty-first Century: An Evolutionary Approach', *Mershon International Studies Review*, 1, 1999: 109–40.

Mokeddem, M., *Les Afghans algériens. De la Djamaâ à la Qa'îda*, Algiers: Éditions ANEP, 2002.

Molloy, S., 'Security Strategy and the "war on terror"', in R. Dannreuther and J. Peterson (eds), *Security Strategy and Transatlantic Relations*, London and New York, Routledge, 2006.

Monaghan, A., 'Russian Oil and EU Energy Security.' *Conflict Studies Research Centre*, November 2005, Russia Series 05/65, p. 1.

Monteleone, C., *Le relazioni transatlantiche e la sicurezza internazionale*, Milano: Giuffrè, 2003.

Monteleone, C. and Rossi, R., 'Transatlantic Cooperation in Conflict Management', *Jean Monnet Working Papers*, 2004, n. 57, Department of Political Studies, University of Catania.

Möttölä, Kari (ed.), *Transatlantic Relations and global governance*, Washington, DC: Center for Transatlantic Relations Johns Hopkins University, 2006.

Morgenthau, H., *Politics Among Nations*, 5th ed, revised, New York: Knopf, 1978.

Morth, Ulrika, 'The EU as an Ethical Power in the WTO', paper given at CIDEL workshop, Oslo, 22–23 October 2004.

Mueller, J., 'The Catastrophe Quota: Trouble after the Cold War,' *Journal of Conflict Resolution*, 1994, vol. 38: 355–75.

Murphy, P., *The Wolves of Islam. Russia and the Faces of Chechen Terrorism*, Washington, DC: Brassey's Inc. 2004.

National Strategy for Homeland Security Washington, Office of Homeland Security, July 2003.

Netanyahu, B. (ed.), *Terrorism: How the West Can Win*, New York: Farrar, Straus and Giroux, 1986, pp. 16–17, 23.

Neumann, I., 'European Identity, EU Expansion, and the Integration/Exclusion Nexus', in Cederman, L. E., ed., *Constructing Europe's Identity: The External Dimension*, Boulder, CO: Lynne Reiner, 2001, pp. 141–64.

Neustadt, R., *Alliance Politics*, New York: Columbia University Press, 1970

——'Presidents, Politics and Analysis', paper presented at the Graduate School of Public Affairs, University of Washington, Seattle, 1986.

——*Report to JFK: The Skybolt Crisis in Perspective*, Ithaca, NY: Cornell University Press, 1999.

Niblett, R., 'Choosing between America and Europe: a new context for British foreign policy', *International Affairs*, 83, 4, 2007: 627–41.

Nicolaidis, K. 'The Power of the Superpowerless', in Lindberg, T. (ed.), *Beyond Paradise and Power: Europe, America, and the Future of a Troubled Partnership*, London: Routledge, 2005: 92–120.

Nuttall, S., *European Political Cooperation* Oxford: Clarendon Press, 1992.

—— *'Consistency' and the CFSP: A Categorization and its Consequences*, EFPU Working Paper no. 2001/3, LSE European Foreign Policy Unit; http://www.lse.ac.uk.

Nye, J., *The Paradox of American Power: Why the World's Only Superpower Can't Go It Alone*, Oxford: Oxford University Press, 2002.

——*Soft Power: The Means to Success in World Politics*, New York: Public Affairs Press, 2004.

Obaid, N., Cordesman, A., *Saudi Militants in Iraq: Assessment and Kingdom's Response*, Washington DC: Center for Strategic and International Studies (CSIS), December 19, 2005.

Oudraat, Chantal de Jonge, 'US Attitudes evolve about EU Security Ambitions', *European Affairs*, Summer/Fall 2007.

Owen, J., "How Liberalism produces Democratic Peace", *International Security*. vol. 19, n. 2, Fall 1994.

Peterson, J., 'The US and the EU in the Balkans: America Fights the Wars, Europe Does the Dishes', paper presented to the 7th biennial International Conference of ECSA, Madison, 2001.

Peterson, J. and Pollack, M.(eds) *Europe, America, Bush: Transatlantic Relations in the Twenty-First Century*, London: Routledge, 2003.

Pérez, García, 'La PESD en el proyecto de tratado constitucional', in Pueyo, Jorge, ed., *Constitución y ampliación de la Unión Europea. Crisis y Nuevos retos*, Santiago de Compostela: Tórculo, 2003, pp. 316–17.

Perovic, J., *The North Caucasus on the Brink*, Zurich: ISN, 2006, p. 7.

Pew Global Attitudes Project, 'The Great Divide: How Westerners and Muslims View Each Other', released 06.22.2006; http://pewglobal.org/reports/pdf/253topline.pdf.

Phares, W., "Projecting Future Jihadi Terrorism Five Years After 9/11" September 8, 2006, in http://counterterrorismblog.org/2006/09/projecting_jihadi_terro.php.

Pollack, M. and Shaffer, G. (eds) *Transatlantic Governance in the Global Economy*, Lanham, MD: Rowman and Littlefield, 2001.

Pouliot, V., 'The Alive and Well Transatlantic Security Community: A Theoretical Reply to Michael Cox', *European Journal of International Relations*, 12, 2006: 119–27.

Putin, V., *First Person*, London: Hutchinson, 2000.

Ransom, H., *Central Intelligence and National Security,* Cambridge, MA: Harvard University Press, 1958.

Rawls, J., *Teoría de la justicia* y *Liberalismo político* and *El Derecho de Gentes y Una revisión de la idea de razón pública*, original 1999, Spanish translation, Barcelona: Paidós, 2001.

Reagan, R., National Security Strategy of the United States 1988, Washington DC: The White House, 1988, p. 1.

Rees, Wyn, 'The External Face of Internal Security', in Hill, Christopher and Smith, Michael, eds, *International Relations and the European Union*, Oxford: Oxford University Press, 2005.

Rees, W., Aldrich, R. J., 'Contending Cultures of Counter-Terrorism: Transatlantic Divergence or Convergence?' *International Affairs*, vol. 80, no. 4, 2005: 905–24

Reus-Smit, C., 'Constructivisme', in Scott Burchill, Andrew Linklater, Reichard Devetak, Jack Donnelly, Matthew Paterson, Chrisitan Reus-Smit and Jacqui True (eds), *Theories of International Relations*, 3rd edn, Basingstoke: Palgrave, 2005, pp. 196–97.

Risse, T., *Cooperation Among Democracies*, Princeton, NJ: Princeton University Press, 1995.

——'A Liberal World Order: The Democratic Security Community and U.S. Power', paper presented at the conference *American Unipolarity and the Future of the Balance of Power*, Woodrow Wilson Center, Washington, DC, 19 May 2000.

——'US Power in a Liberal Security Community' in Ikenberry, G.J. (ed.) *America Unrivalled: The Future of the Balance of Power*, Ithaca, NY: Cornell University Press, 2002, pp. 60–83.

Rhodes, E., "The Imperial Logic of Bush's Liberal Agenda," *Survival*, vol. 45, no. 1, 2003: 131–54.

Richards, J., *Terrorism in Europe: The local aspects of a global threat*, Jihad Monitor Occasional Paper no. 7, April 10, 2007, p. 7, in http://www.jihadmonitor.org.

——*Europe and the nature of the terrorist threat in 2007* June 30, 2007, in http://www.gees.org.

Risse, T., 'US Power in a Liberal Security Community' in Ikenberry, G.J. (ed.) *America Unrivalled: The Future of the Balance of Power*, Ithaca, NY: Cornell University Press, 2002, pp. 260–83.

Robinson, R., Gallagher, J., Denny, A., *Africa and the Victorians: The Official Mind of Imperialism*, London: Macmillan, 1961.

Rodman, P., *Uneasy Giant: The Challenges to American Predominance*, Washington DC: Nixon Center, 1999.

Roe, P., 'Former Yugoslavia: The Security Dilemma That Never Was?' *European Journal of International Relations*, vol. 6, 2000: 373–93.

Roger, P., *The American Enemy: A Story of French Anti-Americanism*, Chicago, IL: University of Chicago Press, 2005.

Rosecrance, R., *The Rise of the Trading State: Market and Commerce in the Modern World*, New York: Basic Books, 1986.

Rossi, R., *Peace Interventions and Armed Conflicts Recurrence*, paper delivered at the ECPR General Conference, Marburg, 16–21 September 2003.

——'Trading States in a New Concert of Europe', in Helga Haftendorn and Christian Tuschhoff (eds) *America and Europe in an Era of Change*, Boulder, CO:Westview Press, 1993, pp. 127–46.

Roy, O., 'Why Do they Hate Us? Not Because of Iraq', *New York Times*, 22 July 2005

Ruggie, J. G., 'Multilateralism: The Anatomy of an Institution', in Ruggie, J. G. (ed.), *Multilateralism Matters: The Theory and Praxis of an Organizational Form*, New York: Columbia University Press, 1993a, pp. 3–47.

——'Territoriality and Beyond: Problematizing Modernity in International Relations', *International Organization*, 46(1), 1993b: 139–74.

—— *Constructing the World Polity: Essays on International Institutionalization*, London: Routledge, 1998.

Rummell, R., 'Speaking with One Voice – and Beyond', in Pijpers, A., Regelsberger, E. and Wessels, W., eds, *European Political Cooperation in the 1980s – A Common Foreign Policy for Western Europe?* Dordrecht: Martinus Nijhoff, 1988: 118–42.

Russett, B. and Antholis, W., 'Do Democracies Fight Each Other? Evidence from the Peloponnesian War', *Journal of Peace Research*, no. 4, 1992.

Salmon, T., Shepherd, A., *Toward a European Army? A Military Power in the Making?* Boulder, CO and London: Lynne Rienner, 2003.

Sanger, D., 'Witness to Auschwitz evil, Bush draws a lesson', *New York Times*, 1 June 2003

Sarotte, M. E., 'Transatlantic Tension and Threat Perception', *Naval War College Review*, vol. 58, no. 4, Autum 2005.

Schiff, A. L., *Fire and Water: Scientific Heresy in the Forest Service*, Cambridge, MA: Harvard University Press, 1962.

Schimmelfennig, F., 'Liberal Identity and Post-Nationalist Inclusion: The Eastern Enlargement of the European Union', in Cederman, L. E., ed., *Constructing Europe's Identity: The External Dimension*, Boulder, CO: Lynne Reiner, 2001, p. 182.

Schroeder, P., *The Transformation of European Politics, 1763–1848,* New York: Oxford University Press, 1994.

——'Does the History of International Politics Go Anywhere?', in David Wetzel and Theodore Hamerow, eds, *International Politics and German History,* Westport, CT: Praeger, 1997: 15–36.

Schulze, K. E., *Mission Not So Impossible: The AMM and the Transition from Conflict to Peace in Aceh, 2005–2006*, Case study for the Madrid Report of the Human Security Doctrine, 2007; http://www.lse.ac.uk/depts/global/studygroup/studygroup.htm

Sciolino, E. and Grey, S., 'British Terror Trial Traces a Path to Militant Islam', *The New York Times*, 26 November 2006, in www.nytimes.com/2006/11/26/world/europe/26crevice.html?_r = 1&ref = worldDomestic Structure and Preventive War: Are Democracies More Pacific?" *World Politics*, vol. 44, 1992: 235–69.

Sedivy, J., in Lindstrom, Gustav and Schmitt, Burkard, eds, *One Year On: Lessons from Iraq*, Chaillot Paper no. 68, Paris: Institute for Security Studies, 2004, p. 107.

Shafir, E., Simonson, I., Tversky, A., 'Reason-Based Choice,' *Cognition*, vol. 49, 1993: 11–36.

Shishkin, P., 'NATO Agreement Sought', *The Wall Street Journal* Europe, 28 July 2004.

Simon, W. H., 'Wrongs of Ignorance and Ambiguity: Lawyer Responsibility for Collective Misconduct', *Columbia Public Law & Legal Theory Working Paper*, no. 0480, 2004.

Sjöstedt, G., *The External Role of the European Community*, Farnborough: Saxon House, 1977.

Sjursen, H., 'Understanding the Common Foreign and Security Policy: Analytical Building Blocks', in Knodt, Michèle and Princen, Sebastien, eds, *Undertanding the European Union's External Relations* London: Routledge, 2003, pp. 35–53.

——'Changes to European Security in a Communicative Perspective', *Cooperation and Conflict*, vol. 39, no. 2, 2004: 107–28.

Slevin, P. and Priest, D., 'Wolfowitx concedes Iraq errors', *Washington Post*, 24 July 2003.

Sloan, S.R. *NATO, the European Union, and the Atlantic Community: The Transatlantic Bargain Challenged*, 2nd edition, Lanham, MD: Rowman and Littlefield, 2005.

Smith, C., 'US training African forces to uproot terrorists', *New York Times*, 11 May 2004.

Smith, K., 'The end of civilian power Europe. A welcome demise or a cause for concern?', *The International Spectator*, vol. 35, no. 2, 2000: 11–28.

——*European Union Foreign Policy in a Changing World*, Cambridge: Polity, 2004.

Smith, Karen, 'Enlargement and European Order', in Hill, Christopher and Smith, Michael, eds, *International Relations and the European Union* Oxford: Oxford University Press, 2005.

Smith, M., 'The European Union and a Changing Europe: Establishing the Boundaries of Order', *Journal of Common Market Studies*, 34/1, 1996: 5–28.

—— 'Competitive Cooperation in EU–US relations: Can the EU be a Strategic Partner for the US in the World Political Economy?', *Journal of European Public Policy*, 5(4), 1998: 561–77.

——'European Integration and American Power: Reflex, Resistance and Reconfiguration', in Slater, D. and Taylor, P. (eds) *The American Century: Consensus and Coercion in the Projection of American Power*, Oxford: Blackwell, 1999: 136–48.

—— 'The Framing of European Foreign and Security Policy: Towards a Post-Modern Policy Framework?' *Journal of European Public Policy*, vol. 10, no. 4, 2003: 556–75.

——'Trends in European Foreign and Security Policy since September 2001', *Studia Diplomatica*, vol. 59, no. 1, 2006: 27–44.

——'Between Two Worlds? The European Union, the United States and World Order', *International Politics*, 41(1), 2004: 96–117.

—— 'Taming the Elephant? The European Union and the Management of American Power', *Perspectives on European Politics and Society*, 6(1), 2005: 129–54

—— 'European Foreign Policy in Crisis? EU Responses to the George W. Bush Administration', *European Political Science*, 5(1), 2006: 41–51.

Smith, M., 'The Shock of the Real? Trends in European Foreign and Security Policy Since September 11 2001', *Studia Diplomatica* LIX(1), 2006, pp. 27–44.

Smith, M. E., *Europe's Foreign and Security Policy: The Institutionalization of Cooperation,* Cambridge: Cambridge University Press, 2004.

——'Toward a Theory of EU Foreign Policy-Making: Multi-Level Governance, Domestic Politics, and National Adaptation to Europe's Common Foreign and Security Policy', *Journal of European Public Policy*, vol. 11, no. 4, 2004: 740–58

Snyder, G., 'The Security Dilemma in Alliance Politics', *World Politics*, vol. 36, no. 4, 1984: 461–95.

——*Alliance Politics,* Ithaca, NY: Cornell University Press, 1997.

Snyder, J., "Imperial Temptations," *National Interest*, no. 71, 2003: 29–40.

Snyder, J. L., *The Soviet Strategic Culture: Implications for Limited Nuclear Operations*, Santa Monica, CA: RAND, 1977.

Spencer, S., Fein, S., Zanna, M., Olson, J., (eds), *Motivated Social Perception: The Ontario Symposium,* vol. 9, Mahwah, NJ: Erlbaum, 2003.

Stavridis, S., 'Militarizing the EU: the Concept of Civilian Power Europe Revisited', *The International Spectator*, vol.36, no.4, 2001: 43–50.

——'European Security and Defence After Nice', *The European Union Review*, vol. 6, no. 3, 2001: 97–118.

Stavridis, S. and Pruett, D., *European Political Cooperation at the United Nations: A critical assessment 1970–1992*, Reading Papers in Politics no. 20, The University of Reading, Department of Politics, 1996.

Steffenson, R. *Managing EU–US Relations: Actors, Institutions and the New Trans-atlantic Agenda*, Manchester: Manchester University Press, 2005.

Steinberg, F., 'Europe's Place in Economic Globalisation', *Working Paper 34/2007 Real Instituto Elcano*, 5 November 2007.

Streit, C. K., *Union Now. A Proposal for a Federal Union of the Democracies of the North Atlantic* New York: Harper & Brothers, 1938.

Sudam, M., 'Yemen says oil site attacks linked to al Qaeda', *Reuters*, 16 September 2006, in http://news.yahoo.com/s/nm/20060916/wl_nm/security_yemen_attack_dc&printer = 1

Talbott, S., *The Russia Hand, A Memoir of Presidential Diplomacy*, New York: Random House 2003.

Taglialone, J., 'France and Russia ready to use veto against Iraq war', *New York Times*, 6 March 2003.

Taliaferro, J., *Balancing Risks: Great Power Intervention in the Periphery*, Ithaca, NY: Cornell University Press, 2004.

Tetlock, Philip, *Expert Political Judgment: How Good is It? How Can We Know?* Princeton, NJ: Princeton University Press, 2005.

Tetlock, P. and Levi, A., "Attribution Bias: On the Inconclusiveness of the Cognition-Motivation Debate," *Journal of Experimental Social Psychology*, vol. 18, 1982: 68–88.

Thornhill, J., 'Sarkozy in call for "hard core G6" to lead EU', *Financial Times*, 26 September 2005, p. 14.

Transatlantic Trends, *Transatlantic Trends Survey*, years 2003, 2004, 2005, 2006, available http:\\www.transatlantictrends.org (accessed on June 30, 2007).

Trachtenberg, M., *A Constructed Peace*, Princeton, NJ: Princeton University Press, 1999.

Tucker, R., *The Radical Left and American Foreign Policy*, Baltimore, MD: Johns Hopkins University Press, 1971.

UN General Assembly, 'A more Secure World: Our Shared Responsibility', *Report of the High-level Panel on Threats, Challenges and Change*, A/59/565, 2005.

Vanhoonacker, Sophie, 'The Institutional Framework', in Hill, Christopher and Smith, Michael, eds, *International Relations and the European Union*, Oxford: Oxford University Press, 2005.

Vaughn, B. (ed.), *Terrorism in Southeast Asia*, Washington, DC: Congressional Research Service (CRS) Report for Congress, Order Code RL34194, 11 September 2007.

Vigalondo, F., *La arquitectura de la seguridad en el proceso de integración europea: observaciones obtenidas a partir de un modelo interpretativo basado en fundamentos teóricos de J. Habermas*, DEA Unión Europea, University of Zaragoza, unpublished.

Vinocur, John, Schroder gives support to Bush's Mideast plan, *International Herald Tribune*, February 27, 2004;

—— U.S.–German reasons to reconcile Schroder and Bush find mutual interest, *International Herald Tribune*, March 1, 2004.

Voss, J. F., Dorsey, E., 'Perceptions and International Relations', in Singer, Eric y Hudson, Valerie (eds), *Political Psychology and Foreign Policy*, Westview Press, 1992.

Youngs, Richard, *The European Union and the Promotion of Democracy – Europe's Mediterranean and Asian Policies*, Oxford: OUP, 2001.

Waever, O., 'European Security Identities', *Journal of Common Market Studies*, vol. 34, no. 1, 1996: 103–32.

—— 'The EU as a Security Actor: Reflections from a Pessimistic Constructivist on Post-sovereign Security Orders' in Morten Kelstrup and Michael C. Williams (eds) *International Relations Theory and the Politics of European Integration: Power, Security and Community*, Routledge: London, 2000, pp. 250–94.

Wagner, W., 'The Democratic Control of Military Power Europe', *Journal of European Public Policy*, vol. 12, no. 6, 2005: 1005–1021.

Wallace, W.,"Europe, the Necessary Partner", *Foreign Affairs* 80, 3, 2001: 16–34.

—— 'Political Cooperation: Integration Through Intergovernmentalism', in Wallace, Hellen and Wallace, William and Webb, Carole (eds), *Policy Making in the European Community – 2nd edition*, Chichester: John Wiley and Sons, 1983, pp. 373–402.

Walt, S., *Taming American Power*, New York: Norton, 2005.

Waltz, K., *Theory of International Politics*, Reading, MA: Addision-Wesley, 1979.

——'America as a Model for the World? A Foreign Policy Perspective,' *Political Science and Politics*, vol. 24, 1991.

——'A Necessary War?' in Harry Kriesler, ed., *Confrontation in the Gulf*, Berkeley, CA: Institute of International Studies, 1992: 59–65.

——'The Emerging Structure of International Politics', *International Security* vol. 18, no. 2, 1993: 44–79.

——'Structural Realism after the Cold War', *International Security*, vol. 25, no. 1. 2000: 5–41.

Warner, Rex, trans., *The Peloponnesian War*, Harmondsworth: Penguin, 1954.

Weidenfeld, W., *Partners at Odds. The Future of Transatlantic Relations. Options for a New Beginning* Brussels: Verlag Bertelsmann Stiftung, 2006, p. 43.

Welsh, Jennifer M., *Canada-United Kingdom Colloquium*, School of Policy Studies, Queen's University at Kingston, Quebec City, Canada, 18–21 November 2004, 2005.

Wendt, A., *Social Theory of International Politics,* New York: Cambridge University Press, 1999.

Wessels W., "Theoretical Perspectives. CFSP beyond the Supranational and Intergovernmental Dichotomy", in D. Mahncke, A. Ambos, C. Reynolds (eds), *European Foreign Policy. From Rhetoric to Reality?* College of Europe Studies, no.1, Brussels: P.I.E.-Peter Lang, pp. 61–96.

Whaley, B., *Codeword Barbarossa,* Cambridge, MA: MIT Press, 1973.

Whitlock, C., 'Salafist Group Finds Limited Appeal in Its Native Algeria', *Washington Post Foreign Service*, 5 October 2006.

——'Converts To Islam Move Up In Cells', *Washington Post Foreign Service*, 15 September 2007.

Whitman, Richard, 'Muscles From Brussels: The Demise of Civilian Power Europe?', in Elgström, Ole and Smith, Michael, eds, *The European Union's Roles in International Politics: Concepts and Analysis* London: Routledge, 2006.

Wilkinson, P., *International Terrorism: The Changing Threat and the EU's Response*, Chaillot Paper no. 84, European Union Institute for Security Studies, Paris, October 2005.

Wohlstetter, R., *Pearl Harbor: Warning and Decisión,* Stanford, CA: Stanford University Press, 1962.

Wolfers, A., *Discord and Collaboration,* Baltimore, MD: Johns Hopkins University Press, 1962.

World Public Opinion, 'World View of US Role Goes From Bad to Worse', 22 January 2007, available at http://www.worldpublicopinion.org/pipa/articles/international_securi ty_bt/306.php?nid = &id = &pnt = 306&lb = btis (accessed on 30 June 2007).

Wyllie, J. H., 'Measuring Up: The Strategies as Strategy', in R. Dannreuther and J. Peterson (eds), *Security Strategy and Transatlantic Relations,*London and New York: Routledge, 2006.

Zakaria, F., 'Realism and Domestic Politics: A Review Essay,' *International Security*, vol. 17, 1992: 177–98.

Zielonka, J., 'Constraints, Opportunities and Choices in European Foreign Policy', *Paradoxes of European Foreign Policy. Policies without Strategy. The EU's Record in Eastern Europe*, EUI WP, no. 97/66, 1997: 10–11.

——'Transatlantic Relations Beyond the CFSP', *The International Spectator*, vol. 35, no. 4, 2000: 27–40.

Index